MIDDLE EASTERN
AMERICAN THEATRE

Michael Malek Najjar is an associate professor of Theatre Arts at the University of Oregon. He holds an MFA in Directing from York University and a PhD in Theatre and Performance Studies from UCLA. His research focuses on Arab American and Middle Eastern American theatre and performance. He is the author of *Arab American Drama, Film and Performance: A Critical Study, 1908 to the Present* (2015), and the editor of *Heather Raffo's Iraq Plays: The Things That Can't Be Said* (2021), *The Selected Works of Yussef El Guindi* (2018), and *Four Arab American Plays: Works by Leila Buck, Jamil Khoury, Yussef El Guindi, and Lameece Issaq & Jacob Kader* (2014). With Jamil Khoury and Corey Pond, he is the coeditor of *Four Plays of the Israeli-Palestinian Conflict* (2018). He is an alumnus of the Lincoln Center Theater Directors Lab, Directors Lab West, and the RAWI Screenwriters Lab-The Royal Film Commission Jordan. He has also directed mainstage productions with Golden Thread Productions, New Arab American Theatre Works, and Silk Road Rising.

Also available in the Critical Companions series from Methuen Drama:

CRITICAL COMPANION TO NATIVE AMERICAN AND FIRST
NATIONS THEATRE AND PERFORMANCE: INDIGENOUS SPACES
Jaye T. Darby, Courtney Elkin Mohler, and Christy Stanlake

THE DRAMA AND THEATRE OF SARAH RUHL
Amy Muse

THE THEATRE OF AUGUST WILSON
Alan Nadel

THE THEATRE OF EUGENE O'NEILL: AMERICAN MODERNISM ON
THE WORLD STAGE
Kurt Eisen

THE THEATRE AND FILMS OF CONNOR MCPHERSON:
CONSPICUOUS COMMUNITIES
Eamonn Jordan

IRISH DRAMA AND THEATRE SINCE 1950
Patrick Lonergan

PRISON THEATRE AND THE GLOBAL CRISIS OF INCARCERATION
Ashley Lucas

*For a full listing, please visit www.bloomsbury.com/series/criticalcompan
ions/*

MIDDLE EASTERN AMERICAN THEATRE

COMMUNITIES, CULTURES, AND ARTISTS

Michael Malek Najjar

Series Editors: Patrick Lonergan and Kevin J. Wetmore, Jr.

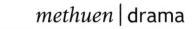

methuen | drama

LONDON · NEW YORK · OXFORD · NEW DELHI · SYDNEY

METHUEN DRAMA
Bloomsbury Publishing Plc
50 Bedford Square, London, WC1B 3DP, UK
1385 Broadway, New York, NY 10018, USA
29 Earlsfort Terrace, Dublin 2, Ireland

BLOOMSBURY, METHUEN DRAMA and the Methuen Drama logo are trademarks
of Bloomsbury Publishing Plc

First published in Great Britain 2021
This paperback edition published 2022

Cover design: Charlotte Daniels
Cover image: *444 Days* by Torange Yeghiazarian, Golden Thread Productions, 2013.
Harry (Michael Shipley) and Laleh (Jeri Lynn Cohen). Directed by
Torange Yeghiazarian. Photograph by David Allen Studio

A catalogue record for this book is available from the British Library.

A catalog record for this book is available from the Library of Congress.

ISBN: HB: 978-1-3501-1703-7
PB: 978-1-3501-9259-1
ePDF: 978-1-3501-1705-1
eBook: 978-1-3501-1704-4

Series: Critical Companions

Typeset by Deanta Global Publishing Services, Chennai, India

To find out more about our authors and books visit www.bloomsbury.com
and sign up for our newsletters.

For Rana and Malak

CONTENTS

Contents

ILLUSTRATIONS

ACKNOWLEDGMENTS

A book like this is not possible without the assistance, advice, and support of an entire village. I would first like to thank Mark Dudgeon, Lara Bateman, Joseph Gautham, and the entire outstanding editorial and production team at Methuen Drama. My deepest gratitude and regards to the series editors Patrick Lonergan and Kevin J. Wetmore, Jr. who have been invaluable to me as guides throughout this process. Their encouragement and support helped me immensely, and I could not have completed this volume without them. Thanks also to my colleagues in the Department of Theatre and the College of Arts and Sciences, University of Oregon. Also, I would like to express my gratitude to the Oregon Humanities Center for granting me the 2019–20 Ernest G. Moll Research Professorship in Literary Studies—specifically, Paul Peppis, Jena Turner, Peg Freas Gearhart, and Melissa Gustafson. You opened your doors to me at the OHC and you have made me feel at home.

Of course, I am most grateful to the Middle Eastern American artists, scholars, and practitioners who have, through tireless and often unheralded efforts, created a genre that transcends borders and cultures. I would like to specifically thank Danny Bryck, Catherine Coray, Kareem Fahmy, Lindsay Joelle, Jamil Khoury, Evren Odcikin, Megan Sandberg-Zakian, David Winitsky, Deborah Yarchun, Torange Yeghiazarian, and Pirronne Yousefzadeh for sharing their cultural insights and theatrical histories with me. I also want to acknowledge a host of other theatre producers that have committed themselves to this mission over decades of their lives. Also, I'd like to thank those whose production photographs are included in this book: Michael Brosilow, David Allen Studio, Teresa Wood, Airan Wright, and Juan Zapata. Thanks, too, to the staff at the theatres who arranged the photograph permissions: Laurie Levy-Page, Michelle Mulholland, Corey Pond, and Juan Zapata. There are far too many to mention here, but I've done my best to chronicle their work in this volume. To those artists and theatre companies I may have omitted, I deeply apologize. I hope that, in the future, we can publish more books that celebrate even more of the accomplished artists that comprise this genre.

Acknowledgments

I would like to offer my gratitude to my colleagues on the MENA Theatre Makers Alliance (MENATMA): Shoresh Alaudini, Andrea Assaf, Leila Buck, Catherine Coray, Debórah Eliezer, Yussef El Guindi, Nora El Samahy, Tracy Francis, Kathryn Haddad, Pia Haddad, Denmo Ibrahim, Taous Claire Khazem, Jamil Khoury, Kate Moore Heaney, Evren Odcikin, and Torange Yeghiazarian. I am inspired by your work, and it is my honor to be collaborating with you on furthering this movement.

Lastly, I am forever indebted to my family and friends for their support. Thank you, Dina, for being such a supportive and loving sister. To my beautiful wife, Rana, and my precious daughter, Malak, I hope you find this book worthy of the time away from you that I spent writing it. Finally I dedicate this to my late mother, Samia Assad Najjar, who passed away in 2019. She was a guiding force in my life, and I will be a forever grateful son for all that she did for me.

PREFACE

Throughout history, political figures and governmental policies focused on differences between communities to stoke animosity and hatred. Such is the case in the current political climate where immigrants and refugees are scapegoated, religious and cultural differences are suspected, and individuals speaking different languages and practicing different cultural values are attacked. So it is with Middle Eastern Americans. Since 2000, this vast and diverse group have been misunderstood and assailed with growing frequency. In North America, those who espouse beliefs that differ from so-called American values are considered foreign "others" who are a danger to society. Middle Eastern Americans are expected to assimilate, leaving behind the cultural riches they brought to North America. Many are born with cultural names that they might Anglicize for the outside world due to prejudice, lack of social cohesion, or simply because they are too difficult to pronounce. This duality extends itself greatly when one faces rising tensions between the culture of their birth and the culture of their upbringing. When conflicts between the US and Middle Eastern nations occur, Middle Eastern Americans feel particularly vulnerable. This vulnerability is heightened when there is a domestic incident involving terrorism. Even when there are no Middle Easterners connected with the terrorism, the entire Middle Eastern American community is scapegoated as somehow being complicit with these heinous acts. In addition, Middle Easterners are frequently dramatized in Hollywood films and television programs mercilessly terrorizing Americans. Generations of Americans have been exposed to such images, and these also cause more fear and suspicion, especially for those who dress in traditional or religious clothing. Synagogues, mosques, churches, and temples are attacked; hijabs are ripped from women's heads; religious cemeteries are desecrated; and governments ban travel.

It is from this crucible that Middle Eastern American theatre is forged. The stories in these works are born from topics that include the difficulties of growing up bi-culturally in a Middle Eastern American household, struggling to find a place to belong in society, life-altering visits taken to the Middle East, dealing with the blowback from US military interventions, or backlash from terrorist incidents carried out on American soil. Middle Eastern American theatre artists utilize their writing, acting, directing, and other performance skills to contest the notion that they are somehow the abject "other" in American society. They employ their artistic talents to give voice to those who are suffering due to the vicissitudes of foreign policies that include economic sanctions, direct military interventions, occupations, and drone wars perpetrated in the Middle East. For these artists, the people "over there" are not just faceless masses shaking their fists and chanting violent slogans seen on television news. For these artists, the people of the Middle East are relatives, friends, and colleagues that suffer and die due to foreign policies often funded by their own tax dollars. These plays and performances imbue humanity to those individuals and societies dehumanized by politicians that believe they come from what some deem "shithole countries." Unfortunately, these countries are the territories where larger nations fight their proxy wars, dictatorial governments are sustained by foreign capital, occupations are funded for decades, and coups depose democratically elected leaders. The rich resources of the Middle East have led to the creation of great wealth, but also to the misery of many who have died in wars to secure those riches. Of course, there is much blame found within these countries, but the overwhelming forces that have led to such circumstances such as colonialism and global proxy warfare, not to mention the devastating effects of global warming and pandemics, created a massive migration from the region and a refugee crisis of epic proportions.

The dramatic and comedic works of Middle Eastern American writers often run counter to the hegemonic narratives pushed by governmental bureaucrats who foment desert wars and financial crises in the name of military supremacy and monetary gain. These artists recognize the need for positive action, creative solutions, and dialogue to solve the intractable problems facing the Middle East. They believe that human beings are more valuable than money or politics because, when the sanctions are imposed, and the bombs fall, it will be the innocent civilians who will ultimately suffer. Of course, these artists are not monolithic. They hail from many nations and countless communities that are sometimes in direct conflict with one another. These communities have traditions that are hundreds, if not thousands, of years old. The Middle East was the "fertile crescent" where some of the greatest human civilizations rose and fell. The contemporary Middle East is suffering through changes that began with colonialism and religious conflict hundreds of years in the making. Now the nations of the

Middle East are facing seemingly intransigent difficulties that will take generations to solve.

The aim of this book is to introduce readers to some of the voices that comprise a burgeoning genre of American theatre often ignored by the mainstream theatre establishment. I have included plays from artists who reside in the United States and in Canada in English translation. I apply the word "American" here to include all the Americas, not only the United States. I must note that my inability to read and/or translate Spanish and French has limited my inclusion of plays mainly to North America and to those translated into English. It would be better if future editions of books like these could encapsulate the Americas from Canada to South America. Also, it is impossible to include every playwright, director, designer, and theatre professional that is working in this genre. The plays I have included here are representative plays and are by no means the only works that exist. Many of the works included here were generously shared with me by playwrights who self-identify as Middle Eastern Americans. Other plays were found in pre-published scripts, anthologies, or videos. Some might criticize the inclusion of certain works and decry the exclusion of others. To this critique I can only say that, in the future, I'm sure entire volumes will be written about these artists and theatres. I must add that, to fully appreciate these plays, one must see them in production. A playscript is to a fully staged production what a blueprint is to a physical building; you cannot fully understand the magnitude of these dramas until you see them fully realized onstage with actors, direction, design, and all the other elements that comprise live theatre. In the case of the one-person monodramas studied here, the actors/playwrights that created these works are such gifted performers that descriptions of their work are a paltry substitute for seeing them perform live onstage.

My hope for this Methuen Drama Critical Companions volume is to introduce theatre students and audiences to the playwrights, directors, designers, and companies that comprise this rich field in the hopes that these plays will receive more scholarship, publishing, funding, and productions in the future. Middle Eastern American theatre is in the same state that other great theatre communities (such as African American, Asian American, Latinx, and Native American) were in decades ago when they, too, were trying to create an entirely new genre. More of these plays must be published, produced, and studied if this genre is to reach its fullest potential. Progress will be gradual, difficult, and oftentimes frustrating. I believe that these artists, and those that follow them, will continue to shape the theatre of the Americas for generations to come.

This book focuses on artists who believe in empathy, solidarity, and celebration of culture. I have met, and worked with, many of the artists included in this book and I can tell you that they see their theatre work as a vital part of who they are as individuals and theatre makers. These artists frequently travel to the Middle East and return with important stories about a terribly misunderstood region. These multitalented writers and performers bring great humanity to their work, and they share that humanity with audiences. They are important harbingers of the events we are seeing in our time and, if we listen closely to them, we might have a much deeper understanding and appreciation of the Middle East, but also of our wider world.

INTRODUCTION
POLYCULTURALISM, TRANSNATIONALISM, AND DIASPORA

Middle Eastern Americans have been a vital force in the United States since the great migrations starting in the late nineteenth century. The Middle East (or Near East) is a term that encompasses a massive area that includes the countries Bahrain, Cyprus, Egypt, Iran, Iraq, Israel, Jordan, Kuwait, Lebanon, Libya, Oman, Palestine, Qatar, Saudi Arabia, Sudan, Syria, Turkey, the United Arab Emirates, and Yemen. Some include South Asian countries like Afghanistan or Pakistan on this list as well. Furthermore, if one adds the nations Tunisia, Algeria, and Morocco in North Africa, there is a vast and virtually limitless definition to the peoples, cultures, and religions that are present.

To understand the scope, imagine a group that includes Armenians, Ashkenazi Jews, Turks, Egyptians, Bedouins, Yemini Arabs, Muwahhidun/ Druze, Qashqai, Baluch, Turkoman, Hazaras, Pashtuns, Tajiks, Iranians/ Persians, Marsh Arabs, Kurds, Lurs, Moroccan Arabs, Berbers, Haratins, and Sephardic Jews. Then, imagine the multiplicity of religious and ethnic groups that constitute each of those communities. The nation-state identification is only one of the umbrella concepts that can define Middle Easterners; one must then go further to get a deeper sense of who these people are and what they believe. For instance, when discussing Islam, we begin by dividing this group into Sunni and Shi'ite Muslims. From there, we must break down the larger into smaller groups such as the Sunni schools of the Hanafi (found in the Middle East and Pakistan), the Malikite (found in western and northern Africa), the Shafite (found in Egypt, East Africa, Malaysia, and Indonesia), and the Hanbalite (found primarily in Saudi Arabia). For the Shi'ites, one should consider the Twelve-Imam Shi'ites (also known as "imamism" found in Iran and Iraq as well as the Gulf Emirates, Chinese Turkestan, Afghanistan, Pakistan, and India) and the "Seveners" or the Ismailis (who are concentrated in India, Pakistan, Central Asia, Iran, East Africa, Europe, and North America). Other groups splintered from the Ismailis as well, namely the Druze, and are often subsumed into the "Muslim" category even though the Druze consider themselves an entirely distinct group which lays claim to elements of Judaism, Christianity, Islam, and Vedic philosophy.

This brief example demonstrates that there is a complex tapestry that makes up the people of the Middle East that is often overlooked by many who are content to identify people of this region generally by religion (i.e., "one is Muslim") or by nationality (i.e., "one is Israeli"). These generalizations are problematic because they presuppose that all the people in a group are similar. The late scholar Edward W. Said, whose book *Orientalism* changed the way many academics approach the study of the so-called East, wrote:

> The point I want to conclude with now is to insist that the terrible reductive conflicts that herd people under falsely unifying rubrics like "America," "the West," or "Islam" and invent collective identities for large numbers of individuals who are actually quite diverse, cannot remain as potent as they are, and must be opposed, their murderous effectiveness vastly reduced in influence and mobilizing power. (Said 1994, xxviii–xxix)

As a displaced Palestinian refugee himself, Said understood more than anyone that reductive labels have dangerous power that can lead to pernicious ideas such as "the clash of civilization" and imperialist wars of conquest. Even the title "Middle East" is a highly contentious Eurocentric term, as European geographers originally called the region the "Near East" given its proximity to Europe. According to Karen Culcasi, the term "Middle East" was coined by British general Thomas Edward Gordon in 1900 to refer to Afghanistan, Persia, Russia, and British India. Two years later, US Navy captain Alfred Mahan used the term in relation to British imperial interests. By 1921, Winston Churchill officially institutionalized the term with the establishment of the Middle East Department of the British Colonial Office (Culcasi 2010, 585). Cartographers have contradictory maps regarding the location of the Middle East and the countries found within its borders. While some include North Africa, others include countries of South Asia such as Afghanistan and Pakistan. This has led to the coining of the term "The Greater Middle East," which then extends from Morocco to Pakistan. Further difficulties arrive when one attempts to define the region by certain ethnic or linguistic identifiers such as "Arab," which then excludes many in the region who do not identify as such.

Dividing the world in discrete regions that are theoretically unified by human and physical geographical traits is a commonly accepted way in which to order and understand our world. Whether we are referring to "Western Europe," "Southeast Asia," or the "Middle East," all world regions have been created, imagined, and naturalized through various historical, economic, and political discourses. What is unique about the Middle East is that pejorative discourses about this place are wide-spread and readily accepted. (Culcasi 594)

Ultimately, the term "Middle East" carries tremendous cultural baggage that includes colonialism, Orientalism, and perverse notions of the region that have been perpetuated through scholarship, popular entertainment, and the arts.

Middle Eastern American Communities

The complex nature of the Middle Eastern American community lies in the differences not only between the people of different home nations or religions but also within the same religious groups themselves. For instance, Sephardic Jews, or Jews that developed communities on the Iberian Peninsula around 1000 ACE, and who have a distinct Judeo-Spanish language called Ladino, also had communities in the former Ottoman Empire (North Africa, the Middle East, Eastern Mediterranean, and the Balkans). These communities practice Sephardic customs that were imparted by Iberian Jews in exile over the past centuries. Mizrahi Jews, on the other hand, come from Middle Eastern ancestry and do not trace lineages to the Iberian Peninsula. Their lineage comes from Persia, Babylonia, and Yemen. Sephardic and Mizrahi Jews were expelled, or migrated, after the events of the 1948 Arab-Israeli War and moved primarily to Israel or the United States. Those Mizrahi Jews who left after the 1979 Islamic Revolution in Iran settled in Southern California and New York. Unlike Ashkenazi Jews, who were primarily from Europe and who primarily spoke Yiddish, Sephardic and Mizrahi Jews have been struggling for visibility among the American Jewish community. In the book *Sephardi and Mizrahi Jews in America*, Saba Soomekh writes,

No longer are Sephardic and Mizrahi Jews dealing with antisemitism and second-class citizenship of their homeland, but now they must cope with how to preserve and navigate their culture, language, history, and heritage of their traditions while dealing with assimilation—not only into a dominant American society, but into a dominant Ashkenazi society. (Ross, Soomekh, and Ansell 2016, xiii)

There are also the Chabad-Lubavitch Jews, who are concentrated in Brooklyn, New York, where the Chabad rabbinic dynasty lived, and where the last Chabad rebbe/spiritual leader first immigrated after fleeing persecution in Europe during the Second World War. This community encourages "Mitzva Tanks" in which groups of Chabad men and boys take to the streets in vehicles to encourage secular Jews to perform "mitzvah," or good deeds, to become more connected with their heritage.

Similarly, many believe that there is a monolithic Iranian American society, but this is also composed of many subgroups, some of whom have no connection to Shi'ite Islam whatsoever. As mentioned earlier, there are Mizrahi Jews that called Iran home, but there are also other groups such as the Baha'is. The Baha'is trace their history to a leader named the Bab (1821–50), who considered himself the gate to the Hidden Imam. After his execution, many of his followers were killed or exiled, and the remaining went into hiding. The exiled leader, Mirza Husayn-Ali Nuri (1817–92), also known as Baha'u'llah, attempted nonviolent opposition to the Iranian State, and relations improved somewhat. However, there continued to be killings of Baha'is and other persecutions that exist to this day (iranbah aipersecution.bic.org). The Baha'i community in the United States grew steadily from the 1890s, especially following the establishment of the Islamic Republic of Iran in 1979. Another Iranian group, the Lur, is found in Iran and Turkey. They speak an Indo-Iranian dialect closely related to Persian/Farsi (ibid.). Yet another group is the Kurds, who hail from several contemporary Middle Eastern countries, including Iran, Turkey, Iraq, and Syria. The Kurds are an indigenous people of Western Asia, who are now the world's largest non-state nation (Hassanpour 2005). Of course, there are different Muslim sects within the Shi'ites, who are the largest Muslim group in the country.

Arab Christians have existed in the Middle East since the Pentecost, and they are sometimes conflated with Muslim Arabs. According to the United States Conference of Catholic Bishops, there are seven Catholic Churches in the Middle East: the Latin, Maronite, Melkite, Armenian, Chaldean, Coptic, and Syrian Churches (USCCB 2010, 1). Since the turn of the twenty-first century, there has been a precipitous decline in the Middle Eastern Christian population. Pressures on Christian communities due to lack of economic opportunities, political instability, and anti-Christian extremism have drastically decreased their populations (ibid.). The Palestinian-Israeli conflict, with its security wall, expanding Israeli settlements, and checkpoints, has created a difficult situation for Palestinian Christians caught between Israeli and Muslim Palestinian interests. The US occupation of Iraq and the ensuing rise of Isis has reduced the Christian population in that country from 1.4 million to an estimated 250,000 in 2020 (Green 2019). In 1970, Lebanon was 62 percent Christian and by 2017 that population had decreased to 36 percent (State Department 2017). Coptic Christians, especially those found in Egypt, have also faced increased persecution in recent decades.

Other groups, like Armenian Americans, are often considered European Americans and not Middle Eastern Americans. However, plays that deal specifically with the Armenian Genocide are often staged at Middle Eastern American theatre companies. The events of the plays harken back to the Middle East itself since many Armenian villages were in present-day Turkey. Therefore, some Armenians were, at one time, technically Middle Easterners. This is not to mention the fact that many Armenians are still Middle Easterners with vibrant communities in present-day Lebanon, Israel, Iran, Cyprus, Syria, and Jordan.

Middle Eastern Americans and the Transnational Belonging

Middle Eastern Americans often claim hyphenated identities that include transnational belonging. The idea of transnationalism is a complex identity formation that includes notions of integration, assimilation, and acculturation in American society with ongoing ties and interactions with their societies of origin. Daniel Naujoks writes that, regarding countries of origin, there are three distinct types of membership: ethnic, national, and civic. Ethnic membership denotes those who identify with other co-ethnics in the host country and around the world; civic membership denotes identification with the home state, central state, or region; and national membership is membership with people living in the home country (either all people or subgroups of those people). Although Naujoks is clear that none of these markers is unequivocal or uncontested, they provide a complex understanding of the various factors that comprise diasporic individuals and their sense of transnational being (Naujoks 2010, 4–5).

Middle Eastern Americans, like other diasporic groups, are sometimes torn between their various identities. Like other groups who come from nations that are in conflict with the United States, these citizens feel the particularly difficult push and pull factors in their lives that often lead to day-to-day dilemmas. Some immigrants from nations that are, or were, embroiled in horrific civil wars immigrate to the Americas bearing the psychological and physical trauma they endured. Others, who survived wars that were either waged by the United States or by allies of the United States, face a peculiar schism—how to live in a country that has opened its doors to them and allowed them citizenship and a better way of life, while simultaneously causing the grievous situation that forced them to immigrate from their home nations. Many Middle Eastern Americans hail from countries that suffered the civil wars that devastated countries like Lebanon, Yemen, Syria, Libya, and Algeria. Others come from nations that had a direct military conflict with the United States such as Iraq. Still others are from countries that are facing occupation such as the Palestinian population living in the Palestinian territories. Yet others are facing the brutal crackdowns imposed by those who are backed by the United States such as immigrants from Egypt and Bahrain. Increased tensions and threats of military conflicts with Middle Eastern nations have also caused great distress such as the worsening ties between the United States and Iran. Amnesty International cites the fact that, since the so-called Arab Spring in 2011, conditions in Middle Eastern countries have worsened. More than 250,000 people have been killed and more than 11 million have been displaced from Syria; the so-called Islamic State has killed scores of civilians and prisoners in Syria and Iraq. Over 8,000 have been killed and 42,000 injured in Yemen; 2.5 million people need humanitarian assistance and protection in Libya, and 22,000 people have been arrested in Egypt (Amnesty International 2018).

These conflicts have a devastating effect on the Middle Easterners living in European and North American nations. According to Lindencrona, Ekblad, and Hauff, post-traumatic stress disorder and other common mental disorders are common problems among refugees. Exposure to severe traumatic events in the refugees' lives explains a higher prevalence of mental disorder. Furthermore, research has shown that so-called post-migration stressors, such as those experienced in the resettlement process, are contributors to the increase in mental distress in refugee populations, particularly those exposed to torture trauma (Lindencrona et al. 2008, 121). Other studies show that many refugees knew friends or family members who were victims of violence, many were imprisoned themselves, and being imprisoned many suffered physical and psychological torture (Hondius 2000, 626).

Middle Eastern Americans have endured generations of trauma from the events of the pre–First World War conflicts, through the two world wars, colonialism, civil wars, political upheavals, mass migrations, occupations, and contemporary wars fought with drones, suicide bombings, and other military means. Therefore, these immigrants sometimes have hybrid identities and/or dual loyalties that can cause conflicting attachments. The connections they have with their family and friends overseas, who are sometimes caught in various conflict zones, cause great strain for Middle Eastern Americans. Of course, those Middle Eastern Americans who settled in the United States long ago, and their descendants, often have only a symbolic ethnicity, or nostalgic allegiance to the so-called old country. Some are so far removed that they rarely think of their Middle Eastern roots as anything more than a remnant of their family's history. For others, the bond is extremely strong with families traveling to the Middle East on a regular basis with their children to maintain language and cultural ties to the home country. Some nations actively promote connections to the homeland, like those who take the "Birthright Israel" trip, which is open to those who "identify as Jewish and are recognized by such by their local community or by one of the recognized denominations of Judaism," who have at least one Jewish birth parent, or who have completed Jewish conversion through a recognized Jewish denomination (Birthright Israel). Others who are persecuted in their home countries, such as those who adhere to the Bahá'i Faith in Iran, find other ways of remaining connected such as the Bahá'i Institute for Higher Education (BIHE), which is committed to educating and empowering Bahá'i youth in Iran by enlisting volunteers worldwide to take courses that help BIHE graduates to secure graduate studies at over ninety-eight prestigious universities and colleges in North America, Europe, Australia, and India (bihe.org).

To make matters worse, there have been periodic persecutions of Middle Eastern Americans throughout recent history. In the post-9/11 era, hate crimes and bias incidents spiked in the United States. According to the Council on American-Islamic Relations (CAIR) *Civil Rights Report 2017*, there was a 57 percent increase in anti-Muslim bias incidents over 2015. This was concurrent with a 44 percent increase in anti-Muslim hate crimes in the same period. From 2014 to 2016, anti-Muslim bias incidents jumped by 65 percent. In that two-year period, CAIR finds that hate crimes targeting Muslims surged 584 percent. There was also a rise in anti-Arab and anti-Semitic hate crimes. In 2015, law enforcement agencies in the United States reported 4,029 single-bias hate crime offenses based on race, ethnicity, and ancestry and of those 1.2 percent were classified as anti-Arab bias (FBI). There was a 6.8 percent increase in reported hate crimes against Arabs from 2014 to 2015. Additionally, anti-Jewish crimes have also spiked. The Anti-Defamation League's annual "Audit of Anti-Semitic Incidents" found significant and sustained increases in anti-Semitic incidents since 2016: "There was a massive increase in the amount of harassment of American Jews, particularly since November 2016, and a doubling in the amount of anti-Semitic bullying and vandalism at non-denominational K-12 schools." This is not to mention other ethno-religious South Asian American groups, such as the Sikhs, who are also attacked by domestic terrorists. One shooting incident at the Wisconsin Sikh Temple in 2012, which led to seven fatalities and the wounding of many others, was carried out by a US Army veteran with a white supremacist history (Williams 2012; CNN 2012).

Some of this persecution is fomented by misleading governmental information. The Department of Homeland Security issued a report stating that "three out of four individuals convicted of international terrorism and terrorism-related offences were foreign born" (DOJ, DHS 2018). However, critics have pointed out that the report was based only on an official list of terrorism cases produced by the Justice Department that limited those categories to "international terrorism." However, codirector of the Liberty and National Security Program at the Brennan Center for Justice at New York University, Faiza Patel, wrote that the Justice Department report failed to show that 73 percent of terrorism fatalities were caused by far-right extremists. Furthermore, half the convictions on the list are "terrorism-related" such as lying to authorities, selling untaxed cigarettes, forced marriage, and female genital mutilation. According to Patel, "the Trump administration is determined to ignore the complexity of the threat and to keep the focus on immigrants and Muslims because that suits its nativist agenda" (Patel 2018). Unfortunately for Middle Eastern Americans, the lack of governmental resources and the ongoing fearmongering of politicians and governmental agents continue to adversely affect this community.

Middle Eastern Americans and the US Census

Middle Eastern Americans have not had specific representation in the US Census since its inception in 1790. The first six inquiries in the 1790 Census included the following descriptions: "Free White males of 16 years and upward (to assess the country's industrial and military potential)," "Free White males under 16 years," "Free White females," "All other free persons," and "Slaves." The US Census Bureau currently lists those people who have origins from the Middle East or North Africa as "White." Although many scholars have outlined the history of this formation of whiteness by Middle Easterners, mostly accomplished through litigation from the courts, it is clear that the omission of a racial question that specifically mentions Middle Eastern Americans has deprived that constituency of the benefits of collecting information on race as proposed by the US Census Bureau: "Race data are also used to promote equal employment opportunities and to assess racial disparities in health and environmental risks."

This issue with the US Census has been a long-standing one, with some Middle Eastern Americans advocating for an individual category on the census that will include them while others, fearing governmental persecution, argue against such a move. For instance, during the Second World War, the United States used census data to deny land rights and to locate and displace more than 100,000 Japanese Americans to incarceration camps because Japanese immigrants were considered "aliens ineligible for citizenship" (Zaho 2014, 39). Advocates for the inclusion of this census data cite the fact that this group would have the opportunity to have policy makers understand the needs of Middle Eastern Americans and to appropriate more resources to health, education, voter protections, and resources for language (Chow 2017). Furthermore, some conservatives believe the categories on the US Census constitute "faux pan-ethnic groups" that "divide us as a people and which have no basis in science, culture, ethnicity or language" (Gonzalez 2017). Others, like Senior Political Analyst Michael Barone of the *Washington Examiner*, believe that race and national origin are often not congruent, and therefore there is no need for the race and ethnic questions on the US Census. Barone believes the solution lies either in the two-question format used in recent decades (such as "Are you Hispanic?" and "What is your race?") or in asking about national ancestry (Barone 2017). The MENA Advocacy Network was established to represent all communities from the MENA region within the US Census. Maya Berry, the executive director of the Arab American Institute, wrote in a 2016 article titled "A New MENA Category: The Reality and the Headlines,"

> What this category is about is visibility—visibility for a group of Americans that are seen only by our government when it comes to counterterrorism programming, and miss out when it comes to education, health care research, or English proficiency classes, to name a few examples. Improved data collection can have a real impact on people's lives. (Berry 2016)

All of this is to say that there is little consensus about the definition of Middle Eastern/North African Americans, and that even a seemingly straightforward notion such as a MENA census checkbox can cause great debate. As of January 2018, the Census Bureau has announced that the 2020 Census would not include a new "Middle Eastern or North African" category. According to the Arab American Institute,

> For the Arab American community, and many other stakeholders, the decision to cut the "Middle Eastern or North African" category from the 2020 Census is a severe blow. Years of undercounting have deprived our community of access to basic services and rights, from language assistance at polling places, to the allocation of educational grants for cultural competency training and language assistance, to greater access to health information and research. (Barry 2018)

Actions like these by the US Census Bureau further complicate how Middle Eastern Americans are treated and perceived in the United States. With such disagreement among the Middle Eastern American communities due to fear of further governmental persecution, a future MENA census category seems to be more of an aspiration than a reality.

The Polycultural and Middle Eastern Americans

Given the great diversity of the people of this region, and of the artists who identify as Middle Eastern Americans, the notion of "polyculturalism" is a useful framework for understanding this genre. In the book *Everybody Was*

Kung Fu Fighting: Afro-Asian Connections and the Myth of Cultural Purity, Vijay Prashad writes,

> Polyculturalism, unlike multiculturalism, assumes that people live coherent lives that are made up of a host of lineages—the task of the historian is not to carve out the lineages but to make sense of how people live culturally dynamic lives. Polyculturalism is a ferocious engagement with the political world of culture, a painful embrace of the skin and all its contradictions. (Prashad 2001, xi–xii)

Unlike multiculturalism, which wishes to claim a direct lineage from a place, polyculturalism allows for the notion that people may descend from multiple lineages and that humans are not necessarily categorized by nationality, culture, or religion. The notion that cultures influence one another over time, and that cultural borrowing is a norm, is the one that defines the polycultural ethos. Robin D. G. Kelley explains,

> "Polycultural" works better than "multicultural," which implies that cultures are fixed, discrete entities that exist side by side—a kind of zoological approach to culture. Such a view obscures power relations, but often reifies race and gender differences. (Kelley 1999)

Polyculturalism prizes diversity, acknowledges that cultures are "dynamic, interactive and impure," and views cultures as being in flux and connected (Haslam 2017). When one adds various other factors such as sexuality, sexual preference, and connection (or lack thereof) to the cultural groups to which one belongs, the notions of multicultural homogeneity become much less stable. In their book *Middle Eastern Lives in America*, Amir B. Marvasti and Karyn D. McKinney note,

> While the creation of a panethnic Middle Eastern identity might seem like an important step to overcoming the discrimination that members of this group face, it would be overly optimistic to assume that there is unanimous agreement on this course of action. There are many internal divisions among members of this group that block the aspiration of a panethnic identity. (Marvasti and McKinney 2004, 160)

If the internal divisions were not enough, there is also a desire by some in this community to fully claim "whiteness" to advance their position in

American society. In his book *Whitewashed: America's Invisible Middle Eastern Minority*, John Tehranian writes that Middle Eastern Americans have had a complicated and difficult relation to whiteness throughout their history in the United States.

> The negotiation of the Middle Eastern identity is mediated by a two-fold process that moves both from the top down and from the bottom up. From the top down, society at large engages in a practice that can be described as *selective racialization*. From the bottom up, Middle Easterners, both privileged and damned by their proximity to the white dividing line, engage in persistent (and frequently effective) covering of their ethnic background. These two social forces combine to create a pernicious stereotyping feedback loop that enervates the political strength of the Middle Eastern community, heightens its invisibility, and leaves little effective resistance to the growing assaults against its civil rights. (Tehranian 2010, 72)

The fact that Middle Easterners themselves are not homogeneous and (more often than not) claim tribal/religious, rather than national, identities makes this entire notion of polyculturalism an even more fraught enterprise. For instance, the nation of Lebanon, which was carved out of Greater Syria by the French in 1920, and which is only 10,500 square kilometers in size, contains 18 different religious sects. However, within those larger groups are multiple subgroups that all contain multiple ethnic and tribal affiliations. During, and after, migration to the United States there has been a great deal of intermarriage which further complicates the possibility of finding any type of consistent or pure lineage. In other words, the Lebanese were polycultural long before they ever reached the shores of the Americas and, in the ensuing years, that polyculturalism continues to flourish with greater diversity within this small population. When one considers the multiplicity of religions, ethnicities, cultures, nations, and tribes that constitute Middle Eastern persons, the awe-inspiring diversity of these cultures becomes too complex to grasp.

For the most part, however, Middle Eastern Americans tend to begin with an explanation of their national backgrounds such as "Turkish American" and "Iranian American." Others might identify as "Persian" instead of Iranian, or "Maronite" instead of Lebanese. As one continues to probe for more information, one realizes that there are multiple layers of identities that make up those who claim Middle Eastern heritage and identification is based less on ethnography and more on political or religious associations in the current moment. Furthermore, Marvasti and McKinney note that there should be a distinction made between Muslim immigration and Middle Eastern immigration, since those two waves took place during different eras and with different populations. Middle Eastern American artists focus their attentions on the various social, cultural, and ethical implications that face this group, creating literature that examines notions of being polycultural and transnational in America.

Middle Eastern American Literature

According to Susan Atefat-Peckham in the introduction to her book *Talking Through the Door: An Anthology of Contemporary Middle Eastern American Writing*, Middle Eastern American writing has several major traits: political marginality, the importance of tradition in "alien" environments, ethnic denial, isolation, the power of the extended family and the community, integration and assimilation of children into the dominant culture, loss of mother tongue, the difference between what America represents and what it is in reality, and the widening gulf between immigrant parents and their descendants born in the United States (Atefat-Peckham 2014, 18). Of course, many of these aspects are shared by a variety of diasporic American literary communities. I would add that there are other defining aspects that make Middle Eastern American works even more specific. These include

- **Transnational Conflict:** The Middle Eastern region has been at odds with the United States since the Barbary Wars of 1801–5 and 1815–16. With the heightened tensions since the foundation of Israel in 1948, and the subsequent wars with multiple Arab states since, the United States has been in various forms of conflict with Middle Eastern and North African states for generations. These conflicts are often reflected in Middle Eastern American literature.

- **Islam:** Since so many of the nations in the region identify as Muslim, and since the United States has been a nation that touts its Judeo-Christian values, there has been great anxiety and fear regarding Muslims in the United States. This has been the case since the first recorded Muslim, Estevanico, set foot in the so-called New World in 1528. Since the earliest times, the United States has maintained an anti-Muslim stance that is sometimes reflected in literary production. Of course, not all those hailing from the Middle East are Muslims (as a matter of fact, Indonesia hosts the largest Muslim population in the world), but the perception that the majority from the region are Muslim is pervasive and difficult to change.

- **Anti-Semitism:** There has been a strong anti-Semitic fervor in the United States from its earliest history. As Arabs and Jews are both Semites, the fear of their infiltration and miscegenation has led to terrible anti-Semitic violence. This, too, is reflected in the literature of Middle Eastern Americans.

- **Omission of Literature:** It is striking that one could attend multiple levels of education in the United States and may never read a Middle Eastern American writer. For some reason, writers from the Middle East, or of Middle Eastern descent, simply do not occupy the same hierarchical structure in American academia as other international or diasporic writers. This also extends to bookstores, where early Arab American writers are sometimes shelved under "Spirituality" or "Eastern Religion" rather than with other American novelists or poets.

Some contemporary writers in this genre include Elmaz Abinader, Kathryn K. Abdul-Baki, Hala Alyan, Diana Abu-Jaber, Sara Deniz Akant, Rabih Alameddine, Mona Awad, Albert Issac Bezzerides, William Peter Blatty, Michelle Chalfoun, Hayan Charara, Miriam Cooke, Firoozeh Dumas, Safia Elhillo, Laila Halaby, Mohja Kahf, Pauline Kaldas, Porochista Khakpour, Lena Khalaf Tuffaha, Laila Lalami, Shahriar Mandanipour, Khaled Mattawa, Azadeh Moaveni, Azar Nafisi, Orhan Pamuk, Patricia Sarrafian Ward, Marjane Satrapi, Samia Serageldin, Naomi Shihab Nye, Leora Skolkin-Smith, Dalia Sofer, and Ayelet Waldman. With more Middle Eastern American writers publishing their works, teaching these works in academic settings, and gaining more widespread recognition there is a heightened awareness of this genre and the cultures represented therein.

Middle Eastern American Diasporic Cultural Production

One of the diasporic identities that define Middle Eastern Americans is that of a "diasporic-cultural identification," defined as an attachment to cultural traditions, values, and culture as identification with the ethnic group and with the nation itself. Therefore, a form of ethnic and transnational group bonding takes place that retains a strong attachment to culture and heritage (Naujoks 2010, 7). Middle Eastern American artists have taken it upon themselves to incorporate their ethnic and diasporic identities not only as influences on their work but rather as the primary focal point of their cultural production. These artists, who regularly identify with hyphenated identities, see their ancestral homelands as equally valuable in their lives and experiences as their identities as Americans. This bifurcated identification serves both as a site of strength and pain, since it situates them in the interstitial, in-between space they inhabit. On the one hand, they are legally Americans through birth or through legal citizenship; however, they retain the markers of their ethnic/transnational belongings physically and/or emotionally. This transnational condition is one that demands that they adhere to the notion that they are fully invested in their Americanness, while simultaneously experiencing the pressures of belonging to their ethnic group and the concomitant cultural and religious expectations that accompany that identification.

For many, turning to cultural production is the way they address this inner schism they face. For Arab American scholar Carol Fadda-Conrey, Arab American cultural production,

> constitutes a formative moment in self-iterations (literary and otherwise) that insist on portraying Arab-Americans through a transnational and anti-homogeneous lens. This formative moment has mobilized more vocal, assertive, and unapologetic claims to transnational enactments of Arab-American identities that problematize the assimilative pressures inherent in dominant performances of US citizenship and belonging. (Fadda-Conrey 2014, 140–1)

Middle Eastern American theatre artists are committed to telling stories of those who are often neglected, unseen, or omitted from American theatre cultural discourses. These writers and performers, who have cultural (and sometimes citizenship) ties to their ancestral homelands, are not content to allow others to tell their stories, nor are they content to have their stories told in a stereotypical or damaging manner. The dehumanizing stereotypes that pervade contemporary American culture's depiction of Middle Eastern Americans are both pervasive and self-perpetuating. Marvasti and McKinney write, "Fears of the ethnic others are manifested in cultural notions that they possess every characteristic that we do not. These characteristics then become stereotypes, and one can trace through the history of the United States how many of the same images are applied to different groups" (Marvasti and McKinney 2004, 108). Middle Easterners are portrayed in a variety of damaging and stereotypical ways including money-obsessed Jews, avaricious and sex-mad Arab oil sheikhs, turbaned sultans with scimitars, burka-clad suicide bombers, scantily clad belly dancers, and snake charmers to name a few. These one-dimensional portrayals are what Jack G. Shaheen labeled as "The New Anti-Semitism," which he defined as new,

> not because stereotypical screen Arabs are new (they aren't) or because anti-Semitism against Jews is dead (it's not). I use the word "new" because many of the anti-Semitic films directed against Arabs were released in the last third of the twentieth century, at a time when Hollywood was steadily and increasingly eliminating stereotypical portraits of other groups. (Shaheen 2001, 6)

Benshoff and Griffin write about the "veiled and reviled" nature of Middle Easterners in American film. They note that the regularity of images of Middle Easterners in films is in contrast with the relative scarcity of Middle Easterners in Hollywood itself. Instead, Arab characters are sexualized, Orientalized, or depicted as terrorists.

> rarely have Arabs been shown becoming part of the fabric of either European or American communities. There has been an attitude among many that people of Arab heritage cannot assimilate into Western society [. . .] just as Irish and Italian Catholic Americans were once considered unable to assimilate because they supposedly held a stronger allegiance to the pope than the president, so too do many today assume that Arab Americans pledge allegiance to the Muslim faith and not to the United States. (Benshoff and Griffin 2009, 72)

Jews also had difficulties with the racial stereotyping in Hollywood films, especially in the early twentieth century. Despite many becoming leaders of major studios during the classical Hollywood era, Jews in Hollywood were still encouraged to assimilate, change their names, and sublimate their Jewishness due to prejudices that were rampant in a larger white society

(Gabler 1988, 4–5). Iranian Americans, who often refer to themselves as Persians to distance themselves from the connection with the current Islamic regime that is ruling the country and from the ongoing conflict between the United States and Iran, also sometimes sublimate their identities due to prejudices against them through manipulation of their names and through accent reduction (Tehranian 2009, 76–89).

Inherent to all these issues, of course, is the conflation of one's religious affiliation, national origin, and racial identification. For instance, Tehranian writes that many Iranians or Arabs of Jewish backgrounds often pass or cover by exploiting what many perceive (or misperceive) as Jewishness. Other Iranians affiliate themselves with being "Persian" rather than "Iranian" since Persia has a perception of a long-lost civilization of empire, complex artistic history, and Zoroastrianism (as opposed to Islam) (Tehranian 2009, 85). Middle Eastern American artists also struggle with many issues regarding how they are perceived by artistic organizations. Many believe that they are either pigeonholed as Middle Eastern American artists who can only write about topics that pertain to their cultural backgrounds, or they must suppress their identity and write plays that will somehow appeal to the mainstream. This either/or dichotomy frustrates many of these artists since they know that most professional theatres will only program one "ethnic" play per season (if at all), and that all the various writers of color will be vying for that coveted position. When their plays are chosen, they then must deal with the fact that, most likely, a director not affiliated with that culture will direct that play and, by doing so, may not bring the requisite cultural background or sensitivity to the production. One playwright lamented the fact that, even after their play was chosen and produced by a mainstream theatre, the banner outside the theatre had completely miswritten the Arabic title. These pressing issues are central to the state of Middle Eastern American artistic production and require a comprehensive approach that can address these situations. Playwright/actress Heather Raffo states,

> one personal marker of success would be if I someday get asked to write about something other than Iraq. I think our value as MENA artists is how we move through the world, what we understand about it, and how we have been bridging seemingly incommensurable cultures. This talent can be brought in many ways into the American theatre beyond just the telling of Middle Eastern stories. (Considine 2017)

So, while these artists are in demand for their perspectives on the Middle East, it seems the only topic theatre companies are interested in producing are these Middle Eastern perspectives.

Some of the central questions that face MEA artists are the following: Can one be a Middle Eastern American theatre artist *and* an accepted "American" artist? What are the difficulties inherent to self-identifying as Middle Eastern American artists? How can MEA artists simultaneously write Middle Eastern stories without sacrificing the ability to be considered a playwright who can write about different topics in different genres? Can or should an MEA artist from one region write about another region? How can the MEA term be more inclusive of all the various tribal, religious, cultural, social, and political groups that constitute the Middle East and its diaspora?

The following chapters are meant to introduce these diverse artists, examine their cultural production, and explore how these artists navigate the perilous landscape of professional American theatre without compromising themselves in the process. This is the challenge facing MEA artists as they continue to write, act in, direct, and produce plays that deal with the exigencies of being both artists of color and self-identifying as Middle Eastern Americans. For many of these artists, this is less a burden than a calling because they are weary of how mainstream film, television, and theatre has misrepresented their cultures. Therefore, the need to create these works becomes a powerful and necessary opportunity to contribute to a growing body of literature and performance even if the social and economic climate is often unwelcoming of their work. For the few theatres that support this work, the desire to tell these stories outweighs the lack of financial and material reward that other mainstream theatres garner through works that are more widely recognized and attended.

However, the rewards for these artists lie in their ability to tell the stories of those who came before them and were unable to speak about the experiences and atrocities of the past. Regarding Arab American drama, Rashad Rida writes, "For it to be meaningful, it must signify more than plays written by someone whose ethnicity is Arab and who lives in America. It must involve a perspective that is in some meaningful way affected by Arab culture" (Rida 2003, 158–9). Middle Eastern American artists tell stories of the European Holocaust and the Armenian Genocide survivors, of those who died in wars like the Lebanese and Syrian civil wars, of those who fought and died during the so-called Arab Spring uprisings, of Palestinians dealing with the trauma of occupation, of Middle Eastern Americans who face homophobic persecution by those inside and outside their communities, and of migrants desperate to reach Europe to flee wars and persecution in Africa. All these stories are ones that these artists attempt to address as a way of dealing with the bitter reality of life in the diaspora. By hearing these perspectives, audiences can gain a greater view into these fascinating cultures and the people within them. Most importantly, they can gain empathy with those who have suffered so much yet fought for a new life in a new land known as America.

Middle Eastern American Theatre

Each diasporic community has its own cultural production. The factors that dictate the diasporic cultural production of each group varies due to the group's history in the United States, the types of literature these groups produce, and the cultural centers where most of the artistic production is found. While there are many similarities in this cultural production, this kind of literature is the output of diasporic communities that are struggling with many of the same issues including leaving homeland, attempting to survive and thrive in North America, issues surrounding marriage and endogamy, and navigating attitudes regarding sexuality. Each playwright addresses these issues differently based on their own perspective within their cultural group. The four major groups mentioned here are by far the largest groups producing theatre, but they are not the only ones.

Arab American Theatre

Arab American theatre is also a problematic umbrella under which to place those who come from, or are descendants of immigrants from, the twenty-two Arab nations. Of course, not everyone who is from this area considers themselves Arab. There are many minority groups that live within the Arab nations that do not consider themselves Arabs such as the Maronites of the Levant, the Kurds, the Amazigh/Berbers, or the Yazidis, to name a few. The shared Arabic language is one of the hallmarks of what constitutes an Arab, yet not all Arabic speakers are of that group. Others point to Islam as a unifying factor, but not all people from the Middle East are Muslims and not all Arabs are Muslims either. Steven Salaita words it this way:

> Arab Americans are Muslim (Shia and Sunni and Alawi and Isma'ili), Christian (Catholic and Orthodox, Anglican and Evangelical,

and Mainline Protestant), Jewish (Orthodox and Conservative and Haredi and Reform), Druze, Bahai, dual citizens of Israel and twenty-two Arab nations, multi- and monolingual, progressives and conservatives, assimilationists and nationalists, cosmopolitanists and pluralists, immigrants and fifth-generation Americans, wealthy and working-class, rural and urban, modern and traditional, religious and secular, White and Black, Latin American and Canadian. We also occupy the many spaces between these binaries. Sometimes Arab Americans are non-Arabs such as Circassians, Armenians, Berbers, Kurds and Iranians. We are likely to inhabit any American industry and are represented across the social and political spectrums of the United States. (2007, 1)

Given that expansive definition, it is nearly impossible to neatly categorize this group. Their early great migration to the United States, starting in the 1800s, was mainly of Syrians from Greater Syria, and was mainly composed of Christians. This changed over time with different waves of immigration, and now Arab American immigrants are from a diversity of Arab states and of many faiths and traditions.

The early Syrian/Lebanese American writers Kahlil Gibran, Ameen Fares Rihani, and Mikhail Naimy were all playwrights in addition to their more well-known works as poets and novelists. Gibran, Rihani, Naimy, and other Syrian/Lebanese immigrants created a writing group known as The Pen Group in 1920. This group aimed to "lift Arabic literature from the quagmire of stagnation and imitation, and to infuse a new life into its veins so as to make of it an active force in the building up of the Arab nations" (Nu'aima 1974, 154). The Pen Group, which also included members Elia Abu Madi, Nasseeb Arida, Wadih Bahout, William Catzeflis, Rasheed Ayoub, Abdul-Massih Haddad, and Nudra Haddad, is credited for the Arab literary movement known as al-Nahda, or The Arab Cultural Awakening, which lasted from 1870 to 1950. The group disbanded shortly after Gibran's death in 1931. Although these plays were never produced in the United States, they did mark the beginnings of Arab American dramatic output in the early twentieth century. In his essay "Issues of Identity: In Theater of Immigrant Community," Ala Fa'ik writes that early Arab American immigrants created and produced plays about Arab history in their cultural clubs and organizations. The Egyptian Arabic periodical *Al-Mushir* reported on an 1896 performance of a play titled *Andromak* that was performed in New York by the Syrian Youth Society, "which had a large audience of 'Syrians' and Americans" (Suleiman 2006, 488). At Ellis Island there is a large photograph of seventeen actors in costume with an inset of a young man's face titled "Amateur Drama Group of Lebanese Immigrants, Utica, New York, ca. 1910. This company performed until the 1940s" (Faris and Yamna Naff). There were other scattered performances by Middle Eastern Americans in the ensuing years between the 1940s and the 1970s. For instance, Lebanese American comic and actor Danny Thomas performed "Ode to a Wailing Syrian," where he wore a tablecloth over his head, spoke Arabic, and lamented the death of Syrians due to famine and revolt against the Ottomans. This performance piece was a comedy, and was Thomas's calling card for Hollywood. Another performance was Lebanese American playwright S. K. Hershewe's comedy about a Lebanese girl falling for a Jewish boy in his play *An Oasis in Manhattan*, which premiered in 1965 at the Stage Society Theater in Los Angeles starring Alan Reed and Vic Tayback (*Los Angeles Times* 1965). Tayback later revived the play in Los Angeles where he starred in the leading role.

By the 1980s there were more concentrated approaches to theatre by Arab American immigrant communities, mainly by nonprofessional troupes. The Baghdad Theatre, founded in 1985 by Salah Kulato in Detroit, had produced fifteen plays by 1999 (Ameri 2000, 246). Another Detroit company, Firqat al-Yaoum (Today's Cast), founded in 1987 by Hussam Zorro, had produced eight plays by 1999. These companies performed in an Iraqi Arabic dialect that focused on immigration and the difficulties immigrants faced in the United States (Ameri 2000, 246). Another Detroit company, the Arab Theatrical Arts Guild (ATAG), was founded in 1998 to promote an interest in the performing arts within the Arab American community. They produced plays by American and Arab playwrights (Ameri 2000, 247).

The Arab American Children's Theater Company, founded in California in 1989, produced plays such as *The Festival* by Hammam Shafie with music composed by Faheem Said. Shafie explained that the goal of the Los Angeles-based company was to provide "a place where kids learn to experiment, explore, and perform their culture, heritage, history, and values which makes it real for them" (Fa'ik 1994, 113). The Kanaaqeel Theater Group, founded in 1998 in Los Angeles, also worked to "explore cultural issues of importance" (Kayyali 2006, 130). Another company from Los Angeles, founded by Arab American anthropologist and filmmaker Fadwa El Guindi, was Al-Fanun Al-Arabiya (Arab Arts). Their most prominent production, written by Ahmed Ahmed and Fadwa El Guindi, was titled

Mahjar, produced in May and June of 1996 at the Ruby Theatre at The Complex Hollywood, California. The play was described as

> [an] original Arab-American bilingual dramatization, in two acts, of life in America as told and lived by Arabs in the community, blending American with traditional & classical Art theater forms with poetry by Khalil Gibran & Maya Angelou and music by Jihad Racy & Marcel Khalife [. . .] MAJHAR is not about any one family, any one country, any one Arabic dialect, or any one experience. Arab-Americans everywhere will find their story embedded in MAHJAR. (*Mahjar* 1996)

Gradually more plays by, and about Middle Eastern Americans, were created in the 1990s. One production, *Ghurba*, by writer/director Shishir Kurup, was a Los Angeles Festival production performed at MacGowan Hall at UCLA in 1993. Taken from testimonies by Arab Americans living in Southern California, the play "wove oral histories into a complex tapestry, then added fragments from the sayings of Jesus, the poetry of Sufi mystic Rabia Al-Adawiya and the writings of Palestinians Mahmoud Darwish and Edward Said. Even a W.B. Yeats play, 'Purgatory,' has been mixed into Kurup's text, alongside Arabic music and dance" (Stayton 1993). The play was coproduced with Cornerstone Theater Company and Al-Funun Al-Arabiya. The play received good reviews and *The Daily News* critic Daryl H. Miller wrote, "There is no plot, really—just the unfolding pageant of life. In the process, the audience is treated to traditional songs and a taste of the vendor's sautéed eggplant [. . .] one can't help but be charmed by the energy and sincerity of its cast of professionals and everyday people" (Miller 1993). Chapter 1 will focus on the Arab American theatre companies that were founded in the post-9/11 period. Suffice it to say Arab American theatre is a genre that is one of the oldest among Middle Eastern American communities.

Iranian American Theatre

For Iranian Americans, there were many changes in Iran during the twentieth century from the Constitutional Revolution of 1906, to the Islamic Revolution of 1979. In addition, Iranians come from many different religious traditions, despite wrongly considered by many to be predominantly Islamic. Many Iranians are proud of their rich literary history that includes the great poets Omar Khayyam, Hafez, Saadi, and Rumi. According to Daniel Grassian, there is a great deal of diasporic literature and Iranian literature translated into English in the form of fiction and memoirs. Iranian and Iranian American literatures have been marginalized in the United States, especially in the academy. Grassian states that Iranian diasporic literature is characterized by a sense of alienation combined with a longing for a lost life in the homeland. That said, "many diasporic Iranian writers and diasporic Iranian characters, both first- and second-generation Westerners, strive to be and sometimes succeed in becoming something more than alienated exiles" (Grassian 2013, 5). In addition, Iranian American literature does not neatly fit in the category of Asian American literature or postcolonial literature. Western media persists in stereotyping Iranians as fanatical, violent, and anti-American, or depicting Iranian Americans as spoiled rich immigrants living in Southern California. Films also continue to perpetuate historical inaccuracies regarding past conflicts. Benshoff and Griffin write that the film *300* "seemed almost designed to exploit and capitalize on current anti-Arab and anti-Muslim feelings in American culture; its grotesque stereotyping encourages audiences to hate and fear its Persian characters while simultaneously inflaming and justifying white masculine violence" (Benshoff and Griffin 2009, 74). This is but one of the many films that continually denigrate Iranians/Persians being produced and distributed in mainstream entertainment.

However, Iranian Americans are actively fighting against these stereotypes. The generation of Iranian diasporic writers born from the early 1960s to the early 1980s, known as "the Burnt Generation," dealt with the strife of the Iran-Iraq War, the rise of the Islamic Republic, and a bleak economic environment. However, this generation was very technologically savvy, highly educated, and more willing to embrace democratic reforms. The generations that followed that were born and raised in North America continue to write about the difficulties of being othered in North American society, conflated and confused with Arabs, and treated with scorn after 9/11 even though no Iranians had anything to do with the attacks. That said, diasporic Iranian writers and Iranian Americans continue to write about their unique experiences in the United States.

With so little known about Iran and so much presumed about it in the Western world, Iranian and Iranian diasporic literature serve a crucial role of educating the Western public about Iran as a country, and, if the texts find their way (legally or illegally) through or by Iranian censorship, providing insight into the West for those living in Iran. (Grassian 2013, 18)

Indeed, even within Iran itself the theatre scene is rich, vibrant, and transgressive. In her article "Dramatic Defiance in Tehran: Reflections on a Society of Contradictions," Torange Yeghiazarian writes that governmental authorities still regulate what can or cannot be staged; however, the productions she witnessed there were aesthetically and politically challenging. Theatre students in Iran see the theatre as a powerful tool for changing society. "For these students," Yeghiazarian writes, "the practice of democracy and cultural change begins in the theatre workshop" (Yeghiazarian 2012, 90). That said, many theatre artists have fled Iran due to persecution and censorship; the question remains whether they will be allowed to return and work in theatres there in the future. Iranian artists who have left Iran including Parvis Sayyad, Farzaneh Taidi, and Arbi Avanesian have brought the same political and social activism to the works they stage in the Americas. Between their works, and the works of Iranian Americans, there is a rich artistic community that continues to shape the Middle Eastern American theatre aesthetic. Chapter 1 will highlight several Iranian American theatre groups including Darvag Theater Group.

Jewish and Israeli American Theatre

In his book *Beyond the Golden Door: Jewish American Drama and Jewish American Experience*, Julius Novick writes that, although there has not been a paucity of Jewish playwrights, after the Second World War many of these playwrights did not concern themselves with writing Jewish protagonists with Jewish themes: "Instead, like the Jewish studio heads who ruled Hollywood, like the Jewish creators of *Archie* and *Superman* comics, they conjured up worlds where everybody is ethnically neutral, with an Anglo-Saxon name, except perhaps for some secondary comic types capering in the background" (2008, 1). Jewish American playwrights like George S. Kaufman, Moss Hart, and Lillian Hellman rarely created Jewish characters in their major works. It is Novick's contention that writers are not necessarily expected to write about their backgrounds: "I reject the idea, tenaciously held in some quarters, that a writer who is a member of a minority group has some kind of moral duty to be always the representative of that minority group" (2008, 3). Therefore, the notion that one must bring one's ethnicity into their writing seemed not to be a preoccupation with these earlier playwrights.

Despite Novick's claim, in her introduction to the anthology *Fruitful & Multiplying: 9 Contemporary Plays from the American Jewish Repertoire*, Ellen Schiff writes that Jews have been writing plays about Jews since the 1920s. Plays written about Jews were not always positive representations. "It is exoticism rather than racism that once distinguished drama about Jewish life. Well into the second half of the century, Jewishness on stage continued to be regarded as foreign" (1996, xvi). In Schiff's view, by the second half of the twentieth century, Jews became very comfortable writing about their American Jewish experiences. Schiff also states, "In no sphere have Jewish artists contributed more to the Jewish image in American culture than the theatre" (1996, xvii). Schiff also distinguishes between the American Jewish and the Yiddish stage. American Jewish theatre has the objective of "representing Jews or Jewish life intelligibly to the theatergoing public," whereas Yiddish theatre has a different style, tone, and point of view. In her book *Yiddish Empire—The Vilna Troupe, Jewish Theater, and the Art of Itinerancy*, Debra Caplan explains that Yiddish theatre emerged in the 1870s, but it was quickly dismissed by Jewish intellectuals. However, within decades, it became one of the most important and influential theatre forms. Yiddish theatre was simultaneously transgressive and regressive. On the transgressive front, the Yiddish theatre attempted to bring fewer elite audiences into the theatre to access a broader audience, which would include non-Jewish spectators. However, Yiddish theatre also introduced plots, characters, and motifs of ancient Greek tragedy (Caplan 2018, 405). This replaced polytheistic Greek gods within a monotheistic Jewish theology. Also, the writers would emphasize biblical and national themes to make them familiar to Jewish audiences. They also revised the "morally ambiguous material characters to align with the more familiar archetype of the overly devoted *Yidishe mame* of the Jewish stage" (ibid., 406). Of course, Yiddish theatre provided great music, performance, and humor as well and many of the actors in this genre went on to become stars of the stage and screen.

Later Jewish American playwrights, however, were more attracted to the art theatre models of Euro-American theatre. The playwrights of note such as Clifford Odets, Neil Simon, Paddy Chayefsky, Herb Gardner, David Mamet, Wendy Wasserstein, Tony Kushner, and Jon Robin Baitz created plays that were written in English, set in realistic settings, told Jewish stories, and expressed the intelligence, humor, and drama of a community that continued to refine the art and create some of the greatest works of contemporary American theatre. Schiff notes that the major themes in this genre include the family play, a focus on Jewish heritage, an exploration of what it means to be Jewish, the quest to be a Jew, and plays that center Israel as their theme. In his book *Acting Jewish: Negotiating Ethnicity on the American Stage*, Henry Bial writes that, from 1947 to the early twenty-first century, performances created by Jews for mass consumption occupy the space he calls "acting Jewish," which is a formulation of Jewish American identity based on "double coding." This is a performance that communicates one message to Jewish audiences while simultaneously communicating another (often contradictory) message to gentile audiences (Bial 2005, 3). In Bial's view, Jewish Americans may have the means of production that other groups might not have, but they must "reform" their performances because of real, or perceived, anti-Semitism. "Acting Jewish" then is a dialectic tension between being too specific and being universal; there is the desire to assert the specificity of Jewish experience yet simultaneously speak to a universal human condition (ibid., 4). Bial focuses on several historical periods: 1947–55 (the era of *Death of a Salesman*), 1964–71 (the era of *Fiddler on the Roof*), 1968–83 (the works defined by Barbra Streisand and Woody Allen), 1989–97 (the era of *Angels in America*, *The Sisters Rosensweig*, and *The Old Neighborhood*), and the current state of Jewish theatre, which seeks to create an imagined community that is defined as an interaction between the spectator and the performance. Bial reminds readers that "Jewish" and "American" needn't be mutually exclusive categories since they are not fixed or static identities.

> Acting Jewish as a formulation of identity should thus be understood as a processual, provisional, and always already contested performance that circulates between the two worlds of essentialism (insistence on the authentic) and postmodernism (all authenticities are equal, which is to say nothing is authentic). (Bial 2005, 15–16)

As these critics point out, Jewish American theatre is a diverse, ever-changing landscape that continues to define the American theatre as a whole.

Regarding Israeli American theatre, Holly Hill writes that "Though their members may not be or may not identify themselves as Israeli-American or Middle-Eastern-American, there are established Jewish theatres in the U.S. that have welcomed Middle Eastern/Middle Eastern-American issues and artists" (Hill and Amin 2009, xxvii). According to actor/playwright Danny Bryck, there are a few important ideas that should be considered when utilizing the moniker "Israeli American." First, one should not conflate being Jewish with being Israeli or Middle Eastern; to do so runs the risk of categorizing all Jews as having Middle Eastern heritage, or of being Zionist in orientation. There are also Jews who are Middle Eastern or have Middle Eastern roots (such as Mizrahi/Sephardi Jews) who are not Israeli, so to conjoin all of these communities into an Israeli identity might erase those histories. Also, Bryck notes, there is the issue of locating Israel and Israeliness within the larger landscape of Middle Eastern identities, given Israel's perception by some in the region as a settler colonial state (Bryck 2019).

Whether these plays are categorized as "Middle Eastern American" plays is debatable. Some playwrights gladly embrace the moniker, while others may not. Regardless, the topics that are explored in many of these plays, especially those that focus on issues related to the Middle East, are very much in alignment with the genre and its specific characteristics. In his *Howlround* essay "Jewish Theater: Every Good Question Deserves Another Question," David Winitsky, artistic director of New York's Jewish Plays Project, attempts to define Jewish theatre. He begins by postulating that many would first think of plays and productions like a Yiddish *King Lear*, *The Diary of Anne Frank*, and *Fiddler on the Roof*, or "your orthodontist in *Little Shop* at the local JCC" (Winitsky 2014). He claims that all the tools for Jewish theatre are present: millennia-old traditions of argument and dialogue, mysticism and magic, a love for the intellectual and the idealistic, a deep attachment to texts, cultural history filled with great stories, tragedy, and lots of humor. That said, Winitsky believes there are several subjects that seem to dominate contemporary Jewish theatre: dysfunctional families and the Holocaust, realism, and a disconnect between the artists who create theatre and the theatre community for which the art is created.

> As Jewish artists—and in some ways American Jews overall—distance themselves from core parts of their cultural inheritance, we start to get a Jewish theatre that is too general, too devoted to the easy joke, the pat historical record, or the cultural stereotype to stir the kind of emotions we want our audience to feel. (Winitsky 2014)

This, he finds, coupled with a Jewish community that has shifted right, conservative, and with unswerving support for Israel, has led to a lack of support for the artists that challenge the status quo. To remedy this, he proposes several solutions: a greater embrace of the mystical from the ancient texts, an invitation to collaborate with more non-Jewish artists, a deeper discussion about Israel/Palestine, less focus on topics of anti-Semitism and the Holocaust, and a focus on the present over the past. Chapter 1 introduces several important Jewish American theatres that are actively promoting these ideas, and creating a new body of Jewish American theatre.

Turkish American Theatre

Perhaps the genre that is least documented is that of Turkish American theatre. According to John J. Grabowski, initially there was a small immigration of Muslim Turks from the Ottoman Empire to the United States. The period from 1890 to 1924 saw the greatest emigration of Muslim Turks, and members of the non-Muslim millets from the Ottoman Empire to ports in New York, Boston, and Providence, Rhode Island (Grabowski 2008, 18). This emigration was mainly economic and political: there were good wages found in the United States, American Protestant missionaries encouraged their pupils to emigrate, and the Ottoman administration's compulsory military service for non-Muslims led many to escape (İpek and Tuncer Çağlayan 2008, 29). The number of Ottoman subjects who migrated to the United States was between 500,000 and 1,000,000. The strict immigration regulations imposed after the Second World War led to very small numbers, and since the 1970s, the number of Turkish immigrants to the United States has risen to more than 2,000 per year. The total population of Turkish immigrants in the United States is estimated at 100,000 to 400,000 persons. Many immigrants settled in or around large urban centers such as New York, Boston, Chicago, Detroit, Los Angeles, San Francisco, and Rochester (Altschiller).

In her book *Towards Turkish American Literature*, Elena Furlanetto describes Turkish American writers as "binational writers of Turkish origin with strong biographical and literary ties to the United States" who engage with issues related to Turkey, but also the relationship between Turkey and America (2017, 11). Although Furlanetto focuses on writers that are oriented more toward Turkey than the Americas, she does call this a strongly bicultural literature written in English that engages with issues regarding ethnicity, identity, and dual citizenship. Also, the novelists she includes such as Halide Edip Adivar, Shirin Devrim, Selma Ekrem, and Elif Shafak write literature that do not reproduce immigrant success stories, or migrant fiction that focuses on the balancing of two cultural traditions. Instead it is a cosmopolitan literature of elite frequent travelers who write from a vantage point not necessarily accessible to working, or low-income classes (ibid., 19). For her part, Verena Laschinger writes that "Turkish American" does not represent a timeless, static, or essential ethnic category but, rather, a social construct that is carved out of political, social, and ideological conflicts. Like other Middle Eastern American groups, Turkish American authors also deal with issues of deep-seated prejudices against Turks and a proliferation of anti-Turkish images (Laschinger 2016, 114).

Regarding Turkish American theatre specifically, there are several prominent playwrights and directors who identify as such and have created works of note since the late twentieth century. The most famous of these would be Sinan Ünel, whose plays *Pera Palas*, *The Three of Cups*, and *The Cry of the Reed* are fine examples of Turkish American playwriting produced at the highest levels of American theatre. Another prominent playwright, Melis Aker, has also written exemplary plays in this genre including *Field, Awakening*; *When My Mama Was a Hittite*; *Guilded Isle*; *Manar*; and *Dragonflies*. Turkish American director Evren Odcikin has directed at many major American theatres, was named Interim Associate Artistic Director at Oregon Shakespeare Festival, and is a founder of Maia Directors. In addition, Turkish American Repertory Theater & Entertainment (TARTE) is a Northeastern American company that is devoted to Turkish and American classics and new works. Its Artistic Director Ayse Eldek-Richardson was born in Turkey but immigrated to the United States in the late 1990s and her company has produced works for decades. These are by no means the only Turkish American theatre makers working in the American theatre, but they represent some of the highest quality work from their community.

Issues Facing Middle Eastern American Theatre

The Middle Eastern American literature genre has been studied but rarely within the context of theatre. In their anthology *Salaam, Peace*, Hill and Amin describe Middle Eastern American theatre through the lenses of hyphenated identities and the events of 9/11:

> The tragedies of 9/11 might have silenced Middle Eastern-American theatre artists, but voices rose through the clouds of outrage, condemnation and suspicion that threatened them individually and communally. (2009, xiii)

For her part, Amin categorizes those who share the moniker "Middle Eastern-American" as

> artists who do not necessarily have a unified vision or constitute a movement within American theatre so far, but have become visible, for both positive and negative reasons, only after 9/11, because of their ethnic background. While attention suddenly focused on them as "the other," many of those artists struggle with that categorization and refuse to be studied/viewed only from that thin prism, which, according to them, is an oversimplification of their situation, after all they *are* U.S. citizens. (x)

One of the biggest issues facing this community is self-representation. The need for self-representation has grown, and Middle Eastern Americans believe they are the ones who are best suited to bring their historical, cultural, social, and artistic stories to American audiences. In the book *Etching Our Own Image: Voices from Within the Arab American Art Movement*, Holly Arida writes, "Without self-definition, we are misunderstood. [. . .] While this effort is not uniform, the artists within it have in common the capacity to etch their own images, to use artistic media to create their own impressions of who they are as artists and as Arab Americans" (Ameri and Arida 2007, 1). Silk Road Rising co-founder and co-artistic Director Jamil Khoury writes,

> I believe that Arab American theatre makers and filmmakers and writers and novelists and musicians and visual artists and dancers and stand-up comedians are poised to lead our community and emancipate us from our cultural dystopia and political powerlessness. Until the larger American public connects with our stories, connects with us on a human level, emotionally, spiritually, intellectually, and viscerally, we will remain [. . .] detested and despised. (Khoury 2013)

Khoury also cowrote an essay with Golden Thread Productions artistic director Torange Yeghiazarian for *American Theatre* titled "Middle Eastern American Theatre, on Our Terms." They summarize the convenings of Middle Eastern American theatre artists over two years. There are two documents in the article: one titled "Dear Producers and Artistic Directors of the American Theatre" and another titled "A Middle Eastern American Theatre Artists Bill of Rights." In the former, they address play selection, casting, cultural competency, and facilitating conversations. They urge American theatre producers to consider the many "excellent plays" that exist in the genre that explore every possible aspect of contemporary theatre. They also urge producers to reach out to the Middle Eastern American theatre artists that are outside their established casting/hiring networks. "Bottom line: You all should be working with more Middle Eastern American actors, directors, dramaturgs, and designers," they write. They also offer their services in reaching out to these artists, and if they cannot cast the play with such artists, they ask that the producers of the play attempt to honor the intentions of the playwright. As for cultural competency, they urge producers to work with culturally competent consultants that have embodied knowledge and lived experience with the community that the play addresses. Furthermore, they argue that the artists must have agency to impact decision making for the production. Because plays that deal with Islam or the Middle East are often politically charged, they believe that "a respectful, honest, and meaningful conversation" must be facilitated despite how difficult the subject matter may be.

In the "Middle Eastern American Theatre Artists Bill of Rights," they outline several "self-evident truths" regarding these artists:

1. The right to tell their own stories in their own words without the burden of representing an entire community's experiences.

2. The right to define their own cultural identities free of stereotypes, coercion, policing, and the right to embrace myriad cultural identities simultaneously.

3. The right not to conform to the preconceived notions of cultural identity, and to resist culturally imposed political and social judgments for stories that reflect individual truths and understandings.

4. The right to bring complicated and nuanced interpretations to the works.

5. The right to be free of performances of preconceived notions of identities or acquiescence to hypersexualized or systematic violent representation of Middle Eastern/American bodies.

6. The right to examine the less serious aspects of their communities, religious traditions, and identity politics without being censured or the expectation of being role models.

7. The right to tell stories that criticize aspects of US or Middle Eastern governmental policies without the threat of being accused of anti-Americanism, racism, or self-loathing.

8. The right to tell stories even if they are not necessarily about Middle Eastern identities.

9. The right to remind "artistic decision makers" of concerns regarding the authentication of cultural heritages, to hear concerns related to identities, and the reminder that Middle Eastern artist participation does not automatically denote approval of all culturally specific choices that are made in a production.

The document ends with a postscript that explains the problematic colonial history of terms such as "Middle East" and "Middle Eastern." For clarification, they write:

We understand our respective backgrounds in terms of rich pluralism and interconnectedness. We also define "America" and "American" in the broadest possible ways to include the continents of North and South America. Furthermore, at this time in history, it's important that we include American Muslims of all cultural, ethnic, and racial backgrounds, as members of our Middle Eastern American communities. (Khoury and Yeghiazarian 2017)

This article, born of several gatherings of Middle Eastern American theatre artists, outlines the various topics, concerns, and frustrations that are discussed in meetings that involve this genre. Of course, theatres are not obligated to follow these guidelines, but they at least voice the concerns of artists that have traditionally been omitted in the American theatre.

Despite the solidarity in the Middle Eastern American theatre movement, there are still contentious issues. Casting is by far the most controversial. Should a Middle Eastern role be played by a non-Middle Easterner? The opinions vary. Some state that the onus is on the producer to find Middle Eastern/American actors to play such roles, and if they cannot find those actors, they should refrain from producing the play at all. Others believe that every effort should be made to find the said actors, but if they cannot be found or hired, then non-MEA actors can fill those roles. Still others believe that it is more important that these plays are produced anywhere than to not be produced only because they cannot be cast with the "correct" actors. Playwright Yussef El Guindi, for instance, commends theatres that wish to cast plays "authentically," but has often found his plays are cast with actors who can "pass" as Middle Easterners. He writes that he prefers to cast the best actors for the roles in his work rather than casting actors who may not be as trained or experienced only because they "fit" the casting requirements.

> I know that sounds rather selfish, but shouldn't my focus be on trying to realize what's on the page in the best manner possible? Wouldn't that raise the profile of our stories, and our place in the wider cultural conversations, presenting quality work in all areas of production, so the audience doesn't feel like they're attending out of obligation to some liberal idea of exposing themselves to different cultures and perspectives? Which is a great impulse, but can also feel more like homework than entertainment. (Syler and Banks 2019, 58)

El Guindi states that when he feels the pressure to only cast within the community, it tends to drive him to write plays that do not contain characters from communities from which he cannot "authentically" cast. In other words, he would prefer to have his plays produced with non-Middle Eastern American characters rather than not performed at all because the "right" actor cannot be cast in the role.

For her part, Torange Yeghiazarian writes about how the San Francisco Bay Area now has many good actors of Middle Eastern heritage for its casting pool, but that in the early years that casting pool did not contain many actors of that heritage. For her company Golden Thread Productions, producing plays with Middle Eastern narratives has always been a top priority due to the underrepresentation of these narratives in American theatre. Furthermore, she believes that the Middle Eastern characters that do exist in American theatre are often demonized or dehumanized. "But how do we bring more Middle Eastern narratives to theater stages in the US," she asks, "when there are very few Middle Eastern actors?" (ibid., 64). For the Golden Thread Productions annual ReOrient Festival, the casting challenges increase since there are both Middle Eastern and non-Middle Eastern characters often represented in the plays: "I sometimes wonder if, in the fight for greater and more 'authentic' representation of communities of color, we have lost sight of theater's intrinsic ability to help us connect by reaching beyond ourselves" (ibid., 69). Like El Guindi, Yeghiazarian believes that if there is to be a critical mass of Middle Eastern

American theatre in the United States, leniency in casting is ultimately necessary.

> Of course we want more opportunities for Middle Eastern artists; but if we are limited to only writing about or playing characters from our own cultures, then we are creating a different kind of cultural ghetto where a community of color is only permitted to represent its own. We need to expand our definitions of community and artistic purview, not make them narrower. (ibid., 70)

The debate about casting these plays is ongoing. Because this genre is relatively new to the professional American theatre, these tensions are inevitable. As more Middle Eastern American artists enter training programs, universities, and find work in professional theatre these issues may subside. For now, it seems that casting in play production will remain problematic for the foreseeable future.

Major Themes of Middle Eastern American Theatre

In deciding how to examine these plays, it seemed best to do so thematically rather than by national/ethnic origin. Several themes are common to most of these works. Of course, not all plays fit these categories, and many works contain multiple themes. However, the plays included in this critical companion feature the following ideas:

Return to the Homeland Plays

Plays found in this genre are about Middle Eastern Americans who are usually second- or third-generation Americans who partake in a journey back to their ancestors' or parents' countries or regions of birth. This type of "birthright" play is one that compels the protagonist to leave the comfort (or discomfort) of their American life in order to travel overseas to their ancestral homelands. These characters sometimes have positive return experiences, whereas others have negative ones. In their desire to return lies the notion that they can somehow better understand themselves by reconnecting with their cultural heritage. However, by doing so, they often find they are more alienated both from their "American" and "ancestral" selves. Protagonists in these plays confront the limits of their belonging:

linguistic (being unable to fully communicate in their second language), cultural (lacking the requisite cultural knowledge to navigate their homelands), social (making unintended social gaffes), and political (being seen as suspect for having allegiances to both cultures). Also, they find that their condition living abroad, and the attitudes they bring to the homeland, is deeply challenged by those who live their lives there. These protagonists, in their positive desire to learn more about themselves and their cultures, experience an epiphany—they realize they are neither fully "American" nor are they of their parents' culture; they are hybrids who are doomed to be fully unaccepted in both cultures.

In the book *The Limits of Whiteness: Iranian Americans and the Everyday Politics of Race*, Neda Maghbouleh writes that second-generation youth who are born in the United States are exposed to the same media depictions of their cultural homelands as other Americans. Simultaneously, they are raised with their parents' stories about growing up and coming of age in those same countries. Where the American media images of the homeland are often of malevolent and terrible places, their parents' deterritorialized narratives create what she calls "inherited nostalgia," or imaginary portraits of life that often omit the suffering and deprivations of war and the pain of being in the diaspora. Therefore, young people often travel to the homeland with optimism, excitement, and anticipation. However, after navigating the difficulties of procuring the necessary paperwork, enduring invasive security checks both at home and abroad, challenging social and gendered norms (especially for women and girls who must alter their dress before arriving), and having negative interactions with family and authorities in the homeland many discover they are "too Iranian for America, too American for Iran" (2017, 128). When the young people Maghbouleh interviewed returned from their trips to Iran, they were faced with the challenge of how to navigate both homes and identities without sacrificing either (ibid., 132). Upon return to the United States, the racializing experience young people face changes them. They had to come to terms with the fact that, in America, they were not fully accepted since they were not "white" and, when traveling to their ancestral homelands, they did not belong there since they did not contain the linguistic, cultural, or social knowledge of that place.

The irony of this situation is that the lack of acceptance they feel fuels their artistic production. In other words, they wrote the plays they wrote *because of* and not *despite* their experiences overseas. This positive artistic result born of a negative experiential one is a fascinating by-product of their inner journey. In a cruel twist of fate, these playwrights find their artistic voice while sometimes losing their cultural identities and the supposed cultural belonging they seek.

Persecution Plays

The plays in this category are ones that depict Middle Eastern Americans being persecuted by government and society. These plays, born of decades of ethnic and/or religious persecution in America, often tell the stories of those who fall victim to larger forces that seek to destroy them because of their allegiances to their ancestral homelands, their religious practices, or their desire to assert themselves in their American communities. These plays reflect the fact that there has been systematic governmental surveillance, persecution, interrogation, incarceration, and ongoing Arabophobia and Islamophobia in the Americas.

The first major study addressing the negative representation of Middle Eastern subjects in the media is Edward W. Said's seminal 1970 essay "The Arab Portrayed." In the essay, Said writes of the misrepresentation of Arabs specifically, but many of the assertions he makes in the essay are completely applicable to Middle Easterners in general. He writes about the American consciousness of the Arab, which is rife with images of Arabs as terrorists, sexual degenerates, or regressive nomads. "If the Arab occupies space in the mind at all, it is of negative value," Said wrote. "He is seen as the disrupter of Israel's continuing existence, or, in a larger view, a surmountable obstacle to Israel's creation in 1948" (Said 1970, 5). Indeed, the beginnings of the transition of Middle Easterners from benign sheikhs and harem girls to pernicious terrorists and suicide bombers began after the 1967 Arab-Israeli War. Prior to this time there were many stereotypical Middle Eastern or Muslim types found on American stages. Barbary Pirates were among the first stereotypes in plays like *Slaves in Algiers; or, A Struggle for Freedom* (1794), *Slaves in Barbary* (1810), *American Captive, or Siege of Tripoli* (1811), and *Young Carolinians; or, Americans in Algiers* (1818). Another trope was the immigrant wishing to assimilate such as *Anna Ascends* (1922), and characters added for ethnic color in *The Time of Your Life* (1939). In the Rodgers and Hammerstein musical *Oklahoma!* (1943), the Middle Eastern/Persian peddler Ali Hakim is seen as a cunning businessman and sexual inveigler who tries to have his way with the women in the musical. Of course, there were always Orientalized dance performances by various troupes in the 1930s–1950s such as the O.W. Pond Troupe of Arabs or the Circassian Slaves (Salem 1999, 272–83).

The portrayals after 1967 became more pernicious. This shift in dramatic representation represented a wider shift in anti-Arab, anti-Muslim consciousness. Suddenly Middle Easterners that were at one time considered exotic or sexy transmuted into violent and terroristic characters. In his book *"Evil" Arabs in American Popular Film: Orientalist Fear*, Tim Jon Semmerling writes, "The political events of the early 1970s gave the American popular consciousness a new nemesis, villain, and culprit that deserved to be defeated" (2006, 17). Throughout that decade, he writes, American fear and feelings of impotence gave rise to images of "evil" Arabs who undermined America by using democracy as a weapon against Westerners.

> The Arabs and the Middle East did not and do not always respond to our desires as we expect them to in our political designs and schemes, i.e., our ideologies and myths. Put another way, this ambivalence of the "evil" Arabs upsets the entire binary system of our Orientalist project. (23)

Therefore, images of terrorists, avaricious oil sheikhs, burqa-clad suicide bombers, and other vile Middle Easterners infiltrated images on stage and screen. Even in recent American dramas like *Bengal Tiger in the Baghdad Zoo, Ruined*, or *The Happiest Song Plays Last*, Middle Easterners are portrayed either as helpless victims or as deceptive comrades who would mercilessly kill American soldiers or steal diamonds that could potentially save the lives of the protagonists. When Middle Easterners are unjustly killed in foreign wars by American soldiers in these plays, those soldiers return home to perform acts of self-atonement rather than face charges in international courts for their crimes.

Middle Eastern American playwrights have written plays that examine the persecution of Middle Easterners in America, especially in the post-9/11 context. The plays in this category are examples of how Middle Eastern Americans view themselves as the ones that have been persecuted by governments and societies, and how that persecution has led to what Hatem Bazian calls "virtual internment" whereby Middle Eastern Americans are automatically guilty by association for the actions of actual terrorists. Bazian defines this as a mentally induced state that targets this community through the legal system, immigration laws, and the media (Bazian 2004, 6). The playwrights in this category explore the lives of characters living in this state of fear and paranoia and explore how it affects their lives in the diaspora.

Diaspora Plays

Diaspora plays are plays by Middle Eastern American playwrights that take place primarily in the Americas and deal with life as "the other" in an American society that is dismissive or discriminatory toward them. The protagonists in these plays suffer from the traumas they experienced in the homeland and seek to establish a new and better life in America, yet they are haunted by the experiences they left behind. These diasporic characters are ones who seek refuge in America from the political, social, religious, and civil strife of their homelands. It is their belief that they can make a new start in a new land but, in play after play, they realize that they simply cannot forget the people and the suffering they left behind. This type of play is one that, as Edward W. Said explained in his essay "Reflections on Exile," highlights the condition of "the age of anxiety and estrangement" exiles face when being "spiritually orphaned and alienated" (2000, 137). For Said, exile is produced by humans for humans and, like death, it tears millions from their necessary traditions, families, and geographies. So it is with the protagonists in these diaspora plays; no matter how much they wish to escape the past and start anew, they are confronted with the specter of those left behind and those lost back in the homeland. Despite this grim backdrop, some of these plays take a darkly comic view of the situation and rely on humor, rather than drama, to tell their stories.

Plays Set in the Homeland

In plays set in the homeland, Middle Eastern American playwrights imagine entire stories that take place back home with the intent of reconstructing lost histories, attempting to address political issues, or imagining a homeland they may not know. In these plays the characters are living in the ancestral homeland, but they are speaking in the vernacular of the communities attending the plays in America. These plays are attempts to translate the experiences of Middle Easterners to American audiences. For instance, there are many Armenian American plays that reconstruct the Armenian Genocide, Palestinian American, and Israeli American plays that address the Israeli-Palestinian conflict, Iranian American plays that focus on lives of

Iranians living under dictatorships, or Arab American plays that focus on the various wars, civil unrests, and political crackdowns that are part of the lives of those living in the Middle East. These plays are born of a desire for those in the diaspora to reconstruct the lives of Middle Easterners. In doing so, they relay important information to American audiences who may not know the tragic histories that comprise some Middle Eastern American lives.

Conflict Plays

One of the largest bodies of plays from Middle Eastern American playwrights concerns conflicts that are taking place in the Middle East. This genre's largest corpus is the decades-old Israeli-Palestinian conflict. These plays come from almost all of the groups and constitute one of the most pressing issues in the minds of these artists and often include the aforementioned categories as well. Topics include returning to Israel and/or Palestine, being challenged as "Americans" while visiting there, and ruminating on their inability to contribute to ending the conflict. The amount of time and effort these playwrights have taken to focus on this topic is remarkable. Playwrights in this genre often tend to humanize the people caught up in this conflict and allow audiences the space to think more deeply about these issues. However, writing about this topic, and getting these plays produced in mainstream theatres, is a difficult task. Many plays that concern the politics of the Israeli-Palestinian conflict are either not produced, are censored by theatres that wish to produce them, or they are given readings but not full productions. In addition, Middle Eastern American theatres complain that they are not funded well enough and they not given press reviews in their communities. Many artists believe that there is a desire by patrons and the press to avoid the difficult topics inherent to this work.

For Middle Eastern American artists, the Israeli-Palestinian conflict is a personal issue since they have a vested interest in peace in the region. Some of these artists have family in Israel and Palestine, have traveled and/or worked there, and know that a wider conflict in the Middle East will most probably impact their families in terrifyingly real terms. Therefore, the urgency to write about this issue transcends their work as playwrights—it is a personal issue that they must dramatize using the tools they know best—their writing, directing, and performing. Palestinian American playwright Betty Shamieh writes, "The cost of ignoring what is happening there—and ignoring how those happenings affect the stability of the entire world—is unbearable"

(Shamieh 2003, 20, 6). Israeli playwright Motti Lerner believes writing and producing these plays can bring about change, though not directly:

> What do I expect from the production of the play? I'm not naïve. I know that it will change neither the fate of the Middle East nor the results of the next elections in Israel. It's very difficult to change people by plays in the theatre. We must be aware of that. But nonetheless, we mustn't lose hope. Books and plays and films do create change. Sometimes the change is very small. Sometimes the change is hidden. Sometimes the change is so deep that we can't see its traces on the surface. But even if this change is very minor, even if it's hidden, it's worth attempting. (Lerner 2015, 152)

As these artists demonstrate, there is a desperate need to address this issue through theatre. The number of plays that addresses this topic is growing, and they come from nearly every Middle Eastern American group writing for the theatre.

Other conflict plays revolve around the various wars and crises that have taken place and continue to plague the region. Plays about the Lebanese Civil War, the Syrian Civil War, and the Algerian Civil War focus on how these wars have damaged the civil society and caused a refugee crisis. The Armenian Genocide is also the focus of plays in this genre. The Arab Spring uprisings also become an important topic for exploration. These are a small sample of the works that focus on the historical and current conflicts that have caused such grief and suffering in the Middle East for generations.

All of these categories—return to the homeland plays, persecution plays, diaspora plays, plays set in the homeland, and conflict plays—are by no means comprehensive of every Middle Eastern American play or musical, but they can provide a helpful set of lenses through which we can understand the people, plays, and styles that exist. These Middle Eastern American artists are often working in obscurity. Many of these plays are either unpublished, have never been produced, or have only had staged readings. This points to the fact that the American theatre establishment has been less-than-receptive to these works, and that these artists are often working against great odds to stage their productions. However, as these works prove, they are all important stories that should be experienced by more audiences in the future.

CHAPTER 1
MAJOR MIDDLE EASTERN
AMERICAN COMPANIES

Much of the success that can be attributed to this genre comes from the various theatre companies and groups that have produced these works on the stage despite lack of funding, resources, and personnel. The founders of these companies have often worked under difficult conditions to assure the production of these plays. In an American theatre landscape that often values large-scale entertainments consisting of musicals or so-called straight plays featuring major film or television stars, these companies rely on arts grants, patron donations, and ticket sales to produce the works. They also rely on various venues that would either donate their spaces, or provide them a reasonable cost, in order to allow them to produce these works. That said, some artists often work for little or no compensation in order to assure the success of these productions.

AJYAL Theatrical Group

Dearborn-based theatre company AJYAL (Generations) Theatrical Group was founded by producer, director, actor, and writer Najee Mondalek in 1988. According to their website,

> Most of AJYAL Theatrical Group' [*sic*] shows poke fun at the everyday lives of Arab-Americans, who have recently become citizens and who are desperately trying to blend into the mainstream of American culture. The plays serve as a forum to help people laugh at their mistakes and mishaps but also to come to terms with social issues facing Arab-Americans, such as their difficulties adjusting to a new culture and lifestyle. These performances, like music, art and other entertainment media, are a very important piece of the fabric of Arab-American culture. (www.ajyal.us)

Mondalek was born in Marjayoun, Lebanon, before the Lebanese Civil War. He immigrated to the United States in 1985 and received his associate degree from Macomb Community College in 1988. He also holds a bachelor's degree in mass communications, and a master's degree in virtual reality, 3D animation, and visualization. While still a student at Macomb Community College, Mondalek began writing plays. In all, Mondalek wrote, produced, and acted in twelve comedies over a twenty-five-year span: *What a Shame* (1989), *Students Nowadays* (1990), *Honest Thieves* (1991), *Smile You're in Dearborn* (1993), *We Became American* (1996), *Come See, Come Saw* (1998), *Happy Bairday* (1999–2000), *Me No Terrorist* (2001–4), *Arab & Broud* (2005–6), *Where Does It Hurt* (2012–13), *The Jubilee Show* (2013–14), *Ghashee w Mashee—The Dumbass* (2015–16), and *Double Trouble* (2018–19). The productions toured throughout North America, Canada, and abroad to Lebanon and Australia. The plays, and Mondalek's alter ego Im Hussein, are well known throughout the Arab American community, and the shows usually sell out wherever they play. Mondalek also records the productions and sells the DVDs on the AJYAL website. The ensemble is made up of several other Arab American actors: Rima Amine, Nader Aoude, Aziz Charabaty, Hassan Haj, Rabih Jaber, Rodney Karromi, Christine Mondalek, Michael Mondalek, Ayman Safaoui, and Rita Srour.

Mondalek (in drag) plays a Lebanese matriarch named Im Hussein (mother of Hussein), a woman who mostly dresses in a floral-patterned, brightly colored *abaya*, a head scarf, and thick-rimmed glasses with caked-on makeup. The character is married to her hapless husband Abou Hussein (father of Hussein), who often dresses in cheap suits, an oversized knit hat, and sports a handlebar mustache. Im Hussein's best friends, Im Elias (mother of Elias) and Abou Elias (father of Elias), round out the main characters in the comedies. The rest of the cast are comprised of colorful characters who are both Arab and non-Arab. The Im Hussein character first appeared in a brief skit in Mondalek's play *Smile You're in Dearborn*. The character was so popular with audiences that Mondalek rewrote the character as a lead role in all his future plays.

Mondalek's plays are written in Arabic and combine English and Arabic into a hybrid language Mondalek calls "Arabeezi." He uses this mixture of Arabic and English to reflect the code switching that many Arabs use in their daily lives. Mondalek uses this hybrid language to great comic effect, especially when his lead character, Im Hussein, speaks with American characters who neither speak nor understand Arabic. The combined use of Arabic and English, the intermittent use of rhyming Arabic proverbs, the colorful costumes and acting, and the use of malapropisms all contribute to creating situations that are both comical and outrageous. Mondalek's plays also include interludes that contain Arabic song and dance, adding to their entertainment for primarily Arab-speaking audiences.

Mondalek's character Im Hussein follows in a long tradition of British and American male actors playing older matriarchs such as Barry Humphries's Dame Edna, Tyler Perry's Madea, Eddie Murphy's Mama Klump, and Martin Lawrence's Big Momma. These entertainers rely on the notion that a strong female character with agency must be large in stature, have a homely appearance, dress garishly, and have the underlying threat of violence. Like Perry's Madea character, Mondalek's Im Hussein contains important cultural knowledge, and he often breaks the fourth wall to speak directly to his audiences about contemporary issues facing the Arab community in the United States.

As a character, Im Hussein has agency. She is the driving force in the comedy and the reason the major events occur. She is also the wittiest, the funniest, and the most forceful character. Whenever her husband talks back at her, she either outwits him with a clever Arabic saying, de-masculinizes him, or even tacitly threatens physical force. In essence, she is the "funny man" and her husband is the "straight man" in this comedic duo (both literally and figuratively). There is no doubt that Mondalek's plays are loved by the Arab American/Arab Canadian community based on their widespread popularity, their packed performances, and their reputation within the community at large. Indeed, it is one of the few live theatrical experiences Arabs in the United States and Canada can attend that include the Arabic language, dance, and music. These performances also provide an opportunity for Arabs to gather, laugh, and share in the situation they are facing living in the diaspora. For Mondalek, the plays are meant to uplift the Arab and Arab American communities:

> Whenever I write my comedies, I always insert good messages. We try to encourage the audience to do your best to feel proud of where you came from and proud you are American now. Follow a good example. Show the public the side of you as Arab or Arab American. Be thankful to this country that opened its arms to welcome you and your family to live a better life. (Virtusio 2015)

According to Mondalek, the plays are performed with 70 percent Arabic and 30 percent English, and the audiences are about one-third Arab American. Despite the humorous nature of the plays, Mondalek inserts some social commentary regarding infertility, drug abuse, the abusive Arab regimes, and the conflict between generations. "Political satire and comedy have always been one of the best tools to explore difficult topics," Mondalek says. "Our theatre will always speak truths for those who hunger [for] them. It will be a cultural space where our community examines itself in a mirror" (Guzman 2016). With full houses across North America and abroad, Ajyal's success is undeniable. Their use of Arabic language, Arabic dances and songs, and the issues they address regarding life in America make them a beloved fixture of the Arab American theatrical landscape.

Alliance for Jewish Theatre (AJT)

The Alliance for Jewish Theatre (AJT), a nonprofit organization, exists to "promote the creation, presentation, and preservation of both traditional and nontraditional theatrical endeavors by, for, and about the Jewish experience" (Alliance for Jewish Theatre). The AJT was formed in 1979 by Richard Siegel and Susan Merson. The company focuses on developing plays that have a Jewish sensibility, create connections between theatre artists, empower theatre artists to tell Jewish stories, and expand the reach of theatre that explores Jewish identity. The group also organizes international Jewish Theatre Festivals, holds annual conferences, and states that its membership includes 225 individuals and theatres in the world. In 2019, the AJT hosted the largest Jewish theatre arts conference in the United States with nearly one hundred artists in attendance. There were workshops, artist panels, and the publication of "Twenty-Five Newish Jewish Plays You Should Know." According to Executive Director Jeremy Alumna, "In Judaism there is a belief that empathy stirs us to great acts of kindness and generosity, and that those actions can repair the pain and suffering in the world. This is what we continuously strive for: Tikkun Olam. And this is what I hope to do with AJT" (Broadway World 2019). Other AJT projects include a virtual theatre project titled "The Telling Monologues/#Passover Telling Project," AJT Pop-Up events meant to celebrate and attract Jewish theatre and performance, and monthly webinars for AJT member artists.

Arab-American Comedy Festival

Founded in 2003 by comedians Dean Obeidallah and Maysoon Zayid, the Arab-American Comedy Festival was created to "showcase the talents of Arab-American actors, comics, playwrights and filmmakers, and challenge as well as inspire our fellow Arab-Americans to create outstanding works of comedy" (www.arabcomedy.com). Obeidallah states,

> We want to show Americans first-hand that Arabs can be funny. I think over the last few years, we have succeeded in showing to Americans that Arab-Americans are funny through our festival and TV appearances. But, frankly, Americans never get a chance to see Arabs from the Arab world being funny. I can't think of a time when I have seen an image of an Arab from the Middle East laughing on American TV—other than maybe when they are playing a terrorist laughing devilishly at his maniacal plans! (Mossalli 2010)

Middle Eastern American comedy has found success since 2000 with various comedy tours and specials such as *Allah Made Me Funny* (featuring Mohammed Amer, Preacher Moss, and Azhar Usman), *The Axis of Evil Comedy Tour* (featuring Ahmed Ahmed, Maz Jobrani, Aron Kader, and Dean Obeidallah), and *The Arab American Comedy Tour* (featuring Ahmed Ahmed, Dean Obeidallah, and Maysoon Zayid). In addition, many of these comics have been able to parlay their success to find opportunities in other types of media. Obeidallah has created a satellite radio program titled *The Dean Obeidallah Show* and is a regular contributor to several news sites, Jobrani has acted in many Hollywood films and television shows, and Zayid has continued her comedy tours as well as worked as a disability advocate. What started out as a desire to break into mainstream American comedy has led these comedians to other venues, heightening their influence and reach beyond the comedy club circuit.

Art2Action Inc.

Art2Action is a company that creates, develops, and produces original theatre, interdisciplinary performances, performative acts, and progressive cultural organizing. They specifically state they support women artists, artists of color, queer or trans artists, and creative allies. The Art2Action

Collective is a group of interdisciplinary artists that work together consistently over time, including the five core/founding members: Dora Arreola, Andrea Assaf, Krystal Banzon, Meena Natarajan, and Jo Novelli. Founding Artistic Director Andrea Assaf "envisioned" the company in 2001, and the first production titled *Globalcities* premiered at the New York International Fringe Festival in 2003. The company was originally incorporated in New York, but is based in Tampa, Florida.

The company boasts three original works: Andrea Assaf's solo performance *Eleven Reflections on September*, Assaf and Samuel Valdez's *Outside the Circle*, and the ensemble multimedia theatre work titled *DRONE*. In addition, they organize and curate the R&R Arts Festival and THIS Bridge: Arab, Muslim & Middle Eastern Artists. They cohosted the National Initiative for Arts & Health in the Military (NIAHM) which focuses on the role of the arts in recovery, transition, and transformation for veterans. In Minneapolis, they also cohost the National Institute for Directing & Ensemble Creation with Pangea World Theatre. In 2020 they hosted their first national online community performance event titled "ONLINE Veterans Community Open Mic" as a means of community building during the COVID-19 pandemic.

Darvag Theater Group

Based in Berkeley, California, Darvag Theater Group has been producing Iranian diasporic theatre since its founding in 1985. "Darvag" is a Farsi word that means "a frog thrashes and croaks to announce the coming of the hoped-for rain" (Hill 2009). The mission of the company consists of "exploring creative expression in theater arts and maintaining a vital living connection with the group's Iranian heritage" (Ehya 2018, 57). Many early Iranian immigrants in the 1960s and 1970s were students who formed campus-based Iranian student organizations that were committed to political activism against the shah's regime. The organizations would perform skits, short political plays, and celebratory dramas that commemorated the Iranian New Year celebration known as Nowruz. Those plays were usually adaptations of Iranian Farsi plays or political plays by Iranian-based playwrights. Following the Iranian Revolution in 1979, which led to the overthrow of the Pahlavi Dynasty in Iran, many Iranians immigrated to Europe and the United States. Unlike earlier immigrants, these post-1979 students were committed to mainly critiques of the Iranian regime, addressing the Iran-Iraq war (1980–8), and focusing on the political persecution faced by many left behind in Iran.

Darvag Theater Group, originally established by ex-student activists in 1984, began in the former *Khaneh ye Iran* (House of Iran) building in Berkeley. In over thirty years, Darvag has produced and staged more than fifty plays in both English and Persian. They also staged plays by non-Iranian playwrights Chekhov, Brecht, Dorfman, and Frayn. They have coproduced plays with Shotgun Players (Berkeley) and Golden Thread Productions (San Francisco). Unlike the former Iranian student organization that focused primarily on political opposition, the Darvag artists utilized theatre, music, literature, and visual arts in order to create an Iranian diasporic community in Berkeley (Ehya 2018, 56). The first play produced by Darvag, *Chamedan* (*Suitcase*), written and directed by Farhad Ayeesh, created the ethos of the early Darvag plays. Later, other Darvag theater artists contributed plays—Mansour Taeed: *Such a Dance* (1986); Sepideh Khosrowjah: *The Beginning* (1985), *If You Leave I Will Be Lonely* (1988, 1990), *A Man, His Four Wives, and His Mother* (1992), *Who Will Give Us a Second Chance* (1993), *The Bird of Dawn* (1997), *The Beginning of a Cold Season* (2002), *In Memory of Kazem Ashtari* (2007), and *It's Not About Pomegranates* (2011); Iraj Mohammadi: *The Visit* (1989), *A Shuttle from North* (1990); Roham Sheikhani: *Three Little Piglets* (1994), *Image Is Everything* (1995), *Satan* (1995); and Hossein Khosrowjah: *Remembering the Unforgettable* (1998).

There were also several seminal directors who worked with Darvag over the years who directed plays by Iranian and non-Iranian playwrights, including Farhad Ayeesh, Jim Cave, Zara Houshmand, Hossein Khosrowjah, Sepideh Khosrowjah, Iraj Mohammadi, Farid Nabavi, Evren Odcikin, Roham Sheikhani, Mansour Taeed, and Bella Warda. One of Darvag's founders and directors, Hamid Ehya, writes,

> Through the prism of Darvag, one can see the entire spectrum of theatrical genres performed by Iranians outside of Iran. Darvag has remained active for over thirty years and has staged more than 50 plays—probably more than any other Iranian theatre group outside of Iran (or even inside). (Quoted in Hill 2009)

The company, which received its nonprofit status in 1995, has obtained several grants, yet most of their productions are funded by ticket sales and donations from the local Iranian community. Their use of Central Stage, a small black box theatre in Berkeley whose mission is to primarily promote Persian arts and culture, allows Darvag to have a consistent performance venue. Several of their plays have traveled nationally, but none have been published in the United States. Given the fraught nature of US-Iran relations, companies like Darvag provide important opportunities for American audiences to experience works by Iranian and Iranian/American writers and directors who can provide insights into life under the Islamic Republic and life as Iranian Americans in exile.

Golden Thread Productions

The San Francisco Bay Area company Golden Thread Productions is described as "the first American theatre company devoted to the Middle East" (Golden Thread Productions). The company was founded by Artistic Director Torange Yeghiazarian, with the assistance of Maria Zamroud, Termeh Yeghiazarian, Gen Hayashida, and Kamshad Kooshan. The name was inspired by the myth of Ariadne, who led Theseus out of the labyrinth with a ball of golden thread. Since its founding, the company has "worked diligently to probe and celebrate the Middle Eastern culture and identity in all its complexity" (Golden Thread Productions). The company's premiere production, *Operation No Penetration*, an adaptation of the classic Greek drama *Lysistrata* in a Middle Eastern setting. Since that time they have produced the world, US, and West Coast premieres of seminal Middle Eastern American plays including *Nine Armenians* by Leslie Ayvazian (2002); Yussef El Guindi's *Back of the Throat* (2005), *Jihad Jones and the Kalishnikov Babes* (2008), *Language Rooms* (2011), and *Our Enemies: Lively Scenes of Love and Combat* (2016); Karim Alrawi's *Deep Cut* (2001), Hafiz Karmali's *Island of Animals* (2006), Denmo Ibrahim's *Ecstasy, A Waterfable* (2009), Mona Mansour's *Urge for Going* (2013) and *We Swim, We Talk, We Go to War* (2018), Amir Nizar Zuabi's *Oh My Sweet Land* (in collaboration with Corinne Jaber, 2018), Saïd Sayrafiezadeh's *Autobiography of a Terrorist*, Hannah Khalil's *Scenes from 71* Years,* Hassan Abdulrazzak's *Love, Bomb & Apples* (2018), Sedef Ecer's *On the Periphery,* and many of Yeghiazarian's own plays including *Abaga* (2001), *444 Days* (2013), *The Fifth String: Ziryab's Passage to Cordoba* (2014), and *Isfahan Blues* (2015). In addition to their mainstage productions, Golden Thread Productions has created the ReOrient Festival of short plays, an annual Women's Day event titled

What Do the Women Say?, the Fairytale Players touring and education program for youth, New Threads Reading Series, and other workshops and special events (Bakalian 2008, 89). The ReOrient Festival has produced plays by many of the prominent Middle Eastern American theatre artists including Melis Aker, Emma Goldman-Sherman, Ken Kaissar, Mona Mansour, Nahal Navidar, Betty Shamieh, and Yussef El Guindi. Other prominent playwrights produced there include Eric Ehn, Israel Horovitz, Motti Lerner, and Naomi Wallace. In addition, Golden Thread has partnered with Silk Road Rising and the Lark Theatre in forming the Middle East New Plays Initiative. The company has been recognized by the American Theatre Wing and by the City of San Francisco. Torange Yeghiazarian has been recognized by Theatre Bay Area, the Cairo International Theatre Festival, and the Symposium on Equity in the Entertainment Industry at Stanford University. She is also one of Theatre Communication Group's Legacy Leaders of Color.

Jewish Plays Project

Jewish Plays Project (JPP) describes itself as a group that "puts bold, progressive, Jewish conversations on world stages" (Jewish Plays Project). As a development vehicle for plays, the JPP is committed to new plays and musicals, and playwrights, who are interested in their Jewish identities, and they engage Jewish communities in the vetting, selection, and championing of new voices. The JPP began in 2012 and has chosen many plays over the intervening years by writers like Martin Blank, Lindsay Joelle, Motti Lerner, Zohar Tirosh-Polk, Misha Shulman, and Deborah Yarchun. The submission guidelines state, "Submissions are open to artists of all backgrounds, denominations, faiths, creeds, religions and other ideals. We believe that Jewish identity and culture are specific manifestations of universal human cravings for spiritual, ethical, moral and worldly joy. 'Matrilineal descent' is neither important nor necessary" (Jewish Plays Project). According to *Jewish Boston*, the JPP has vetted 913 plays from 650 writers in 29 states and 8 countries and has placed 15 plays on stages from London to New York to Tel Aviv (Bolton-Fasman 2019). JPP also holds regional play contests in Houston, Charlotte, Chicago, Fairfax, Hartford, Buffalo, Silicon Valley, and New York as well as a national contest online. JPP artistic director David Winitsky states that the plays JPP chooses cover "the most pressing stories in the Jewish world. Jews taking responsibility for refugees, Jews confronting racial injustice, American Jews and Israel, Jews in the face of anti-semitism, Jews facing off with each other. This is the reason the JPP exists—to find plays that matter, and to champion them as they move onto the best stages in the world" (Broadway World 2020). Companies like JPP are striving to address issues that its founders believe were not central to the missions of previous Jewish theatre organizations, and their use of online resources has created a virtual national network of artists.

The Lark

The Lark is an international theatre laboratory based in New York City "dedicated to amplifying the voices of playwrights by providing transformative support within a global community" (larktheatre.org). Since its founding in 1994, the Lark has hosted three Middle Eastern American Convenings which hosted several hundred attendees. The Lark was also one of the original partners, with Golden Thread Productions and Silk Road Rising, of the Middle East America Playwrights Fellowship, which helped to develop plays by Yussef El Guindi, Mona Mansour, and Adriana Sevahn Nichols. The Lark also hosted Noor Theatre's 48-Hour Play Forum, and presented new works by Mike Mossalam, Arian Moayed, and Lameece Issaq which were commissioned by Noor Theatre with a grant from Pop Culture Collaborative. In addition, the Lark created a home for the Middle Eastern Writers Lab, which was founded by Mona Mansour and Kareem Fahmy, and has a Middle East-US Playwright Exchange Initiative. The Lark has a Middle East-US Playwright Exchange program, directed by New York University Arts Professor Catherine Coray.

Mosaic Theater

Mosaic Theater was founded by the former Artistic Director of Theater J, Ari Roth, who, according to their website, "saw an increasingly polarized landscape filled with reactionary pushback in the face of groundbreaking interfaith dialogue" (Mosaic Theater). After the Edlavitch DCJCC canceling of Theater J's Voices from a Changing Middle East Festival, Roth decided to "deepen his commitment to intergroup dialogue through the arts by stepping out to build a new, mission-driven theater company that would expand upon the values of the festival and resonate more broadly within the nation's capital" (www.mosaictheatre.org). The company partnered with African Continuum Theatre Company, and now performs in the Atlas Performing Arts Center. The company has produced the works of many Middle Eastern American writers including Leila Buck, Aaron Davidman, Hanna Eady, Mona Mansour, Shachar Pinkas, and Shay Pitovsky.

New Arab American Theatre Works

New Arab American Theater Works, based in the Minneapolis-St. Paul area, was founded in 2012 as a collective of Minnesota-based Arab, Arab American, and Muslim theatre artists. Its founder and Artistic/Executive Director Kathryn (Kathy) Haddad has been creating works in the area for over twenty years, first as cofounder and executive director of Mizna (a Minneapolis-based organization dedicated to contemporary literature, art, film, and cultural programming centering the works of Southwest Asian and North African artists). New Arab American Theater Works strives "to benefit underrepresented Arab, Arab American and Muslim artists, locally, nationally and internationally" (newarabamericantheaterworks.org). In addition, the company wishes to give new perspectives to the terms "Arab," "Middle Eastern," and "Muslim" which are often conflated with the words "terrorist," "war," and "oppressive." The company produces full-length plays as well as staged readings of new works including *Gaza Stories* (1995), *Trapped Between Bush and Bin Laden* (2002), *With Love From Ramallah* (2002), *Latitudes* (2008), *A Clown in Exile* (2015), *In Algeria They Know My Name* (2015), *Road to the City of Apples* (2015), *Tales of Time* (2017), *The One Who Returned* (2017), *Turbulence* (2018), and *Zafira and the Resistance* (2019). Haddad's *The Hour of Separation*, part of a Jerome Fellowship granted the playwright, focuses on one hundred years of Lebanese and Syrian immigration history.

Nibras Theatre Ensemble

Nibras, a former New York-based Arab American theatre ensemble, described themselves in this way:

> Nibras is an Arab / American theatre ensemble that is built upon a shared passion for theatre and is united by a common heritage. It is our belief that by fostering an understanding of the Arab experience

in America, we will help to engender a greater understanding for all communities who feel left outside the equation of American society. Through our productions, we hope to aid in the process of inclusion, thereby enriching the colorful tapestry of American culture. Nibras also seeks to create a strong and viable support group for other Arab theater artists. We will work to build a network of young and old, acolytes and adepts, who can all benefit from one another's talent, experience and passion. (Fractured Atlas)

The group's members—James Asher, Leila Buck, Maha Chehlaoui, Omar Koury, Omar Metwally, Najla Said, and Afaf Shawwa—began exploring their Arab American identities in the years following the September 11 attacks. According to *VOA News*, the group began the documentary drama *Sajjil* prior to 9/11, but "its aftermath underscored their efforts to challenge misconceptions and present the diversity of the Arab-American experience" (voanews.com). The production, which debuted at the International Fringe Festival in New York City in 2002, won a FringeNYC Overall Excellence Award for Ensemble Performance that year. The members of Nibras met online via an ArabDrama listserve. According to Said, the eventual members of Nibras became friends online long before they ever met in person: "For most of us, newly crowned 'Arab-Americans' by the agents and casting directors we had been getting to now, it was an opportunity to dip our foot in the waters of being Arab-American without diving all the way in" (2013, 218). For Buck, the Arab American identification was one that provided artistic insight: "I cannot judge why people choose to identify with or write about their Arab-American heritage. For me, it is the reason I write—not an obligation but an inspiration" (Najjar 2004). Regardless of their motivations, the members of Nibras found both a cultural and artistic home at a time when being identified as an Arab American performer was hardly desirable.

After *Sajjil* concluded, there was a feeling of great accomplishment, but not a desire to continue with Nibras. According to Said, "We were ready to take over the world with our company, we felt like we'd found our own voices, our way into our culture" (Said 2013, 228). For Buck, understanding the complexity of her background was important to her as a writer and performer.

What I have come to realize is that it is only by acknowledging and confronting the negative aspects of Arab culture that we can truly begin a dialogue about the positive ones. At the same time I feel strongly that it is important to keep telling simpler, personal stories because that is what is missing in American culture—positive, human portrayals of Arabs. (Najjar 2004)

Nibras never produced another play, but they were involved in several projects including *Aswat: Voices of Palestine* that was sponsored by New York Theatre Workshop in 2007. The group disbanded due to many factors. The artists involved were primarily focused on creating theatre and not administration, marketing, or fundraising. Although there were some "frustrations and frictions along the way," according to Chehlaoui, the major reason for ending the artistic relationship had more to do with the tensions of trying to be an institution, especially after 9/11. "To build anything from the ground up is a challenge," Chehlaoui said. "But to do so in upheaval, while grieving, and feeling threatened on multiple fronts is especially so" (Najjar 2014). Nibras's legacy lives on through the work of its artists, who continued to create theatre long after the company disbanded.

Noor Theatre

Noor Theatre was founded in 2010 by Founding Artistic Director Lameece Issaq, Executive Director Maha Chehlaoui, and Producing Artistic Director Nancy Vitale. The theatre, based in New York City, and company-in-residence at New York Theatre Workshop, described its mission as "dedicated to supporting, developing and producing the work of theatre artists of Middle Eastern descent." The company has several projects which include its Highlight Reading Series, Co-presentation Partnerships with universities and other organizations, and Premiere Productions/48 Hour Forum, where the aim is to "create exceptional work that transcends cultural boundaries and speaks to all people" (noortheatre.org). The word "Noor" means "light" in both Farsi and Arabic.

The company won an Obie Award in 2016. In their acceptance speech for the award, Issaq and Chehlaoui listed many reasons for why the company was founded, including providing a home for talented Middle Eastern American theatre artists, to support and develop the work of artists of Middle Eastern descent, and to create a place where playwrights and directors could tell their own stories and be the center of their own narratives. In addition, the company was a direct response to living in a post-9/11 atmosphere, where Middle Easterners are regarded with suspicion and fear. "We create plays that counter those stereotypes, in the hopes that the work we do just might shift those dangerous misperceptions, or change a heart, or mind" (Noor Theatre 2016). Since their founding in 2010, they produced world premieres of ten plays, including *Food and Fadwa* by Lameece Issaq and Jacob Kader (2012); *Myth in Motion* (with the students of the NJIT/Rutgers Theater program (2013); *The Myth Project*, which included *Phoenicia Flowers* by Noelle Ghoussaini; *The In-Between* by Kareem Fahmy; *I Am Gordafarid* by Pirronne Yousefzadeh; and *Dead Are My People* by Ismail Khalidi, Hadi Eldebek, and Patrick Lazour.

Pangea World Theatre

Minneapolis-based Pangea World Theatre's mission states, "Pangea illuminates the human condition, celebrates cultural differences, and promotes human rights by creating and presenting international, multi-disciplinary theater" (pangeaworldtheater.org). The theatre focuses its "intercultural, sacred theater that stands for intersectionality and justice" in multiple theatrical communities, including Middle Eastern American and South Asian American artists. The company was founded in 1995 by Artistic and Executive Director Meena Natarajan and Artistic Director Dipankar Mukherjee. With a focus on ensemble-based processes interlaced with a global perspective, Pangea World Theatre has defined itself as a theatre that celebrates multiple aesthetics and mediums, community engagement, and leadership in participating Immigrant, Indigenous, and People of Color communities. Their programs include Lake Street Arts!, The National Institute for Directing & Ensemble Creation, Indigenous Voices, Alternate Visions, Race North and South on the Great River, and other educational workshops and residencies.

Silk Road Rising/Silk Road Theatre Project

Silk Road Rising (previously known as Silk Road Theatre Project) bills itself as "America's first theatre and media arts organization dedicated to telling stories of East Asian, South Asian, and Middle Eastern Communities" (silkroadrising.org). Its founding artistic director, Jamil Khoury, and founding executive director, Malik Gillani, established the company in Chicago, Illinois, in 2003. Khoury, who describes himself as "a white Arab

Slovak Pole," was raised in the Antiochian Orthodox Christian tradition. His husband, and cofounder, Malik Gillani, is an Ismaili Muslim. Their theatre, labeled by American Theatre Magazine as one of "A dozen young American companies you need to know" in 2004, has risen in prominence as one of the preeminent Middle Eastern American theatres. Their first production, *Precious Stones*, set the tone for the works to come: plays that focus on playwrights of Asian and Middle Eastern backgrounds that both "enrich the fabric of American storytelling" and "advance civic engagement and public discourse." The company was also founded as a response to the attacks of 9/11 with the aim "to educate, promote dialogue, and heal rifts through the transformative power of theatre." Silk Road Rising has been the professional theatre-in-residence at the downtown First United Methodist Church at the Chicago Temple since 2006.

For Khoury, theatre is a means to a specific end. He says, "We love the art form, but that's not where we're coming from. It's the desire to impact change." Khoury, who was shaped directly by his cross-cultural upbringing, his sexuality, his direct engagement with the plight of Palestinian refugees, and his personal experiences with homophobia and racism, believes in the activist potential of theatre and social media. According to their website, "The legacy of the Silk Road provided us the narrative from which our core values would appear: Discovery, Pluralism, and Empathy" (silkroadrising .org). The company has expanded from one that solely presented theatre productions to one that now creates video plays, community-based performances, and recorded internet and television interviews.

Since its initial production in 2003, Silk Road Rising has produced many plays by Middle Eastern American and South Asian American writers, including *Ten Acrobats in an Amazing Leap of Faith* (2005), *Back of the Throat* (2006), and *Our Enemies: Lively Scenes of Love and Combat* (2008) all by Yussef El Guindi; *Scorched* by Wajdi Mouawad (2010); *Invasion!* by Jonas Hassen Khemiri (2013); *My American Cousin* by Jameeleh Shelo (2015); *Ziryab, the Songbird of Andalusia* by Ronnie Malley (2016); *Mosque Alert* by Jamil Khoury (2016); *Detour Guide* by Karim Nagi (2019); and *Twice, Thrice, Frice . . .* by Fouad Teymour (2019).

TARTE: Turkish American Repertory Theater & Entertainment

TARTE is a Turkish American Repertory Theatre based in the Northeastern United States "whose mission includes the sharing of Turkish culture and literature with American audiences" (tarteusa.com). TARTE performs Turkish and American classics as well as new works. They have also adapted plays, dance theatre, and have created a one-act play festival and children's programs. The founding artistic director, Ayse Eldek-Richardson, was born and raised in Turkey but immigrated to the United States in 1997 where she has worked in theatre, film, and television since. Other artists who work with TARTE include resident choreographer Sevin Ceviker, resident writer Ayse Alagoz, writer Ivan Faute, writer/director Yusuf Yildiz, writer Emre Ozpirincci, and resident performers Defne Halman, Hazar Tuna, Denise Turkan, Feryal Kilisli, Zeynep Desen Uygur, and Hannah Snow. Other associated artists include honorary writer Tuncer Cucenoglu, honorary actor Tolga Savaci, tap choreographer Jule Jo Ramirez, and music mixer Fuat Caner Tokgozol. Some of the plays they have produced include *Lost Sock Laundry* by Ivan Faute, *Of Dogs & Squirrels* by Emre Ozpirincci, *Matrushka* by Tuncer Cucenoglu, and *To love . . .* by Ayse Eldek-Richardson.

Theater J

Theater J, based in Washington, DC, and founded in 1990 as a program of the Edlavitch DC Jewish Community Center (EDCJCC), was established under the leadership of Founding Artistic Director Martin Blank. Its initial space was a 40-seat black box theatre at the original home of the EDCJCC, but in 1997 the company moved to a larger 238-seat theatre named for Aaron and Cecile Goldman. The company describes itself in this way:

> Theater J is a nationally renowned, professional theater that celebrates, explores, and struggles with the complexities and nuances of both the Jewish experience and the universal human condition. Our work illuminates and examines: ethical questions of our time, inter-cultural experiences that parallel our own, and the changing landscape of Jewish identities. As the nation's largest and most prominent Jewish theater, we aim to preserve and expand a rich Jewish theatrical tradition and to create community and commonality through theater-going experiences. (theaterj.org)

Theater J became known for producing works from and about Israel and the Middle East and for their "Voices from a Changing Middle East" Festival. The company states that it produces works by Jewish and non-Jewish writers that "investigate diverse stories about immigrants, language, assimilation, genocide, religion, otherness and other topics that resonate with a diverse set of communities" (theaterj.org). In 2017 Theater J inaugurated the Yiddish Theater Lab, which was meant to revitalize Yiddish theatre and to make those works relevant to contemporary audiences. The company has produced works by renowned Jewish American playwrights such as Richard Greenberg, Tony Kushner, David Mamet, Donald Margulies, Arthur Miller, Itamar Moses, Clifford Odets, Neil Simon, and Wendy Wasserstein. They have also produced work by Israeli playwrights like Boaz Gaon, Motti Lerner, Savyon Liebrecht, and Hillel Mittelpunkt. Theater J has been honored with the D.C. Mayor's Arts Award for Excellence in an Artistic Discipline and has garnered over seventy Helen Hayes nominations and nine Helen Hayes Awards.

Tribute: Reza Abdoh

Reza Abdoh was an Iranian-born theatre director, playwright, and founder of the company Dar A Luz. The company's most renowned productions included *The Hip-Hop Waltz of Euridice* (1990), *Bogeyman* (1991), *The Law of Remains* (1992), *Tight Right White* (1993), and *Quotations from a Ruined City* (1994), all directed by Abdoh. The productions were primarily staged in Los Angeles, New York City, and in various European cities, and some were cowritten with his brother, Salar. Abdoh preferred site-specific, mixed media theatre that crossed the boundaries of theatre and performance art. Considered one of the leaders of the postmodern avant-garde of his time, Abdoh's large ensemble-based productions were "queer, non-Western, antihierarchical, political, and mystically religious" (Bell 1995). Abdoh borrowed from many sources: BDSM, fairy tales, talk shows, video art, classical texts, raves, and previous avant-garde theatrical productions.

Abdoh died of AIDS-related complications on May 11, 1995, at the age of thirty-two. In 2018 MoMA PS1 held a large-scale retrospective exhibition of his theatre and film works, organized by Negar Azimi, Tiffany Malakooti, and Babak Radboy. In her *Artforum* review of the exhibition, Jennifer Krasinski wrote, "It is not an overstatement to say that had Reza Abdoh lived even one more year, had he created even one more production, American theater would look very different now" (Krasinski 2018).

As this chapter demonstrates, Middle Eastern Americans have been creating professional theatre in North America for many decades now.

Representing many communities, these companies seek to foster the work of new writers, change the misperceptions many have about Middle Easterners, offer opportunities to Middle Eastern American artists, and to increasingly diversify the American theatre landscape. Despite their efforts, many of these companies are still not funded sufficiently, and they struggle to get their own communities to fully support them. However, these companies continually defied the odds and produced high-quality works that redefined the theatre landscape.

CHAPTER 2
RETURN TO THE HOMELAND PLAYS

One of the major types of plays by Middle Eastern American playwrights is that of "return to the homeland." Many of the writers in this genre are either from the countries they write about, descendants of immigrants from those countries, and/or dual citizens of those countries. As such, these playwrights (and sometimes performers) find themselves writing plays that explore their journeys from, journeys to, and experiences in their ancestral homelands. These experiences challenge their protagonists (whether the protagonists are themselves, or fictional creations that mirror their own lives and experiences). In some cases, these journeys home are enlightening; however, some are heartbreaking returns that challenge their deepest beliefs. For in these journeys home, they realize their journey away from home has changed them, and their desire to find a place where they belong in their parents' homeland, or even their own, proves that they no longer belong there. This leads to a schism within these characters. Some return with more wisdom, and more pain. Others return with the understanding that they cannot find peace at home or abroad. Some playwrights decide to end their plays with no definable conclusion—they remain in a state of limbo, letting the audience ultimately decide what happens in their future.

When discussing the idea of transplanted immigrants from their homes of origin to their new homelands, Victoria M. Abboud writes, "The 'trans' part of 'transplant,' I argue, is a continuous process, a difficult and arduous task that requires immigrants continuously to negotiate their identities through their pasts and their current situations. The children of immigrants, too, must negotiate this identity and determine the level at which they will acknowledge or own their cultural history and current life's narrative" (Abboud 2003, 373). Unlike previous generations of immigrants, who could not regularly visit their homelands, contemporary immigrants can regularly maintain political, economic, and emotional connections with their home countries through relatively inexpensive modes of transportation and communication. Internet communication has led to a tighter global community, allowing cultural connections to remain stronger than ever. Abboud cites that immigrants experience a "guest-foreigner" dichotomy when coming to a new country, but the same occurs when immigrants, and children of immigrants, return to their respective homelands. On that return, Abboud writes, one must reconcile the memory of what was, with the reality of what has become of their country in their absence. "The immigrant experience [. . .] is filled with complex issues of identity-formation, the sense of longing for a former life, and the difficulty of attaining cultural and linguistic fluency in the new location" (ibid., 391). Carol Fadda-Conrey labels this phenomenon "returns and rearrivals." For Fadda-Conrey, Arab American protagonists experience a revisionary negotiation of their Arab American identity through journeys to their Arab ancestral homelands. She notes,

> Renegotiating the place of the Arab-American body, specifically the female body, in light of such political relations inscribes transformative understandings of the Arab homeland onto the US terrain. For instead of the homeland being regarded as the root cause of Arab-Americans' foreignness in the US, a more complex, transnational, and less binary-based knowledge of this homeland becomes an important conduit for reimagining the place occupied by the Arab-American subject within the US. (Fadda-Conrey 2014, 68)

This lack of cultural and linguistic fluency is the very thing that makes visits back to the homeland so fraught with difficulty. The return to homeland leads to rearrivals that question and rewrite both the inherited and the hegemonic ideas regarding Arab American identity. In addition, they cause a rethinking of citizenship back in the United States. Fadda-Conrey writes that these literary and artistic works "create transformative spaces that are elemental for social and political justice" (ibid., 104).

Neda Maghbouleh writes about the specific issues Iranian Americans face when returning to the homeland. These difficulties include having two passports, and the need to swap them when in transit; young men having to deal with being of age for mandatory military service; and girls and young women having to cover their hair and change into appropriate clothing after entering Iranian airspace. Upon entering Iran, there are other challenges. "For young men in particular, to be viewed with suspicion for *being* Iranian while getting to Iran only to be viewed with suspicion for not being Iranian *enough* once they stepped foot on Iranian soil was particularly vexing" (Maghbouleh 2017, 124; emphasis in original). Further difficulties lie in embarrassment about one's accent, manner of speaking or dressing, and the need to mute one's Americanness in public places. "This involved conscientious choices around when to speak in public settings in order to remove the threat of being 'found out' as an Iranian American" (ibid., 128). According to Maghbouleh, young Iranian men and women are disillusioned when traveling back to Iran because they come away with "gendered ethno-racial experiences that rendered them liminal outsiders within" (ibid., 133). What's more, there have been troubling accounts of Iranian Americans who hold dual citizenship being arrested, with some given lengthy prison sentences. Many who wish to travel back to Iran are nervous about doing so, but some travel agents tell them, "If they are not active in politics, they are safe" (Etehad 2016). Still, many students, journalists, business travelers, and academics are under the threat of arrest for espionage or posing threats to national security. In addition, Iran does not recognize dual citizenship so, if one is detained, it is difficult for the foreign governments to aid with their release. Regarding travel to the United States, Iranians studying in the United States with student visas have been summarily deported back to Iran with little or no explanation. In the process, students are subject to extreme profiling and aggressive interrogations.

Some of these plays focus on young Arab Americans or Jewish Americans going to Palestine and/or Israel. This particular genre is fascinating because it usually takes the form of a young Jewish person going on their Birthright Trip, which is, according to Taglit/Birthright Israel, "A free Israel Adventure, A 10-day journey for Jewish young adults aged 18–32." The website Birthrightisrael has a running tally of those who have taken the trip, which, by early 2020, was at 750,000. The website claims, "Experience Israel on an action-packed journey exploring ancient sites, local hotspots, and natural wonders. Travel with Israeli peers who will introduce you to the vibrant culture, and mouth-watering cuisine that makes Israel a top vacation destination" (birthrightisrael.com). For Palestinians and Palestinian Americans, however, the journey back to Palestine has no website promising exciting journeys, exotic foods, or sunny vacations. In fact, the journey for these travelers is usually fraught with complications that include hours-long interrogations at the airport, taking long and punishing bus rides across the Allenby Bridge/Al-Karameh Bridge/King Hussein Bridge from Jordan, or finding other ways to get to the Palestinian territories that are glutted with checkpoints, curfews, and armed military personnel. Some are turned back at entry points if Israeli authorities discover anything on the traveler's social media accounts that supports the BDS (Boycott, Divestment, and

Sanctions) movement, or any other information the Israeli government believes "wish it harm" (Goodstein 2017).

Palestinian American solo performer, playwright, and comic Jennifer Jajeh's *I Heart Hamas: And Other Things I'm Afraid to Tell You* is another personal journey of a Christian/Catholic Arab American woman who journeys back to her ancestral homeland of Palestine. Jajeh, whose family has lived in the West Bank town of Ramallah for the past 450 years, decided to create the play because she was tired of explaining herself and her beliefs about the conflict. In 2000 she traveled to Ramallah, staying a year and a half, only to return to New York and the 9/11 attacks. "I clearly had post-traumatic stress from living in a war zone," she says. "'Why do these people hate us' is what a lot of people were saying after September 11th. There's such a misunderstanding of Arabs and Muslims in general. . . . There was such a need of humanization of stories" (Girmay 2010). As a Palestinian American actress frustrated with the limited choices of roles available to her, her solo performance became the vehicle whereby she could begin a more playful, less fearful conversation about Palestine. She makes it clear she is not speaking for all Palestinians in the play—only for herself.

Jajeh labels the show "a tragicomic solo show." The play's provocative title, especially considering the US State Department's designation of Hamas as a terrorist organization, and with the ongoing violence between Hamas and the Israeli State, makes it controversial in American theatre. During an opening voice-over, Jajeh asks audiences to consider the conflict in the Middle East from the Palestinian perspective. She also asks the audience to not accuse her of being anti-Semitic because Arabs, as well as Jews, are Semites. After explaining about herself and her family's background, Jajeh describes the history of Ramallah to the audience. She then relates why she traveled to Palestine where she was going not to find her roots, but rather because her life in New York as an actress was at a standstill and she wanted a break and to learn Arabic.

While in Palestine studying Arabic at a university, she meets a Palestinian Muslim man named Hakam. She encounters the same kind of resistance many face when returning to a place their parents are from, but a place they must now understand for themselves. Some tell her that her Arabic is terrible, some tell her she looks Spanish and not Palestinian, and she realizes that the occupation affects everything in her life. Her relationship with Hakam is strained because of the cultural and religious differences that divide them. When Hakam asks her to marry him, she objects saying that he's already married, and she would have to convert and become his second wife.

Despite her desire to find normalcy, she discovers that roads are closed, checkpoints have endless lines of cars, and she takes her position as an American for granted. When she finally confronts an Israeli soldier, she realizes the limits of her privilege. Jajeh describes spitting on an Israeli soldier during a protest and justifies this by telling the audience about the assaults Palestinians face every day, and how they are treated inhumanely by the soldiers. She states that living there is like living in a pressure cooker, and that not everyone there can handle the pressure. She witnesses a child being shot by an Israeli soldier for throwing rocks. She hears about a Palestinian man who runs over a group of Israeli soldiers. The mounting violence leads to her spiraling into depression. She departs Palestine after breaking up with Hakam and coming to an awful realization. After living there for a year and a half, she reached a point where she could actually imagine how someone might carry out a suicide attack. The 450-year history of her family will soon end since most of her family have also fled Palestine, and the Christian community in Ramallah is dwindling. She feels that she is the break in a chain that stretches back 450 years. Despite her desire to leave Palestine behind her she cannot do so, leaving her feeling lost and helpless.

Ken Kaissar's play *The Victims: Or What Do You Want Me to Do About It?* is the journey of a Jewish American man to Israel and Palestine. Kaissar, a Yemenite-Mizrahi Jew, wrote the play based on his own visit to Israel. Kaissar's protagonist, David, is also of Yemenite Jewish heritage. Another subplot, connected to the main plot and David's journey, deals with two Beckettian characters of unknown ethnicity named Jadi and Basee, who live in a nondescript garden, and who are against their mysterious overlord Assav. Kaissar's primary focus on David's journey is mirrored in the conflicts of Jadi and Basee, and their parallel stories eventually merge for the play's climactic ending.

David was born in Israel but now resides in the United States. The first indication of this dual citizenship comes when the Immigration Officer at Ben Gurion Airport, who takes his Israeli passport, tells David his US passport will not be of use to him while in Israel. David tells the man that Israel is his home, but he is instantly rebuked when the Officer asks him why he lives in New York and not in Israel. Instantly, David is confronted with the fact that he may be welcome, but he is also seen with suspicion by his fellow Jews there.

David's stay at the Chalom Herzl Hotel introduces him to Motti, a free-wheeling and casual businessman whose hotel seems to be running on the barest of means: the beds aren't made, there are no towels in the room, and hardly any running water. His experience at a local restaurant is not much better. The proprietor there reminds him that everybody around him is a thief or a terrorist. When David befriends a Palestinian man, Mas'ud, who lives in Huwara within the West Bank, he is invited to dinner at his family home. David's theatrical detour to Palestine is one many Israeli Jews have actually taken recently as "detours" from their Birthright trips to Israel (Turnbull 2019). One group named Breaking the Silence arranges such tours. This group, comprised of veteran Israeli soldiers, "have taken it upon themselves to expose the Israeli public to the reality of everyday life in the Occupied Territories." They claim that their work "aims to bring an end to the occupation" (breakingthesilence.org).

Upon their approach to a checkpoint, David experiences Mas'ud's humiliation. "Do you know what we hate, David?" Mas'ud asks. "We hate living under Israeli occupation. We hate that the Israeli government targets Palestinian civilians. We hate that there is not a moment of peace for us. That there is no freedom. That's what we hate" (Kaissar 2018, 203). David is given another rude awakening when he returns from the West Bank to Israel and is detained by soldiers. When David stands up for his Arab friend when he is accused of potential terrorism, the soldier Yael disabuses him of any notion that Israelis and Palestinians can coexist.

> DAVID: His name is Mas'ud.
> YAEL: Mas'ud? How nice. It'll be handy to know his name when he blows himself up on a bus.
> DAVID: That's a really ignorant thing to say, you know that?
> YAEL: Ignorant? The absentee Israeli is calling me ignorant. Do you serve in the army? Do you risk your life everyday protecting this country?
> DAVID: No.
> YAEL: No. So don't call me ignorant. Enjoy your calm, peaceful life in America. And don't come here to teach me about terrorists. I see it everyday. I know what it looks like. (ibid., 208–9)

By befriending a Palestinian, David transgresses. He comes to the country in a spirit of peace building, but quickly realizes that spirit is one that is born from a privileged position far from the conflict. Yael tells him, "It's easy to be a peacenik from thousands of miles away, Americano. Try being a peacenik here. It won't be so easy for you" (ibid., 209–10). David is further disillusioned when he meets his cousin Elad, who owns a bar and has a Palestinian man named Bassam working for him. After joking and drinking, David asks his cousin to tell him what life is like there. Despite protesting and telling David he doesn't really want to know, Elad explains what he had to do as a soldier to a young Palestinian boy throwing rocks at him.

> What did I do? I picked him up. I stripped him naked. And I tied him to the top of my jeep. And then I drove him all around the village, so that everyone could see him. Eight years old. No one throws rocks at you with a naked 8 year-old kid tied to your jeep. And everyone got the message that you don't throw rocks at a soldier. (ibid., 216)

Elad tells David not to get too comfortable in America because, eventually, Americans will also turn on the Jews. When David asks where that leaves Israel, Elad tells him that Israelis are not going anywhere without a fight and, with nuclear weapons, they will face defeat like Samson: "We may lose. But we won't be the only ones" (ibid., 217). David's most painful experience occurs when the Shalom Herzl Hotel is blown up by a suicide bomber, just minutes before he was to return there. When Mas'ud finds him, David lashes out:

> DAVID: How does this happen, Mas'ud? How does a man just blow himself up to murder others?
>
> MAS'UD: It's terrible, David. What can I tell you? If that man had a life that was worth living, maybe this wouldn't happen.
>
> DAVID: See Mas'ud. When you say things like that, it sounds like you think what he did was justified.
>
> MAS'UD: No David. Please. Don't misunderstand. Killing innocent people is never justified. I wish these things would stop happening. But at the same time, when people can barely feed their families, when they have nothing, no life, no freedom, what do you expect them to do?
>
> DAVID: What do I expect? I'll tell you what I don't expect. I don't expect them to murder innocent people. That's what I don't expect.
>
> MAS'UD: Again, I'm not excusing what he did, David. But . . . it's complicated. No? (ibid., 220)

Kaissar's subplot complicates the issues in the play since it is impossible to tell whether Jadi, Bassee, and Assav are Israeli or Palestinian. All that is known is that they continue to abuse one another in the garden in more violent ways. Even the intervention of an American peacekeeper/envoy named Paula only leads to more chaos and less peace. David finally ejects Paula from the garden, makes Jadi, Bassee, and Assav get into a cage with him, and he throws away the key. Instead of running away, David decides to stay and tells them that they had better get busy dreaming together of a solution to the problem. The final image is one of all four trapped in the cage as the lights fade to black.

Najla Said's solo performance *Palestine* is about a real-life journey Said took with her father, the late Edward W. Said, to Palestine in the late 1990s. There she sees signs of the Israel occupation—settlements, Israeli soldiers at checkpoints, and her family's ancestral home which was then occupied by Israeli citizens. She realizes that, despite being Palestinian herself, she is an outsider there.

> And yet, I realized, they are the ones who suffer on a daily basis in a way I never would. They were victims of the circumstances of their birth in a way I would never be. And they are the ones who would have to deal, not just mentally, but actually, for the rest of their lives, with the consequences of a history that they, like me, might never fully understand. (Said 2013, 165)

Said, who grew up in New York as a self-described "Upper West Side princess," was often confused by many for being Jewish herself. While growing up in Beirut in the 1980s during the civil war there, Said survived several bombings. Later, as an adult living in New York, she witnessed the attacks of 9/11, and found herself in Beirut during the 2006 war. During 9/11, when some were quick to incorrectly blame Palestinians for the attack, she realized that her anonymity was forever removed. She then decided to embrace her Arab American identity and to speak out about the injustices she saw all around her: "Since 9/11 I am officially an Arab, bridging the gap between two worlds that don't understand each other" (ibid., 251). One way she did this was joining the Arab American ensemble Nibras, and writing and performing works from that subject position.

Her solo performance *Palestine* is her way of working through her experiences of being a Christian Palestinian American and being the daughter of one of the most revered and influential Palestinian academics, writers, and activists in US history. The trip to Palestine with her family was, at the time, a forced family vacation. As she travels through Jerusalem, Nablus, Hebron, Nazareth, and Bethlehem, she sees Israeli soldiers everywhere: "I found comfort nowhere but in the faces of the Palestinian children we meet along the way. They, like me, were silent. They very clearly had no control over their surroundings. They were simply born into this history, and just like me, they had no memories of a Palestine other than the one in which they lived" (ibid., 165). The trip to Gaza is even more harrowing. There she experiences what she calls "an enormous concentration camp" with overcrowded refugee settlements, the smell of sewage, and a terrible lack of hope. "I tried to wrap my teenage head around the existence of such a place in the world, where people are trapped like caged animals in the filthiest zoo on earth, while I somehow got to prance around in suede shoes and $150 skirts and then get on a plane and go home" (ibid., 173). This kind of second-generation survivor's guilt is one that pervades many plays of this genre. There is an intrinsic connection with the people in the homeland, but a terrible sense of shame that others are living through difficult circumstances, while the visitor can return to life as normal back in North America: "I wanted to know why I was born lucky. Why didn't I have to live here? Why was I able to pass as a Jew if I wanted? Why did I get to go to the best schools in the world? And why, despite all of this, did I still feel awful?" (ibid., 175). The final leg of her journey takes her to Jordan (for a brief and strange encounter) with Yasser Arafat, and then to her mother's homeland of Lebanon which was recovering from the civil war that raged there. She experiences the lively café and nightclub culture of Beirut, but she also visits places like Al-Khiam prison where the South Lebanese and Israeli Armies incarcerated and tortured prisoners. On her later 2006 trip to Lebanon, she is reminded of the conflicts that embroil the region. She was in Beirut when Hezbollah and Israel fought, and Israeli planes bombed Lebanon. Suddenly, her beliefs as a pacifist and humanist are challenged and she feels rage at the planes bombing the city around her. She feels a momentary rage against the Israelis. Again, she returns to New York, leaving the conflict behind her. She concludes that she is both Arab and American and that she is "bridging the gap between two worlds that don't understand each other" (ibid., 251). Said brings a unique perspective to her work given her family's notoriety, her personal journeys overseas, and her perspective as a Palestinian American woman.

Taous Claire Khazem's one-woman play *In Algeria They Know My Name* chronicles her upbringing born to an Algerian Kabyle (Berber) father and American mother. Khazem grew up in Minnesota and fell in love with an Algerian man. The solo performance chronicles her subsequent marriage and life living and working in North Africa. With only a few bins and a bicycle on stage, Khazem begins by telling the audience about how awkward it was growing up in America with a name hardly anyone could pronounce (Taous is an Amazigh name that means "peacock"). Her parents were divorced, but she recounts that her father would take her to a museum to see a painting titled *The Carpet Merchant*, which was meant to remind her of her Berber heritage. Later, while in college, she makes her first trip to Algeria to attend her uncle's wedding. When she visits her father's village of Tizi Ouzou, she realizes that she has found her people. The Kabyle are a Berber subgroup from Algeria that inhabit mountainous regions. The Kabyle speak a Berber language of the same name. Khazem states she was often frustrated because she only spoke English and French, not Kabyle or Arabic, which led to many difficulties navigating her life in Algeria.

In the play she meets an Algerian actor from Oran named Mohamed. After a short courtship, they decide to marry but, as Khazem says, his family wanted nothing to do with her. Like most single Algerians, Mohamed lived with his family—a mother, three married brothers, one married sister, and two unmarried older sisters. As she says, in Algeria you do not just marry one finger, you marry all ten. Gradually, the family accepts the marriage, but Khazem then faces the very different and complicated traditions that comprise Algerian wedding customs including a massive guest list, expectations of wearing multiple outfits at the reception, and not being present when the Imam actually marries them. She learns of the legal exigencies of marriage in Algeria such as virginity certificates and pregnancy tests. Also, she experiences the charming elements of Kabyle customs such as drinking a glass of milk (a symbol of purity and good luck) and eating dates (a symbol of sweetness), while keeping the date pit as a reminder of their union (another symbol of good fortune).

The next difficulties Khazem faces are professional: trying to have a theatrical career with her husband in Algeria and Tunisia. Her inability to speak Arabic becomes an issue, as some Algerians consider French the language of the colonizer, and therefore speaking it there is not always welcome. She perseveres, starting a theatre company with her husband called Daraja (Bicycle) Theatre and teaching theatre classes to local women. Despite her best efforts, she fails. Like many second-generation children who travel back to the homeland, she says the wrong things and angers the people around her. She observes the fervor of the Arab Spring and finds that Algerians of her generation that grew up with civil war, curfews, and assassinations have little enthusiasm for the revolt. Eventually she finds her place, coaching Algerian women to act and create their own theatre work. It is in the theatre there that she finds that she has finally done something right. By the end of the play she says her Arabic improved, she became her mother-in-law's favorite, and she learned to love eating lamb. Khazem's play is meant to give audiences an experience of her journey from a disconnected, single Algerian American young woman to an older, married woman living in Algeria who has learned not only to love her father's culture but to also fully embrace it in her life.

Leila Buck's solo performance *In the Crossing* is an exploration of her real-life experience of visiting her mother's homeland of Lebanon with her Jewish American husband Adam during the outbreak of war between Hezbollah and Israel. Buck's mother Hala Lababidi was born to a Sunni Muslim father and a Maronite Catholic mother, and her father, Stephen Buck, has filial roots that date back to the Massachusetts Bay Colony of 1636 (Lababidi Buck, xiii). Buck also calls herself "a bridge" in the play, something her mother has called her, since the gift of the bridge is that it can see both sides. Buck has written about this topic before in her other solo works *ISite* and *Hkeele*. Like those plays, Buck evokes the spirit of her Teta (grandmother) and Jeddo (grandfather). She recounts how her grandmother was raised Catholic and her grandfather, Muslim. Her parents met while working at the American Embassy in Beirut, and Leila Buck grew up traveling the world with her parents whenever her father was given a new assignment.

The play takes the format of a conference speech that Buck is delivering for what is called the "National Association for Cross-Cultural Education and Transformation." The play has three characters—a White Anglo-Saxon Protestant woman known as "Moderator"; Leila, a 31-year-old Lebanese American writer, performer, and activist; and an "Audience Plant," who is Jewish American or possibly Israeli. The Moderator tells the audience that Leila's husband Adam, who is a photographer and web designer, is in the tech booth projecting the images that appear behind her. Buck begins with her understanding of being a bridge between cultures, how her parents met, and how she and her husband Adam met in college. She explains that Adam is Jewish and attended Hebrew school but does not share many of the views of Zionist Jews regarding Israel. She also recounts the first Passover she spent with Adam's family and how the Middle Easterners in her life have consistently had misunderstandings about one another's cultures. She tells the audience about how she grew up hearing about the glories of the Lebanon of the 1960s, and the horrors of the Lebanon of the 1970s–1990s. When she and Adam receive news of a friend's wedding in Beirut, they decide to travel there in 2006. Many relatives worried about Adam's traveling to Lebanon, but he ultimately decides to go.

Arriving in Lebanon, they experience the Beirut from the bar culture, to the stylish beach resorts, to the excitement over the World Cup happening that year. Suddenly they are faced with the breakout of hostilities between Hezbollah and Israel. Gradually, the vacation they enjoyed becomes one filled with the mounting fear of being killed by air raids, and the necessity for evacuation from the country. In recounted conversations, Buck explains how Lebanese discuss the frustration of Hezbollah being a fixture in their country's politics, the anger at Israel for their punishing attacks on Lebanese civilians and infrastructure, and the complicity Leila and Adam feel being American citizens who, indirectly through their US taxes, are funding such a war. Images of destruction from the war are projected behind Leila as she embodies a host of characters. While this occurs, the Audience Plant makes snide remarks under their breath at some of the claims Leila makes during her speech. Leila takes the audience through the day-to-day discussions she has with family, friends, and others who debate the justifications and outrages of the war that has suddenly overwhelmed the nation. They urge their friends and family to write their elected officials to call for a cease-fire. Ultimately, they decide to leave the country, through Syria, despite their feelings of guilt for doing so. They arrive in Damascus and later go to Amman, all the time hearing of more bombings and death just three hours away in Lebanon. Later, in London, while visiting Adam's grandparents, Leila is again faced with more complicated feelings regarding what their family suffered from the time of the Holocaust to the events of Hurricane Katrina. There are painful conversations that underscore the shared pain of Arabs and Jews that have spanned over a century now, leading Leila to conclude her speech in the play with the understanding that families are made of blood or marriages, but the connections we make are made by choice and that love heals all wounds.

Just when it seems the play has concluded, the Moderator opens the floor to questions and Leila is confronted by the Audience Plant who berates her for siding with the Lebanese against the Israelis. As the Audience Plant becomes more angered and confrontational, all the Moderator can think to do is sing "All You Need Is Love" by the Beatles, while more images of death and destruction are displayed on the screen behind them. Finally, the character Leila screams, "ENOUGH!!!" and she is left alone to tell of the discussion she had with Adam's grandparents after 9/11 where they realized that the topic of Israel was one they could not discuss with one another because of the painful emotions it stirred for them all. Returning to the conference, Leila tells the Moderator that she understands that both sides have suffered in the conflict, but that the view Americans have of the wars in the Middle East are often skewed to present an American perspective at the expense of those who have suffered and died in the wars there. She says that she is trying to ask audiences to picture the people living in the Middle East, to hear their voices and stories like she does, and she questions if that makes her biased. She returns to why she loves bridges and how hard it is to build them. She states she wants to be the bridge that makes people understand the journey that must be taken collectively to get to the other side because the importance is not in the bridge itself, but in the crossing.

Buck's monodrama is a deep exploration into her roots, her family's history, and the ongoing struggle she faces attempting to exist in two very different worlds. Her return to the homeland, like that of her other contemporaries, is fraught with conflict, war, and painful realizations that she must straddle two very different worlds that are often at odds with one another. Buck has the unique vantage of someone who comes from both cultures and can see the beauty and flaws in each. As a gifted storyteller and performer, she is able to weave the complicated Lebanese, Jewish, Palestinian, and American narratives together in order to create the journey that allows audiences with little experience with Middle Eastern stories "crossing" into worlds they would otherwise never know. Furthermore, by playing all of these characters herself, she physically embodies the conflict so audiences can experience the journey through her and not as passive observers of actors playing characters they may have no connection with whatsoever. Buck writes her own experiences and performs them as well, which takes her storytelling deeper and gives audiences a unique perspective into a world facing unimaginable conflict.

The return to the homeland play is a fixture of Middle Eastern American theatre because so many travel back to the homeland to find meaning in their lives. The connections diasporic Middle Eastern Americans have with their families overseas are deep, meaningful, and rich. As seen in the plays by Jajeh, Kaissar, Said, Khazem, and Buck, the travels back to the homeland have many reasons—some travel with family in a kind of pilgrimage, some travel with a desire to reconnect with family, while for others it is to marry and create a life. In all cases, the journey back to the homeland is often filled with joy and pain, frustration and understanding, fear and love. These plays can give Middle Eastern Americans a shared experience that allows them to have a greater understanding of their unique realities. These plays also offer non-Middle Eastern American audiences the opportunity to better understand the complex reality those living in the Middle East face on a regular basis, sometimes as a result of the actions taken by foreign governments. Essentially, these playwrights and performers are translating their experiences for audiences who they believe should know more about what is being done, both politically and militarily, in the Middle East, in their name.

CHAPTER 3
PERSECUTION PLAYS

Middle Eastern Americans have dealt with different forms of anti-Semitism, Islamophobia, Arabophobia, and other forms of xenophobia since they arrived on the shores of North America in the late nineteenth century. The fact that the United States and Canada were ostensibly established as Christian nations for those of Northern European ancestry has led to a great unease when dealing with those who espouse different religious beliefs, or those who hail from nations outside of the European sphere. To complicate matters further, the nation's founders were intent on the notion that when one became a citizen, they were to cast off any allegiances they might have with their lands of origin. Furthermore, whiteness as the predicating factor for citizenship was the US notion of "free white persons" as outlined in the 1790 Naturalization Act. Therefore, in case after case, those who were outside the bounds of these prescriptions found themselves outside of citizenship and privilege. Middle Eastern Americans, along with many other immigrants who could potentially pass for "white," litigated for their racial status in federal courts in order to gain citizenship. In the book *Between Arab and White: Race and Ethnicity in the Early Syrian American Diaspora*, Sarah M.A. Gualtieri writes,

> Lawyers and applicants marshaled evidence that ranged from skin color to national origin, culture, scientific studies, and popular opinion—or some combination of these factors—to claim whiteness. It was up to the courts to decide which elements should be the basis for determining race and, by extension, eligibility to participate in the privileges of citizenship. (Gualtieri 2009, 2)

Gualtieri writes that, despite victories in court, Middle Eastern Americans were not considered fully "white" but rather somewhere between "black" and "Asian." Later, the 1924 National Origins Act severely restricted the immigration of non-Europeans into the country. Therefore, "whiteness" and "Americanness" were deeply intertwined. Furthermore, one's ability to prove their whiteness was bound to their belonging to the Christian fold.

> Particularly threatening to white southerners was the "inbetweeness" of the new immigrants. The ambiguous racial status of Italians, East European Jews, and Syrians stemmed from the perception that they possessed cultures and habits that were fundamentally at odds with southern traditions and values and that immigrants would not abide by the "white man's code." (ibid., 54)

Nativism ran deep and there were multiple instances of violence perpetrated against Middle Eastern Americans and other immigrants in the early twentieth century. Three Italians were lynched in Hahnville, Louisiana, in 1896: a Jewish man was lynched in 1915; a Syrian family's home was dynamited in Marietta, Georgia, in 1923; and a Syrian grocer was lynched in Lake City Florida in 1929 after his wife was killed by police. Gualtieri quotes one North Carolina senator named F. M. Simmons (1854–1940), who referred to Syrian immigrants as "degenerate progeny of the Asiatic hoards [*sic*] . . . the spawn of the Phoenician curse" (ibid., 4). These are just a few cases of the discrimination Middle Eastern Americans faced in the early twentieth century.

In the book *Colors of Jews: Racial Politics and Radical Diasporism*, Melanie Kaye/Kantrowitz writes about the fact that Jews, along with Irish, Italian, and other "ethnic whites," were viewed as "filthy, diseased, verminous, intellectually inferior, criminal, and morally deficient" (Kaye/Kantrowitz 2007, 11). Although some now see Jews as the model for an American assimilated minority, this extends only to what Kaye/Kantrowitz calls "assimilated Ashkenazi" with stereotypes about Jews primarily revolving around Ashkenazim. The anti-Semitism in North America is as virulent as it is in other places in the world, with ongoing stereotypes such as blood libel, the fear of Jewish conspiracies, and hatred based on Israeli policies.

> In the United States, sectors of the left are blaming Jews for Israeli brutality while sectors of the right blame Jewish money, Jewish homosexuality, and Jewish immorality for everything else. Add in the pro-Zionist Christian Right—the ones who love Jews because the second coming requires our presence—it's hard to know whom to fear most. (ibid., 209)

There is also the ongoing Islamophobia that continues, with the racialization of the religion of Islam. In her book *Detained Without Cause*, Irum Sheikh explains that Muslims have been a part of American history as slaves and immigrants since its outset; however, the image of Muslims as dangerous terrorists subject to detainment and deportation has been rooted in the American imaginary since the Cold War. There has been a long history of anti-Muslim governmental policies including Operation Boulder, Operation ABSCAM, the Registration Program for Iranian Nationals, the Anti-Terrorism and Effective Death Penalty Act, the PATRIOT Act, and the so-called Muslim Ban regarding travel from nations deemed threats to the United States. According to Sheikh,

> The combined impact of foreign policy, global politics, domestic enforcement policies, orientalism, and the shift from the cold war to a holy war has increasingly contributed to creating the image of Muslims as terrorists who are barbaric, savage, fundamentalist, and inhumane. Some political analysts have argued that Islam is the West's new evil empire. (Sheikh 2011, 8)

As these examples demonstrate, Middle Eastern Americans have been facing both governmental and societal persecution for decades. This persecution has led many in the theatre community to write plays about this in order to humanize those who are innocent but perceived as guilty just by their association with their race, ethnicity, or religion.

Governmental Persecution Plays: *Back of the Throat*, *Truth Serum Blues*, and *Zafira and the Resistance*

Playwright Yussef El Guindi has become one of the most prolific and produced Arab American playwright in the post-9/11 era. His plays *Back of the Throat* (2005), *Ten Acrobats in an Amazing Leap of Faith* (2006), *Language Rooms* (2007), *Jihad Jones and the Kalashnikov Babes* (2008), *Our Enemies: Lively Scenes of Love and Combat* (2008), *Language Rooms* (2010), *Pilgrims Musa and Sheri in the New World* (2012), *Threesome* (2015), *The Talented Ones* (2016), and *People of the Book* (2019) have all been widely produced, published, and awarded by the American theatre establishment. El Guindi's breakout play *Back of the Throat* not only established him as a major Muslim Arab American playwright but heralded a series of post-9/11 plays that focused directly on the persecution of Arabs and Muslims in the United States following the attacks of September 11, 2001. The protagonist, Khaled, finds himself at the mercy of a power structure that has predetermined his guilt, which leads to his dehumanization within his own home. The fear, suspicion, and surveillance that hallmark the post-9/11 era, especially against Muslim communities, are dramatized here when two FBI agents named Bartlett and Carl visit Khaled's small apartment and systematically interrogate, threaten, and torture him into confessing to a terrorist attack he did not commit. El Guindi creates a dramatic situation where post-9/11 persecution is viewed as both legitimate and acceptable because of the hysteria and fear of past and future terrorist attacks. El Guindi saw the rising tide of Islamophobia and Arabophobia in the years following 9/11, which prompted him to write the play. He writes, "In this climate, where one feared officials needing to look and act tough and avoid allowing more terrorists through the net, I personally, on a visceral level, found myself fearing a knock on the door. For no logical reason, I should add" (El Guindi 2006, 29).

In the play the agents, Bartlett and Carl, question Khaled about his reading habits, employment history, and social relations. Gradually, the line of questioning becomes more intense and menacing. The agents accuse Khaled of collaborating with a suspected terrorist named Gamal Asfoor. During a series of flashbacks, it is revealed that Khaled's female acquaintances, one of whom was a former girlfriend, have implicated him as someone aiding Asfoor. After the agents violently interrogate and physically abuse Khaled, they leave him with a threat to return the next day to complete their interrogation.

> Here're your choices, Khaled, that you can think about. Either you're innocent. In which case proving that might be difficult. Or you're guilty, in which case telling us now would score you points because we'll find out soon enough. Or: you're innocent of being guilty. You didn't know what you were getting into. Stumbled into it. Through deception. Other people's. Your own stupidity. And that would be okay too. We can work with that. We can work with you to make that seem plausible. (ibid., 49)

Khaled is told that the interrogation is nothing personal. They tell him that what is happening is not profiling, but rather deduction because he happens to come from the place where the troubles are originating. Bartlett tells Khaled,

> You're a Muslim and an Arab. Those are the bad asses currently making life a living hell and so we'll gravitate towards you and your ilk until other bad asses from other races make a nuisance of themselves. Right? Yesterday the Irish and the Poles, today it's you. Tomorrow it might be the Dutch. (ibid., 29)

The terrifying logic employed here is one that simultaneously situates "Americans" as a central, homogeneous group that is constantly being attacked by the foreign Arab/Muslim "other." The fact that each ethnic group must go through a form of state-sanctioned hazing demonstrates that this foreign "other" will never be fully accepted until they conform to some form of American allegiance that dictates that they must strip away all vestiges of their former ethnicity, religion, and culture. Even when Khaled attempts to secure his legal rights as a US citizen, he is rejected outright. Bartlett tells him,

> If I hear another immigrant spew back to me shit about rights, I will fucking vomit. . . . You come here with shit, from shit countries, knowing nothing about anything and you have the nerve to quote the fucking law at me? Come at me with something you know nothing about? [. . .] It's galling.—Sticks in my craw. To hear these people who got here two hours ago quote back to me Thomas Jefferson and the founding fathers. They're not his fucking fathers. (ibid., 36)

The evidence provided against Khaled about his connection with an accused terrorist named Asfoor comes in the form of testimonials by several women who had encounters or relationships with him. The circumstantial evidence against him mounts. The more he protests his innocence, the more violent and aggressive the agents become. Instead of realizing that they are part of a system that creates the violence they perpetuate, the agents blame the victim. Carl tells Khaled,

> You know what I really resent? . . . What you force us to become. To protect ourselves. We are a decent bunch and do not want to be dragged down to your level. But no, you just have to drag us down,

don't you. You have to gross us out with your level of crap. I personally hate this, you know that. I hate it when I have to beat the shit out of someone because then by an act of willful horror, whose effect on my soul I can only imagine, I have to shut out everything good about me and do my job to defend and protect. (ibid., 45–6)

El Guindi's play was one of the first protest plays that addressed the anti-Muslim surveillance state that had developed in the years after 9/11. Its muscular language, raw emotion, and terrifying spectacle set a standard for the plays in this genre. The brutality inflicted on Arab and Muslim bodies in prisons, black sites, and military camps were dramatized for audiences in a way they were not seen prior. El Guindi held up a mirror to American society and asked audiences to question the actions that were committed in their name.

Palestinian American playwright and poet Ismail Khalidi has focused his work on the plight of Palestinians both in Palestine itself and in the United States. His plays include *Truth Serum Blues* (2005), *Tennis in Nablus* (2010), *Foot* (2016), *Sabra Falling* (2017), *Returning to Haifa* (2018), and *Dead Are My People* (2019). Khalidi's plays range from hip-hop-oriented monodramas to historical political realism. The son of noted Palestinian scholar Rashid Khalidi, Ismail Khalidi brings a potent combination of Palestinian history, political activism, poetry, and playwriting to his work.

His solo performance *Truth Serum Blues* dramatized the governmental persecution, intergenerational trauma, and incarceration of Arabs and Muslims imprisoned in black site prisons and other government-sanctioned facilities such as Guantanamo Bay Detention Camp. The play, set sometime between 2002 and 2007, employs multimedia, a chorus of voices, and hip-hop-inflected language and lyrics to tell the story of the protagonist, Kareem. He says he is incarcerated in what he calls "Dubya's Gitmo," a reference to the George W. Bush administration's creation of a site on the island of Cuba that housed suspected terrorists associated with the September 11 attacks as well as those captured during the war in Afghanistan. Kareem jokes about the difference between the Cuba of his imagination—replete with rum, cigars, and the music of the *Buena Vista Social Club*—and the brutal totalitarian prison within which he finds himself. He calls it a mix of Attica and Alcatraz. Kareem knows, however, that the base is vital to US military interests and that, even if a black site like that were slated to be closed, it would ultimately remain open. According to National Public Radio in

2019, in eighteen years the Guantanamo Base cost taxpayers more than $6 billion, and costs $380 million a year to operate despite only housing forty prisoners. There has been only one finalized conviction, and because so many prisoners were tortured there, prosecutors most likely cannot win death penalty convictions. The appeals process will last another ten to fifteen years which may cost billions more. "And the government argues that even if the defendants are found not guilty at trial, it can continue to keep them imprisoned indefinitely" (Pfeiffer 2019). Khalidi reckons that the prison cannot be closed because the crimes committed there cannot be exposed.

The play unfolds with graphic scenes of torture, intercut by flashbacks to scenes with Kareem's Palestinian cousin Waleed. Kareem talks about Palestinian history with recitations of the seemingly endless string of wars, occupations, and dislocations endured by the Palestinian people from the days of the crusaders to the present. We learn that his cousin, Waleed, is a doctor who was accused of cooperating with Hamas. He then adds a chorus of "Intellectual Factors" who appear to be pundits that reduce the Palestinian quest for statehood as one of pathological anti-Semitism and a culture of hatred. In one dialogue Kareem and Waleed discuss why Waleed left the United States. He says that the American inside of him began hating the Arab inside of him, so he smuggled his Arabness back home for safekeeping. For Kareem, born and raised in the United States, there is no going to live in Palestine and no way to go on living in the United States, a country that views him as a terrorist by virtue of being Palestinian alone.

Kareem describes, in detail, the torture he endures in the camp including sleep deprivation, verbal abuse, physical exertion, and broken bones. This is consistent with what is known about how prisoners were treated in US black sites. In her article "The Black Sites: A Rare Look Inside the C.I.A.'s Secret Interrogation Program," *New Yorker* columnist Jane Mayer writes about the use of waterboarding, keeping prisoners for prolonged periods in "dog boxes" or small cages, extreme sensory deprivation, and systematic dehumanization (Mayer 2007). Therefore, Khalidi's play accurately reflects the cruel and inhumane methods deployed by the United States against those suspected terrorists.

In Khalidi's play, Waleed tells how he was verbally attacked and beaten while living in the United States. Kareem begins to look back on US history through the lens of the history of the Black Panthers, the Chicano Movement, the assassinations of Dr. Martin Luther King, Malcolm X, and the history of slavery and the genocide of the Native Americans. The use of "truth inducing drugs" on the protagonist allows for poetic stream-of-consciousness rants about how Arabs and Muslims have faced discrimination for decades, and how Islamophobia and Arabophobia are plaguing society. By the play's end, we learn that Waleed's clinic is obliterated by a US missile strike, and that Kareem feels guilt through his complicity in his cousin's death by being an American taxpayer that indirectly funded the military means of his cousin's murder. Kareem turns himself in to authorities because if he had not, he might have acted out angrily after hearing of his cousin's death. Plays like *Truth Serum Blues* expose the layers of guilt and shame Middle Eastern Americans feel knowing that their tax dollars are funding so many militaristic missions that directly affect their homelands. Khalidi has become one of the leading Palestinian American playwrights who has made it a priority to chronicle the Palestinian experience, and he has consistently done so despite the negative ramifications to his career.

Kathy Haddad's *Zafira and the Resistance* is another play that highlights anti-Arab, anti-Muslim persecution. Haddad is the founder of Mizna, an organization devoted to promoting Arab American culture, a founding member of Pangea World Theatre, a board member of the Loft Literary Center, and the artistic director of New Arab American Theatre Works. Her plays *With Love from Ramallah* (2004), *Zafira the Olive Oil Warrior* (2011), *Zafira and the Resistance* (2019), and *The Hour of Separation* mine Arab American existence in the United States, and how that group deals with issues of separation, exile, and governmental persecution.

Zafira and the Resistance focuses on Zafira, a Minneapolis schoolteacher of Christian Lebanese descent, who must contend with a growing tide of Islamophobia and Arabophobia following a fictional 9/11 scale attack. She is ostracized by her colleagues for eating Middle Eastern foods and scorned by her students who blame her for assigning literature by "dead old foreigners." She has found herself in a climate where teachers are giving extra credit for wearing red, white, and blue to school and her fellow educators are assigning so-called American books for class. An ominous figure called only "The Great Leader" pipes in patriotic music and video messages to the class about fulfilling their duty to country and his special plans to transform public schools into detention centers for detainees. Zafira is called into the principal's office and reprimanded for teaching Arab literature and attempting to convert students to Islam. The principal of the school demands that Zafira spend less time on politics and more time on poetry that is about truth and beauty. Zafira is secretly writing a play about an Arab American superhero whose superpower lies in her olive oil and a belief in her Arab American heritage.

Zafira soon discovers that there are roundups of various Arab and Muslim women occurring in her community. After she confronts a student for recording in her classroom and potentially exposing a young Latinx dreamer named Elisa, she is incarcerated and placed in a converted room in the school with three other women: Noor, a young Palestinian American student; Leylo, an expecting Somali American activist; and Samira, an older Syrian refugee. The women are expected to cook for the school while Zafira's former students are serving as guards. Kenji Tanaka, the child of Japanese Americans who were imprisoned in camps during the Second World War, and who now works as a janitor at the school, joins forces with Elisa and another sympathetic student Marcus to release the women after discovering they will be moved to a potential death camp. During their incarceration, the women confide in one another and find commonalities as women from the Middle East and Africa. Eventually Kenji, Marcus, and Elisa release the women, and they all go on to create a new resistance against the Great Leader's forces that sought to eliminate them.

Haddad's dystopian vision of a nation that becomes consumed by its fear and loathing of Arabs and Muslims is one rooted in the real concerns many Arabs and Muslims in the United States face amid heightened xenophobia, surveillance, and even calls by an American president who wants many immigrants sent back to their home countries if they dare to criticize the government. Haddad's protagonist, Zafira, was born and raised in the United States, yet her proximity to her Arabness and her desire to teach resistance literature are met with scrutiny and contempt by the government-sanctioned powers that run her school. The Great Leader's speeches are rife with calls for students to take back their country and to reclaim their future by working as "resistors." On the other hand, Zafira calls for an Arab American renaissance—a movement to take back those things that define a rich Arab American heritage. In a pivotal monologue, Zafira pleads to the Arab Americans in the audience to join her in a group action and does so by recounting the foods, activities, and population centers that are central to Arab American identity in the United States. Haddad's play is calling for a resistance to the power structures that wish to suppress Middle Easterners living in America in the name of blind patriotism.

Najee Mondalek's comedy *Me No Terrorist* is the story of Im Hussein, a Shi'ite Lebanese Muslim female character living in Michigan with her husband Abu Hussein, her Lebanese Christian friend Im Elias, and her husband Abu Elias. The play was originally scheduled to perform in the fall of 2001 but was postponed by the events of 9/11. The production, directed by Ray Alcodray, was staged in 2002 and toured fourteen cities around the United States, Canada, Lebanon, and Australia.

Me No Terrorist is a comedic take on what happens when an Arab living in America is charged with terrorism. The play opens with FBI agents casing Im Hussein's house while Abu Hussein, Abu Elias, and Im Elias are inside "mourning" her passing. They have all decided to pretend Im Hussein is dead in order to get the FBI to finally leave them alone. Along the way the characters have multiple interactions that involve jokes, puns, play on words, and physical humor. Both lead females—Im Hussein and Im Elias— are played by the two male Mondalek actors. The husbands are hapless, foolish old men who serve as the foils to Im Hussein's incessant insults. Her daughter-in-law, Sharon, arrives and discovers the ruse. Im Hussein is eventually discovered by the agents and, after a case of mistranslation from Arabic to English, she and the others are incarcerated on terrorist-related charges. The next act flashes back and forth between Im Hussein in prison and the various scenes of her arrival in America, her receiving her citizenship, and the various protest scenes outside the courthouse where media and protesters gather to decry her incarceration. The final scene takes place in a courtroom where an Arab American judge hears Im Hussein's pleas and decides to release her due to lack of evidence.

Despite the comedic tone of Ajyal's theatrical productions, there are deeper cultural and political messages within. Mondalek uses multiple opportunities to speak out against the way Arabs are persecuted, attacked, and maligned by foreign governments and the media. He is also critical of his own culture. He speaks about how the Arabs once had a glorious past, but now only seem to know how to fight with one another. He laments the terrible situation facing his native homeland, Lebanon, and how the politicians there are robbing the people of their livelihoods. He also condemns US foreign policy for actions that have left Arab nations occupied, bombed, and ruined. His character Im Hussein dreams of a future where the children will learn from the mistakes of the current generation and change the way Arabs live and interact with one another. Toward the end of the play, a chorus of children draped in white enter carrying the flags of the Arab nations, with traditional Arabic music playing. Mondalek's character praises the life lived in the United States, but also speaks out against foreign policies that have caused such destruction in the Middle East.

Societal Persecution Plays: *Autobiography of a Terrorist, Me No Terrorist, Roar, Mosque Alert,* and *Lubbock or Leave It!*

Saïd Sayrafiezadeh is a memoirist, novelist, and playwright whose plays include *New York Is Bleeding* (2001), *All Fall Away* (2003), *Long Dream in Summer* (2005), and *Autobiography of a Terrorist* (2017). *Autobiography of a Terrorist* includes a protagonist, also named Saïd Sayrafiezadeh, a director, and two actors attempting to stage a play about the Iran hostage crisis of 1979. Through a convoluted series of events they inadvertently stage a play about 9/11 instead. Sayrafiezadeh, a writer of Iranian-Jewish-American heritage, places a fictional version of himself as the playwright of the play within the play. The setting is simply a stage with an oven. The metatheatrical play puts the playwright, Saïd, as the main character having to negotiate his own play with the non-Middle Eastern director and actors.

The play opens with Saïd addressing the audience. He tells them it is not a finished play, but rather "An Iranian-Jewish collage of scenes," and how important it is to speak out now about what is going on in the world. He then thanks the theatre for giving him the opportunity to bring the diversity of Middle Eastern perspectives to the audience as an invitation for discovery. He claims the play is a story about his own unfinished life, what it is like to grow up as a Middle Eastern American in the United States, and how he came to realize and accept that he was an American like everyone else. As he continues to introduce the play, the actors begin discussing his name, how it is pronounced, what it means, and ask him what it is like being Arab in America. He then must explain the difference between Iranians and Arabs, Aryans and Semites, those born overseas versus those born in the diaspora. The character Saïd says that he never intended to be Iranian and that he always accepted that he was a "white" American. In the book *The Limits of Whiteness: Iranian Americans and the Everyday Politics of Race*, Neda Maghbouleh writes that Iranians harken back to an Aryan heritage that she calls "the Aryan myth," a notion that the word "Iran" is derived from the word "Aryan." She writes, "some Iranian immigrants and their offspring believe themselves to be at the top of a racial hierarchy vis-à-vis other immigrant and minority groups in the United States" (2017, 60). Therefore, many second-generation Iranian Americans are raised believing they are "white," yet they are confronted with their "otherness" by the American society around them. Maghbouleh adds,

The idea that Iranians are racial Aryans remains pervasive in Iran and its diaspora, despite a century of successive revolutions, governments, and uprisings opposed to the very regimes that concretized the myth. Perhaps most disturbing to some second-generation Iranian Americans, the myth remains pervasive despite absolute refutation of the racial science on which it was constructed. (55)

Given this historical and cultural background, it is little wonder that the character Saïd is confused by his identity as opposed by his fellow actors in the play within the play.

Saïd recalls how things changed in 1979 with the hostage crisis in Tehran and, and when his Iranian father abandoned him to live with his Jewish mother. He takes the audience through different scenes in his professional life such as having to audition and being asked to have an accent when speaking, wearing cultural clothing like turbans, and having to turn down terrorist roles even when it jeopardizes his career. He finds himself acting out a scene about why the US hostages were abducted and the reasons for the Islamic Revolution in Iran. A scene then plays out where a CIA agent named Kermit Roosevelt interrogates a woman attempting to hide Saïd in an oven. Suddenly, the director appears and introduces himself to the audience, stating that the audience have filed complaints against the playwright. The director assures the audience that the theatre has no desire to offend them, and that the playwright has been removed from his own play. The director then assigns the role of Saïd to one of the white actors on stage and, after a comedic scene ensues, Saïd confronts the director. He tells him the play is about what it is like to be Middle Eastern in America and his journey toward resolution. The director then pulls out Saïd's journal and shares private facts about him with the audience which reveal his sexual habits and other embarrassing events from his life. The director and actors rewrite the script and change everything that Saïd was attempting with his play. Saïd says that Americans pride themselves on speaking out about injustice in other countries, but somehow when that injustice is done in America itself, there is little action or introspection to be found.

The play devolves further with the director, actors, stage manager, and Saïd all debating the veracity, history, and truthfulness of the play being presented. The actors read even more personal events from Saïd's journal including his fear and sadness growing up as an Iranian American, the painful alienation he felt from his father who lived in Iran and who he barely knew, the way children teased and taunted him growing up, and how he was envious of boys and girls with "American names." The actors then start singing "Bomb Iran" to the tune of the Beach Boys song "Barbara Ann." This leads to a more heated debate about American military might and the desire for military intervention overseas. The actors then bring up 9/11 and the time when Saïd's father was incarcerated in Iran by the regime. They begin taunting Saïd about whether he cried on 9/11 and mourned the victims, and whether his play was justification for the attacks. Saïd is forced to justify the words in the journal that are misinterpreted to sound as if Saïd himself agreed with, and was an apologist for, the attacks. The final scene flashes back to his childhood, to the racial epithets hurled at him by his classmates, and how he was forced to urinate on a map of Iran. In a desire to retell the truth, Saïd takes over the role of Saïd in the play and recreates the final scene, only this time he tells of how *he* was a boy playing with his friends who brutally attacked a young Iraqi boy on a playground. The director and actors chastise him for ruining the life-affirming resolution of the play they created by staging a scene that depicts his own self-loathing and how he persecuted a child just for being Middle Eastern. The play ends with the cast dancing together and Saïd offering to buy drinks for everyone involved.

Despite being a hilariously metatheatrical take on a Middle Eastern life in America, the play takes an interesting and complicated look at how Middle Eastern Americans attempt to negotiate their identities in a country that offers confusing messages that celebrate diversity while simultaneously creating an atmosphere of fear and loathing of others. The protagonist of the play searches for resolution, but as the play progresses, he is Orientalized and transformed into a grotesque version of a Middle Easterner in direct contradiction with his own wishes. On this journey, he also exposes his own innate inner hatred and cruelty toward other Middle Easterners. The word "terrorist" in the title refers not to a Middle Eastern American who commits a violent act in the name of some "jihad," but rather Saïd's own terrorism of a small Iraqi boy who he attacks out of a misplaced and misguided need to "fit in" with his friends. His self-loathing, cultivated by decades of ostracization, prejudice, othering, and personal pain, finds itself unleashed on a small Iraqi boy who just wanted to find a friend on a playground. The play's humor masks the deeper pain of its revelatory ending and creates an inverted tale of persecution—one where one Middle Eastern American persecutes another Middle Eastern American out of a perverted sense of their own misplaced need for belonging.

Palestinian American playwright Betty Shamieh's play *Roar* takes place in the immediate aftermath of the invasion of Kuwait by Iraqi forces in 1991. The play focuses on a family of diasporic Palestinian shopkeepers and landlords in Detroit. Ahmed and Karima Yacoub own and operate a "party store" in Detroit, above which they reside. Their daughter Irene, a Palestinian American teenager, has dreams of becoming a famous American singer. When Karema's sister Hala comes to visit from Kuwait following the invasion of Iraqi forces in 1991, the family dynamic unravels. Ahmed begins longing for the relationship he and Hala once had, and for his life as a musician back in Jordan. Hala, traumatically damaged from the events of Black September and the Gulf War, cannot seem to find a place anywhere, especially in Detroit. Abe, Ahmed's brother, is a record producer who passes as Jewish but has lost all ties with his family. The play's resolution comes when Ahmed and Hala run away together to Jordan leaving Karema and Irene searching for a way forward with Abe's assistance. In a recognition of her own post-trauma, Hala tells her niece Irene, "what happened to your mother and her sister affects you in a thousand ways that you yourself will never be able to explain" (Shamieh 2005, 47). Karema copes with this trauma by devoting herself tirelessly to securing financial security. Hala, on the other hand, acts out her trauma by filling her life with meaningless affairs and endless wandering. The diasporic experience for the Palestinian American characters in the play is rife with contradictions. For instance, Karema and Ahmed wanted Irene to be raised in the United States so she could escape the misery of Palestinians living in refugee camps in Jordan. In doing so, Irene has embraced her Americanness and denied her Arabness completely. When Hala first tries to teach Irene Arabic music and song, Irene dismisses the gesture altogether. She tells Hala, "Arabic sounds so ugly. I never speak it in public. It sounds like spitting" (ibid., 30). Later, when Hala tries to teach Irene Arabic music, Irene constantly evades her, preferring instead to sing English songs. Karema also internalizes her own oppression, telling Ahmed not to inform the tenants that he is the owner of the building while on repair calls since people would not rent the apartments if they knew Arabs owned them. Similarly, Abe passes himself off as an Egyptian Jew in order to further his career as a music producer. Ironically, despite the compromises Karema has made in her own life, she considers Abe's actions reprehensible. Gradually, Abe admits that his actions were mistaken and that it cost more than it gave to deny his heritage. Abe tells Irene not to mask who she is because, by doing so, nothing she achieves will be of any worth. As seen in other Arab American dramas, Shamieh is positing that, in order to succeed in America, one's identity as a Middle Easterner must be sublimated.

Only the characters Hala and Ahmed decide that the alienation they face in America becomes too much to bear, which compels them to return to Jordan. The fragmentation of the Yacoub family, first through violence and exile, and then through adultery and dislocation, is complete. Edward W. Said once said, "In a way, it's a sort of the fate of the Palestinians not to end up where they started but somewhere unexpected and far away" (Said, "In Search of Palestine" 2010). The characters are scattered once again, much like the Palestinian diaspora, which has been scattered after the wars in 1948, 1967, 1973, and onward.

Jamil Khoury's play *Mosque Alert* was inspired by the mosque controversies that centered on the Cordoba House/Park 51 Mosque (pejoratively labeled the "Ground Zero Mosque") in New York City. Khoury spent five years writing the play and, after 9/11, he was concerned with the challenges facing America's Muslim communities, especially resistance to the building of mosques in US cities. Khoury sites two Naperville-based mosque controversies as his primary inspirations. Khoury sought "to wed playwriting with public discourse, to blend a 4,000-year-old art form with modern-day digital technology" (Khoury 2016, 3). Khoury solicited input on character development, plot, narrative, civil rights, Islamophobia, and religious pluralism. Out that material a ten-minute play, two video essays, twenty-four video blogs, several digital scenes, live screenings, and other productions were created. In his playwright notes, Khoury expresses his positionality as a playwright focusing his attention on Muslim issues:

> First and foremost I am an artist. I have a particular interest in the dramatization of ideas, theories, and debates, and in creating characters for whom social and political activism informs identities and relationships. I am not Muslim. I'm a mixed blood Arab American of Syrian Christian heritage, raised in the Antiochian Orthodox Church. My husband Malik is Muslim. I write this play as an anti-Islamophobia activist, a supporter of Muslim American civil rights, and an ally to progressive Muslim, feminist Muslim, and queer Muslim communities. *Mosque Alert* belongs to an emerging body of Arab American plays that intersect lived politics and discursive arguments within the everyday lives of characters. (ibid., 5)

The characters include three families: The Bakers, comprised of Ted (the father) and his brother Daniel, Emily (a stay-at-home mom), Carl (a graduate student), and Jen Baker (a college senior). The Khalils family is comprised of Mostafa Khalil (an Imam) and his wife Aisha. The Qabbani Family is comprised of Tawfiq (chairman of the Al Andalus Mosque Board of Directors), Aminah (his wife, and aspiring designer of contemporary fashion for Muslim women), Samar (their daughter, a graduate student who occasionally wears a hijab), and Farid (the son, a recent college graduate).

The play begins with Mostafa giving an address about the proposed Al Andalus Library and Community Center to the town's Planning and Zoning Commission. We later find that Ted and Tawfiq are cutthroat businessmen who see the mosque as a sure thing in the eyes of the planning and zoning officials, and they expect the same from the City Council. Tawfiq is concerned that the proposed mosque will face the same controversies the Park 51 Mosque faced in New York, and his fears are confirmed when he finds that Daniel has launched a site called "MosqueAlert.com" that is against the proposed mosque using vitriolic and anti-Islamic sentiments online. Aisha, Mostafa's wife, is very concerned and does not trust the city planners the way her husband does. Where Mostafa believes he represents his community, and that Muslims are partially to blame for their predicament in America by not coming to the proverbial table, his wife Aisha tells him that Muslims have never been invited to the table, and never will be. While Mostafa shaves his beard to appear less threatening to non-Muslims, Aisha cannot remove her hijab the same way. Meanwhile Emily and Aminah are making plans to launch a new Muslim women's clothing line. Aminah, a Syrian refugee, is concerned about Isis and the destruction of Syria. Carl, who is an "out" gay man, and Samar discuss how parents are trying to matchmake for them when Jen, who has been studying in France for a year, arrives to greet them. Once they all learn of Daniel's website, they decide to confront him and attempt to take the site off the internet. Khoury portrays Samar and Farid as very hip, contemporary Arab American Muslims who join a "coalition of the hated" with Jen and Carl to stop the anti-Islamic website.

Meanwhile, Ted and Daniel discuss the mosque and Daniel reminds Ted that there have been Muslim threats to the country and that he believes the mosques are breeding grounds for anti-American hatred. When Aisha and Mostafa arrive and confront Daniel, both sides realize neither will back down and that the fight to build the mosque will be a long and ugly one. Khoury then takes the audience into an intra-Muslim dialogue about the mosque, which raises the complex issues the characters are facing. Samar wants a progressive mosque while Tawfiq just wants to build a new Islamic center. Farid says he is "unmosqued," and that the mosque isn't for young people. Aminah is trying to hold on to tradition in order to pass culture down to her children, and to be surrounded by those who understand her. Emily, Carl, Jen, and Ted discuss racial profiling of Muslims and their changing relationship to their uncle Daniel. Where Carl sees opposing mosques as un-American, Jen says it is fundamentally French. Ted blames the opposition to the mosque as a community's fear of change; he tells his kids that Naperville was once a place with no minorities and now that more have come, the town has become unrecognizable to them.

It becomes clearer that there are more divisions among the different groups than there are similarities. Aminah says that the "Muslim rainbow," as she calls it, is splintered along religious, ethnic, and national lines. She believes that Muslims need to change their public image by reducing accents and changing from traditional dress to more modern clothing. They begin a mock town hall where they role-play while Mostafa tries to fend off the group's hostile questions. In this scene Khoury brings up all the negative connotations some have about Arabs and Muslims in society which include racial epithets, apprehensions about Muslims with beards and hijabs, and fear of the broadcast of the call to prayer at the mosque. By doing this, Khoury dramatizes that there are such negative stereotypes and that Arabs and Muslims are privy to them and feel the need to constantly explain themselves. Ted and Daniel are also preparing for the town hall, but Ted is coaching Daniel on how they will disagree in public and wait out the process that will eventually defeat the mosque's approval.

The town hall meeting descends into chaos as audience members shout each other down, Mostafa attempts to assuage the crowd, and Daniel uses the opportunity to foment anti-Muslim sentiment and turn public opinion against the mosque. He accuses the Muslims of playing the victim and race card. He then evokes the attacks on 9/11, which leads the audience to start chanting "U.S.A.!" thus ending the act and the hopes of the mosque's future. After the meeting Emily discovers that Ted is a silent investor for a gourmet market that wants the same site as the mosque developers. The loss of the mosque also puts a terrible strain on Aisha and Mostafa's marriage. Mostafa tries to convince her that the loss was not against them but against the ideals of America itself. For his part, Daniel tries to convince Carl and Jen that he did what he did to protect their future from radical Islam, political correctness, and Muslim hatred against gay people. Carl meets with Mostafa asking him to be his ally but realizes that a conservative Islamic cleric cannot support Carl as a gay man; where Carl sees discrimination against gays and Muslims as similar, Mostafa sees a clear difference. Carl cannot understand how Mostafa can propagate notions of coalition building and remain bigoted against gays in the community; yet Mostafa is not willing to change his beliefs regarding homosexuality. Ultimately, Carl sees this as mendacity, stating that a conviction only has value if it's applied consistently. Mostafa tries to convince Carl that he cannot accept his help, and, if Carl does attempt to write something that connects the Islamophobic backlash the Muslim community faces in Naperville with the homophobic sentiment in that community, he would condemn him publicly. Jen also rejects Farid, telling him that after the Paris Charlie Hebdo attacks, she can't be a good ally to the mosque either. Gradually Tawfiq realizes that Ted has been working against the mosque all along as a silent investor on the property. Tawfiq dares to reveal Ted for undermining the mosque with his business dealings and his connection with his brother. Aminah also breaks ties with Emily because of her knowledge of the scandal as well, and Aisha wants to break all ties with the Qabbanis and to get Mostafa to take more of a leading role in the Muslim community by starting a small house mosque instead of the massive downtown mosque he had been planning. Her desire to return to what she calls "Real Islam" is one that recaptures the spirit of why they wanted to build a mosque in the first place—not for prominence and glory but rather for spiritual fulfillment and connection to God (Figure 1).

The final scene has Farid, Jen, Samar, and Carl preparing protest signs together. They decide that they must find a way forward since their parents had made such a mess of the mosque situation. Carl realizes that he can support the right to build mosques and what he calls other "gay-hating houses of worship," but with the knowledge that they are political enemies to his cause as an out gay man. Jen realizes her white privilege and the fact that she is an implicit accomplice to her uncle's hate. Samar tells Carl Muslims are neither angels nor demons and that they have a spectrum of beliefs like any other group. They protest outside of the city hall, celebrating the democracy they share as Americans to speak out against anti-Muslim hate, Islamophobia, and homophobia in Naperville and in America.

Khoury's play takes a specific event that crystalized the anti-Muslim sentiment of the time—the so-called Ground Zero Mosque controversy—and focused his attention on the various sides in the debate against mosques in American communities. By doing so, he dramatizes the many arguments for and against the building of mosques, and he exposes the hatred and

Figure 1 *Mosque Alert* by Jamil Khoury, Silk Road Rising, 2016. Sahar Dika (Samar) and Frank Sawa (Mostafa). Directed by Edward Torres. Photograph by Airan Wright.

bigotry that exists in many communities. By complicating the narrative and exploring the various communities that are affected by these debates, he provides audiences with a dramatic, astute, and informed drama. Like many of Khoury's plays, the play focuses on the intellectual arguments that are often emotionally debated. The play received many strong reviews through its theatrical production, its videos that accompanied the play's development, and the various national and international presentations Khoury held to promote and discuss the work.

A more comedic take on societal persecution is Leyla Modirzadeh's solo performance *Lubbock or Leave It!* The play, which was created in association with Ping Chong & Company, involves a single female actor playing Roxane Khodambashi (also known as Rocky), and a puppet. Rocky is from New York and takes a teaching job in Lubbock, Texas, because she needs a tenure track-teaching job and the economy is bad. This revelation is much to her friends' surprise who are horrified that she would try to find a job in the Lone Star State. As her friends predicted, Rocky runs into all sorts of strange people. One man, Dub, cannot pronounce her name and does not know the difference between an "A-Rab" and an Iranian. The city hardly impresses her either; she finds that Lubbock is the second most conservative town in the United States behind Provo, Utah. Her puppet, Daisy, serves as her inner voice, which Rocky tries in vain to silence. Daisy tells Rocky's sad story about divorced parents, an absent father who became the American Dream immigrant success, a life of poverty with her mother, and her abandonment at the age of thirteen. Rocky tells the audience she took the job for security, and that security means giving up and giving in, for the comfort of being called middle class.

As she teaches her new students, she encounters more homophobia, a sexist faculty, and colleagues that verbally attack one another in faculty meetings. At one point, her department chair tells her he hates his job, hates theatre, and dreads coming to work. Her Iranian Cinema lecture is met with more misunderstanding and Islamophobia. One ROTC student asks her why Iranian women are so ugly, and openly states that America should "nuke them all." When Rocky tells Daisy she wants to quit, Daisy tells her to stay and deal with the problems because she can't afford unemployment. Rocky believes things will get better, but each day brings another round of insults and offenses. Finally, at her first-year review, she gives her resignation. Her chair tells her that whatever she dreamed of when she was younger is unrealistic and that compromise is the key to adulthood. Rocky decides to go back and visit Iran, a place she has not seen since the age of six. The play ends with Rocky on her way back to the homeland.

A comedy like *Lubbock or Leave It!* demonstrates the cross-cultural misunderstandings that many in the diaspora face when attempting to negotiate their place in American society. Rocky is harassed for having a different name, teased about the foods she eats, and finds she does not share the same values as others who espouse American supremacy over foreign countries in the Middle East. The play has a humorous subtext with the Daisy puppet as she chides Rocky for being too fragile, but Rocky's displeasure with living in a place that is anathema to her and her values makes staying there untenable. The idea that Rocky should "grow up" and stay in the job despite the sexism, homophobia, and anti-Iranian sentiment she encounters there makes her feel even more alienated. Like Rocky, some Middle Eastern Americans are caught between the freedoms they enjoy in America and the painful reminders that they are both different and unacceptable to their society. This dichotomy makes some want to return to the homeland in order to find a place where they are not as abject, not as reviled—a place where they might, finally, find acceptance.

The playwrights in this genre are attempting to focus their attention on the social and governmental persecution Middle East Americans face daily. By dramatizing these events, they attempt to explore the deep and painful wounds carried by those who face racism, xenophobia, Islamophobia, and other forms of ethnic and religious discrimination. They also highlight the fact that Middle Eastern Americans come from a variety of nations with a multiplicity of sects, religions, and political affiliations that are misunderstood by the society they inhabit. These factors cause Middle Eastern Americans to withdraw from jobs or situations where they find they do not belong because their "outsider" status makes them feel unwelcomed. The persecution can be governmental or societal, yet both cause tremendous unease within a community struggling to find acceptance. Through dramatic and comedic means, these playwrights and performers dramatize the societal unease their community faces in a time of heightened fear and surveillance.

CHAPTER 4
DIASPORA PLAYS

Another genre of Middle Eastern American drama deals with living in the diaspora. Like the previous persecution plays, these plays deal with many complicated issues, but they are more personal and less about the outside persecution they feel around them (though many have this aspect as well). In these plays, we see diasporic Middle Eastern Americans dealing with issues such as US interventions in Middle Eastern conflicts, having to contend with difficulties concerning identity and immigration, foreign events that directly and indirectly affect Middle Eastern Americans living in the diaspora, and issues regarding perception in the media.

Middle Eastern Americans and the Entertainment Industry: *It's Not About Pomegranates!* and *Browntown*

Middle Eastern Americans in the entertainment industry face a host of problems. These range from being Orientalized, stereotyped, misrepresented and sexualized to being ignored altogether. In his groundbreaking books *The TV Arab* (1984), *Arab and Muslim Stereotyping in American Popular Culture* (1997), *Reel Bad Arabs: How Hollywood Vilifies a People* (2001), and *Guilty: Hollywood's Verdict on Arabs after 9/11* (2008), Jack G. Shaheen critiqued the Hollywood studio system for decades of Orientalizing Arabs and Muslims onscreen. Shaheen chronicled how movies that include insidious images of Arabs and Muslims are consistently depicting this group as a threatening cultural "other." By examining hundreds of films made from 1896 to 2008, Shaheen writes that he was "driven by the need to expose an injustice: cinema's systematic, pervasive, and unapologetic degradation and dehumanization of a people" (Shaheen 2003, 172). He writes that Arabs are repeatedly portrayed as heartless, brutal, uncivilized religious fanatics focused on terrorizing Westerners—especially those who are Christians and Jews. The image is always the same—harems, oil wells, camels, flying carpets, hate-filled terrorists, and oppressed burqa-clad maidens. Shaheen reminds readers of the proud heritage of Arab intellectuals and others who contributed to human civilization, and how they have been stereotyped in ways like other groups such as Asians, American Indians, African Americans, and Jews. He calls this "The New Anti-Semitism," because Arabs are Semites, and because this occurred mainly during the last third of the twentieth century.

> Why is it important for the average American to know and care about the Arab stereotype? It is critical because dislike of "the stranger," which the Greeks knew as xenophobia, forewarns that when one ethnic, racial, or religious group is vilified, innocent people suffer. (Shaheen 2001, 4)

In his later book, *Guilty: Hollywood's Verdict on Arabs After 9/11*, Shaheen continued his analysis of Hollywood films but also focused on the effect of typecasting of Middle Eastern Americans in the entertainment business. Shaheen calls for more Arab American imagemakers to enter the industry and for individuals and organizations to assist them with their careers.

> [T]oday's Arab American actors also have a tough time. Unlike other performers, they rarely are given opportunities to play humane, diverse characters, roles that would contest stereotype. Some directors contend there's a demand for young Arab-American actors. Sure, a demand to play billionaires, bombers, bundles in black, and belly dancers. Casting directors toss them stereotypical scraps and bones. (Shaheen 2008, 58)

Many contemporary Arab American playwrights look to the scholarly works of Edward W. Said and Jack G. Shaheen to contest the ongoing stereotyping Hollywood perpetuates. By doing so they attempt to demonstrate in their plays how their community is often misread and misrepresented as "authentic" Middle Eastern American lives onstage.

Harry M. Benshoff and Sean Griffin write that while there is a proliferation of images of Middle Eastern Arabs, there is a scarcity of Arab Americans on screen. Hollywood films portray Arabs as bloodthirsty, sexualized, or exotic while Arab Americans barely exist. They write, "The linkage of sex, violence, and (non-Christian) religion continues to mark more contemporary stereotypes of Arabs and Arab Americans" (Benshoff and Griffin 2009, 72). Furthermore, they write that many Americans make no distinction between Arabs, Arab Americans, and Muslim terrorists. "Against this complex socio-political backdrop, it is perhaps no surprise that Arab and/or Arab American actors in Hollywood have not had an easy time finding challenging or complex characters to play" (ibid., 74). They conclude that if actors of Middle Eastern heritage often play terrorists or sheiks, they are compelled to change their names and sublimate their identities.

In a 2015 *GQ Magazine* interview by Jon Ronson with Muslim American actors Anthony Azizi, Ahmed Ahmed, Sayed Badreya, Maz Jobrani, and Waleed Zuaiter titled "You May Know Me from Such Roles as Terrorist #4," the actors lamented the many times they were cast in roles as plane hijackers, infidel slaughterers, holy warriors, and any other assortment of terrorists in Hollywood films. Ronson writes,

> I'm sure practically *all* actors, Muslim or otherwise, feel degraded. Most have no power over their careers—what roles they can play, how their performances are edited. But Muslim actors are powerless in unusually hideous ways. The last time one became a big star in America was back in 1962—Omar Sharif in *Lawrence of Arabia*. These days they get offered terrorist roles and little else. And we—the paying public—barely even notice, much less worry about it. Where's the outrage? There is none, except from the actors themselves. These roles are ethically nightmarish for them, and the stress can wreak havoc on their lives. (Ronson 2015; emphasis in original)

The interviewed actors recount how the roles involve all of them dying at the hands of an action hero and being paid handsomely to do it. When they accept these roles, they are ostracized by family and members of the community, and when they refuse these roles, they find very little acting work. These actors have responded by subverting the situation and performing stand-up comedy that satirizes their travails in the Hollywood system (Ahmed Ahmed, Maz Jobrani), or writing, producing, and acting in films that counteract stereotypes (Sayed Badreya, Cherien Dabis). In past decades non-Middle Eastern American actors would be hired to play these stereotypical roles and were given brown makeup and some sort of costume to denote their Middle Eastern background, and they would often mumble some gibberish that was meant to sound like Arabic. What is most troubling now is that *actual* Middle Eastern American actors are being hired who not only "look" the part but speak the languages required of them fluently. This gives these films a kind of cultural authenticity and veracity that producers in the past wanted but could not achieve. These actors now look, sound, and act the part perfectly. Lebanese American actor Haaz Sleiman says, "It's moving in the right direction for Arab actors but very slowly. Look at African-Americans. It took them forever to move ahead. Arabs are the new blacks. We took their place and moved up" (Fleishman 2016). An Egyptian Canadian actor of Coptic Christian background, Mena Massoud, who was cast in the titular role in Disney's 2019 film *Aladdin*, found no opportunities awaiting him after the film was completed. "There's always a wild card or two when you're casting," Massoud said. "I'm usually the wild card. In a room of Caucasian guys, a director might be like, OK, let's see, like two guys who aren't. And maybe they'll be the wild card choice" (Fallon 2019). Despite several actors like Massoud given leading "breakout roles," they find that once Hollywood is through utilizing them for their look, they have little use for them afterward. The plays discussed here are about actors and writers who also endure the fickle nature of theatre, film, and television in America.

Iranian American playwright and actress Sepideh Khosrowjah's play *It's Not About Pomegranates!* is a romantic comedy between Roya, an Iranian American playwright, and Sean, an Anglo-American theatre producer that takes place in a theatre in San Francisco. Roya meets Sean to discuss her play, which Sean's theatre wishes to produce. During their dialogue and monologues, they break the fourth wall to share their inner thoughts about one another. Initially, Sean likes Roya's play, and Roya is attracted to Sean. However, Sean begins to make assumptions about the playwright, and the situation quickly devolves into an essentializing view of Iranian American women. He assumes that Roya, a first-generation immigrant, has challenges speaking English. Then he discusses how there is a large market for "Middle Eastern stuff" as he puts it, and that he is intrigued because the play has a lesbian couple as its protagonists. Sean then goes on to explain how he, too, has Persian friends which gives him insight into her culture. He then insults Roya by telling her that her play is not authentic enough. When she protests his changes, he asks the audience why Middle Easterners are so combative and deduces this is because they have been fighting with one another for centuries. Sean urges Roya to use her Muslim and Iranian background as assets in writing her works. Roya tells him she is a "non-Muslim Muslim," and that she is not interested in writing about pomegranates (a fruit commonly connected with Persian culture), or a "mysterious Persia." Sean gradually accepts her work, but she is convinced he is only interested in issues regarding diaspora and lack of authenticity in her writing. Roya tells

Sean that Tehran is a loud, polluted city with good and bad people, just like anywhere else. She loves her home city but there is nothing magical about it, and there are similarities between the United States and Iran where people fall in love, suffer loss, and love their children.

In Act 2, which takes place the next morning, the audience discovers that they have slept together the night before. Roya claims she was completely drunk and does not know how she got to his apartment, though Sean claims she insisted on joining him. After they argue, Sean tells her that Americans want to understand what is happening to Middle Easterners. Roya tells him that Americans do not really want to understand Iranians, only to confirm their negative views of them that include oppressed Middle Eastern Muslim women. She goes on to say Americans are not at all interested in discovering the truth behind the generalizations they hold.

Sean tells her the world is regressing because of notions of "Otherness" and the rise of fanaticism and fundamentalism. Roya insists that if the world is going backward, it is because humanity has stopped dreaming of a better world. She tells him writers need to create beautiful realities, not give in to "the market" and a desire to give consumers what they want to see. She fears Sean is what she calls a "WAMCCP" or "white American male capitalist chauvinist pig." Roya tells him that she has also been disillusioned by the decades of CIA coups and sanctions that have plagued Iran. It is ironic, she says, that she must defend the Islamic regime in Tehran because of her fears that the United States might invade her country. Her people have suffered enough without the United States dropping bombs on them, and Iranians don't want American interference. Based on what happened in Iraq and Afghanistan, she doesn't believe the United States means well by bringing democracy to foreign lands. In Act 3 they return to the theatre for another meeting. We discover that Sean broke up with Roya because of his fear of an intense relationship. He also tells her the theatre wants to produce her play. Roya tells him they could be friends, but they are two different people from two different worlds. After reciting many clichés about what her future Iranian American play might be, the play ends with the notion that they might be able to be friends after all.

Khosrowjah's play may be a romantic comedy, but it contains many political messages that attempt to educate American audiences about the Iranian American condition. The American character, Sean, is so caught up in the Orientalism he has known his entire life that he cannot see Roya as a fully realized Iranian woman. She, on the other hand, has such trauma after decades of animosity she has experienced from her life in America that she cannot seem to give in to a relationship with someone who cannot overcome his preconceived notions of what an Iranian woman is or should be. The play Roya offers him is a metaphor for the relationship between Americans and Iranians—a contested territory that is both misunderstood and fought over.

Another play that illustrates the Orientalization of Middle Eastern Americans in the film industry is Sam Younis's play *Browntown*. Younis explains that his play is his reaction to his audition experiences as an Arab American actor after earning his MFA in acting and looking for work in New York. He asked himself, "Why am I routinely a candidate for terrorist roles? Why are these terrorists always named 'Mohammed'? Why does that Indian guy keep getting the Arab terrorist parts over me? Why should that upset me? Am I a sellout?" (Hill and Amin 2009, 225). As the play demonstrates, Younis's fears were not unwarranted.

Younis states his play is deliberately set after the US-led invasion of Iraq. The play features two Arab American actors, Omar Fakhoury and Malek Bizri, and an Indian American actor named Vijay Govindu. There is also a casting director named Ann Davis, an actress named Sherry Holloway, and a senior vice president of casting for a major studio named Hamilton Jeffries. The play is set in a casting office in New York City in 2003. The actors are in the office to audition for a film titled "The Color of Terror." Omar and Malek know one another, as they are the ones that are consistently called for the same roles in what they ironically call "Browntown." They call the films they audition for "scary brown-guy" movies where all the characters are named "Mohammed." After reading the script they are auditioning for, Omar says,

> I'm just saying you gotta draw the line somewhere. For Chrissake, this Mohammed's got four wives, he hates all Jews, he drives a Mercedes that he bought with his family's oil money, and he's conspiring with a guerilla group called "Allies for Allah." They may as well put him on a camel and strap a bomb on to him in the opening scene. This is basically the same shit as *True Lies* or *Not Without My Daughter*! There are consequences for perpetuating these stereotypes. (Younis 2009, 235–6)

Malek reminds Omar he was an actor in *True Lies*, but Omar protests that he just wants to play a regular bad guy. When Vijay enters the room to audition for the same part as Omar and Malek, they quickly get upset that an Indian

American actor is auditioning for Arab roles; however, Omar himself was once cast as an Indian character in a play. When Malek reads a stereotypical part replete with an Arabic accent with Sherry, Ann tries to side coach him but does so by getting all sorts of facts wrong about the character (such as Afghanistan and Pakistan as Arab countries, backward moral codes, and societally pervasive misogyny). Meanwhile, in the waiting area, Omar and Vijay discuss South Asian actors they know, and Omar himself makes many stereotypical and culturally inappropriate assumptions about South Asians. Malek enters, disgusted that he must audition for roles that call for what he calls "Brownsploitation," but Vijay tells him actors of color must work and they should quit being too overprotective of their culture. Vijay admonishes them telling them that everyone of color in America must play denigrating roles.

> Blacks have to play gangsters, Latinos play drug dealers, Chinese play tourists, and we both play Al Qaeda operatives on *24*. All actors deal with this shit. Get over it and do your job. (Younis 2009, 243)

Vijay tells them that terrorists exist, and people find them interesting; hence, they are being represented in films and TV. Unwilling to believe Vijay, Omar and Malek resolve to write their own script instead of being forced to act in films that demean them. Omar's audition is also fraught with more of Ann's misperceptions and misdirections regarding "what is really going on in those countries." Ann is most interested when the actors show fury, rage, and fierceness (i.e., her perception of the "angry Muslim"). When they tell Vijay he should audition for Ann with an Indian accent, he tells them he doesn't know one. When they tell him to use his parents' accent, he tells them his parents are from Queens. When they ask him to sound like the character Apu from *The Simpsons*, he tells them he has tried but ends up sounding like an Arab character from *Raiders of the Lost Ark*. Vijay's audition script is filled with angry monologues about revenge, jihad, and violence against infidels. Ann offers Sherry a part as the main character "Chemical Ali's" wife Jumana (who she mistakenly refers to as "Jumanji"). When Ann auditions the actors with one another, she remarks with amazement how well they "delved into the Arab mindset." The casting director Hamilton Jeffries, on the other hand, wants a star playing the lead role, so he opts for casting Colin Farrell. Ann dismisses Omar, Malek, and Vijay who still believe one of them will be cast in the terrorist role, not knowing it was given to the famous Irish actor instead.

Younis's dark comedy highlights how Arabs and South Asians are misperceived by casting agents, how roles written for these actors are typically shallow and rife with ugly stereotypes, and how actors of color turn on one another in an attempt to land roles that they don't even want but are forced to audition for just to keep working. The play is a comedy, but the situation Younis dramatizes is not necessarily that unrealistic. There are many other Middle Eastern American plays, and stand-up comic routines, that directly deal with the difficulties of being included in the American entertainment system including Yussef El Guindi's *Jihad Jones and the Kalashnikov Babes* and the comedy specials *Allah Made Me Funny*, *The Arab American Comedy Tour*, and *The Axis of Evil Comedy Tour*. In the decades since Younis wrote *Browntown*, a few Arab American actors like Rami Malek (*Bohemian Rhapsody*), Tony Shalhoub (*Monk*), and Ramy Youssef (*Ramy*) have achieved some prominence in Hollywood. That said, there are still only a handful of actors of Middle Eastern descent who can find consistent work playing multidimensional roles.

Living between "Here" and "There": *444 Days*; *This Time*; *Twice, Thrice, Frice . . .*; *Reading Hebron*; *Noura*; *Dragonflies*; *Suitcase*; and *Living in the Hyphen-Nation*

Another playwright who explores the difficulties of living in the diaspora is Iranian Armenian American playwright, director, and actress Torange Yeghiazarian. Yeghiazarian was born in Iran of Armenian heritage to a family of theatre performers who were musicians, actors, and night club proprietors. Her family moved to the United States in 1978. Yeghiazarian worked as a clinical microbiologist for fifteen years before obtaining her master's degree in theatre arts from San Francisco State University. She has authored many plays including *Abaga (The Future)*, *Dawn at Midnight*, *Publicly Resting*, *Behind Glass Windows*, *Operation No Penetration*, *Lysistrata 91!*, *TORCH!*, *Isfahan Blues*, *444 Days*, *The Fifth String: Ziryab's Passage to Cordoba*, and *Call Me Mehdi*. In 1996 she founded Golden Thread Productions in San Francisco. The company has been recognized by the American Theatre Wing and the City of San Francisco. Yeghiazarian was honored by the Cairo International Theatre Festival in 2016 and by the Symposium on Equity in the Entertainment Industry at Stanford University in 2017.

Yeghiazarian's play *444 Days* is set in December 2006 at Lucile Packard Children's Hospital in Palo Alto, California. The cast includes Laleh, an

Iranian woman in her forties who is a former hostage taker from Iran; Harry Rubin, an American professor from Columbia University in his fifties, and a former hostage himself; Olivia, a hospital nurse in her fifties; and Hadyeh, a 25-year-old woman in a coma. The play reflects on the 444-day hostage crisis of 1979 and the Iranian group named "Students Following the Imam's Line" who took sixty-six Americans hostage at the American Embassy in Tehran. The Islamic Revolution toppled the Iranian Monarchy. With the fall of the shah and the rise of Ayatollah Khomeini, US and Iranian relations immediately deteriorated and has remained unsettled since that time. In the play, Yeghiazarian writes that the play is inspired by actual events, though the story is fictional.

At the opening the audience sees Hadyeh lying in bed after being in a coma for three weeks with Laleh sitting by her side. Harry enters and chides Laleh for being in town for a month without contacting him. Protesters are outside the hospital protesting Laleh's presence there. Olivia, the nurse, is upset that Laleh, a former hostage taker, is at the hospital, and laments that Laleh comes from a place where people chant "Death to America." Harry went to Iran in the 1960s as a Peace Corps volunteer. Amin, Hadyeh's father, is an offstage character that is not seen. We discover that Harry is Hadyeh's biological father, and that his older son, Michael, could be a possible bone marrow transplant candidate. Harry begs Laleh to allow Michael to be a bone marrow donor, but Laleh (who has never told her husband Amin about Harry) is unwilling lest Amin find out about Hadyeh's true parentage.

Olivia and Harry discuss the hostage crisis and Harry tells her about the 1953 coup that ousted the then Iranian prime minister Muhammad Mossadegh known as Operation Ajax. Mossadegh, who nationalized Iran's oil industry, became a pariah to the United States and the United Kingdom so they conspired to overthrow him and restore the monarchy under the shah. The coup was successful and there was a return to foreign control of Iranian oil. Many blame the coup for radicalizing the Iranian populace against the United States, and for leading to the eventual rise of the Islamic Republic (Allen-Ebrahimian 2017). Olivia has no knowledge of the coup, and supports the US invasion of Iraq, blaming the Iraqis for not being more grateful for the US removing their president. When Harry reminds her things are more complicated, she responds that regular Americans only need a roof over their heads and food on their tables, not political discussions. Laleh informs Harry they found a donor and will proceed with an operation, which happens to be on Christmas Eve. It is Michael, Harry's son, who Laleh had been in contact with for years without Harry's knowledge. Michael does not show up on time, which makes Laleh panic. Olivia chastises Laleh for the revolution and the anti-American sentiment Iranians hold. Laleh responds that the United States holds the power and expects other nations to bow to its wishes or suffer the consequences. Laleh compares the United States to a giant elephant that is so big, strong, and remote which consumes the world's resources while others pay for that with their lives. In her view, the United States ruins other nations' futures in the name of security and justice while leaving foreign lands destroyed.

In a surprising turn, Hadyeh rises from her bed and delivers a monologue to the audience. She tells of her mother teaching her soccer when she was younger, how her father Amin refused to move to the United States, and how she likes Harry with his Persian spoken with a funny American accent. Harry tells Olivia that he believes Amin is a spy who is trying to pass on master codes of Iran's nuclear program to the Chinese. Laleh discovers that Harry has stopped Michael from coming to the hospital unless Laleh admits that she and Amin are passing on the nuclear codes. Amin dies in the hospital, and Laleh tells Harry she must return to Iran to bury him there. Harry and Laleh reconcile. Harry asks her to promise that she, Hadyeh, and he can stay together and start a new life. She does. After Harry leaves, Laleh burns a piece of paper and disconnects the tracheal tube that connects Hadyeh to the ventilator. The lights fade to black as the monitor continues beeping.

444 Days attempts to reconcile the present situation many Iranians face with the past actions committed during the revolution. Through the love triangle, Yeghiazarian dramatizes an American hostage and an Iranian hostage taker whose time together yielded a young woman now dying of cancer. The play subtly educates audiences about the US interventions in Iranian history including the 1953 coup, the US-sanctioned chemical weapons attacks by Iraq on Iran during the war from 1980 to 1988, and the hostile takeover of Iranian oil fields by the US and UK companies (Regencia 2018). Yeghiazarian attempts to complicate the history surrounding the US hostage crisis and to depict America (via Harry) and Iran (via Laleh and Amin) as nations that were caught up in geopolitical struggles that ultimately led to an acrimonious and antagonistic relationship that has lasted decades. The complicated nature of Iranians living in diaspora and having to contend with the violence that has been perpetrated is reflected in the painful relationship that Laleh, Harry, and Hadyeh share. By utilizing a present-day trauma with flashbacks that illuminate the past relationships, Yeghiazarian attempts to reframe the debate regarding the Iran Hostage

Crisis. *444 Days* is a human story that reminds us that there are a multitude of factors that determine how, and why, the acrimony between the United States and Iran has increased. The play also demonstrates that there are real, devastating human consequences to foreign interventions committed in the name of democracy.

The play *This Time* by Sevan K. Greene, which was inspired by stories from the book *Not So Long Ago* by Amal Meguid, and developed in collaboration with Egyptian Canadian director Kareem Fahmy, is a play that takes place in different time periods and different nations. The protagonist, Amal, is seen both as a sixty- to seventy-year-old woman living in Toronto and as a forty- to fifty-year-old woman living in Egypt. Her daughter Janine and her son Hatem are dealing with her present difficulties, which they realize are deeply rooted in her past. Other characters are Nick, a thirty-year-old Canadian who woos a younger Amal while she lived in Egypt; Monsieur Joseph, a thirty-year-old Middle Eastern owner of a fabric store; and Tom, a twenty-year-old man. We meet Younger Amal in 1962 as a married mother of two at a socialite party in Cairo. She meets Nick, a handsome Canadian teacher who is obsessed both by women and liquor. Nick instantly falls for her despite her protestations, and the couple are destined for a tortured love affair. In the present, an older Amal is living with her divorced daughter Janine (who was born of Amal's broken marriage). Janine, separated from her own husband, has decided to move out of her home and start anew, consumed by anger toward Amal for leaving her father and brother decades earlier. For her part, Amal is now an elegant older woman who swears Nick is hiding in the bushes outside her daughter's home. As the play progresses, we see the passion and dysfunction of Nick and Amal's love affair and marriage, and how Amal's decision to leave her children has permanently ruined her adult relations with both of them.

The play follows the characters living through the various Egyptian regimes from Nasser to Sadat to Mubarak. Amal chooses her affair with Nick, leaving her husband and her son Hatem and daughter Janine behind, and moving to Canada. As an older woman, abandoned by Nick and left with two children who are spiteful for the way she left them behind when they were young to be with her lover, Amal contends with being alone as an older woman living in a country she barely understands. Janine's hatred for her mother leaving her as a young girl finally erupts. Amal tells her daughter that, eventually, she will have to balance regret with freedom. The play's climax intertwines the past and the present as Janine and her mother Amal finally learn to recognize and love one another. Greene's play offers a fascinating view into an Egyptian woman's life of the past and the present: a woman who gave up her filial and societal expectations regarding marriage and the role of "a good Arab wife" in order to run away with the man she loved. Although Amal's life did not work out the way she intended, she decides to live her life without regrets because her freedom was ultimately more important to her. Greene's portrayal of Amal dispels facile stereotypes some might have about Arab women as oppressed subjects in a patriarchal society. Amal is a bold and courageous female character that defies all expectations put upon her by her society, and by the audiences who would like to view her as an oppressed Arab woman.

Fouad Teymour is a Chicago-based Egyptian American playwright and professor of engineering. His play *Twice, Thrice, Frice . . .* is an all-female, three-character play that explores Islam and marriage. Amira is a forty-year-old Iraqi American visual artist and real estate agent. She is married to a doctor named Hassan who travels to Iraq to volunteer to help refugees. The couple has been unable to conceive children. Khadija is a forty-something Palestinian American woman who is a conservative Muslim mother of two married to a professor named Ramzi. Samara is a thirty-year-old Egyptian American woman who wears a hijab and believes in Islam as a guiding factor in her life. At first, the three women get along very well and form a tight intra-cultural group. The play is set in "America pre-Trump election" as late as mid-2016.

At the start of the play the women discuss their career ambitions and their family life. Samara wants to return to school for an MBA while Khadija tells her how it is important for her to be married and have children. Khadija is a mother figure for Samara, who was orphaned at a young age. Amira and her husband Hassan are strictly anti-polygamy, while Samara and Khadija are more open to the idea. Samara believes in polygamy because there are interpretations of Islam that condone the practice, while Khadija believes in polygamy for other reasons including the couple's inability to produce children. Regardless, Khadija dismisses the notion because the practice is unlawful in the United States. When Amira discovers that Khadija's husband is seeing another woman, and that other woman is Samara, the women's relationships are strained to a breaking point. Samara accuses Amira of being unfaithful for painting nude women and sending the paintings to other men, while Amira is outraged that Samara would marry Khadija's husband at a mosque. When Khadija discovers Samara and Ramzi's marriage, she questions everything about her life, including the Islamic precedent that would allow such a marriage. The plot becomes even more complicated when Samara reveals she is pregnant with Ramzi's child. By play's end Khadija decides to divorce her husband, Amira and Hassan decide to adopt an Iraqi child, and Samara raises her child with Ramzi.

Teymour's play explores the ramifications of Islamic tenets that are sometimes practiced in the Middle East yet banned in North America. By personalizing this notion of Islamic polygamy, Teymour takes an abstract conversation and dramatizes it in a way that is not often reflected in American theatre. He brings together three Muslim Arab women from three different cultural contexts (Iraqi, Palestinian, and Egyptian) and finds the commonalities among the women including their love of Arab food, smoking the *argeeleh* (or hookah), and their devotion to the religion of Islam. However, the way their devotion to the religion manifests is vastly different. For instance, Amira does not wear hijab, while Samara and Amira are strict about their adherence to covering. Also, the play wrestles with the notion of adherence to Islam within a vastly different context than it was originally prescribed, namely in the diaspora. How does one contend with religious tenets that are perfectly acceptable in the homeland, but not permitted in the diaspora? The three women are trying to negotiate their allegiance to culture, religion, and homeland in a place and time when those things are not only unknown but often completely discouraged. This leads to painful personal negotiations and conflicts that tear relationships apart and cause deep distress. The play ends on a hopeful note, however, when we see the three women content in their new lives: Amira excited about the prospect of becoming a mother to an adopted child; Khadija ready to become a single-mother divorcee; and Samara eager to start her life with a new baby and a marriage to Ramzi. At a time when women wearing hijab are looked at with suspicion, Teymour's play gives these characters dimension and allows audiences who may never personally know Muslim women a view into the interpersonal conflicts that this community faces.

Canadian playwright Jason Sherman's 1996 play *Reading Hebron* concerns a specific event that occurred in 1994—the Cave of the Patriarchs/Ibrahimi Mosque/Hebron Massacre of Muslim worshippers by American Israeli settler Baruch Goldstein. The massacre claimed the lives of 29 and injured 125 other Muslim Palestinian worshippers. Goldstein was killed on the spot by the survivors. The play takes place in Canada. The protagonist, Nathan, is a Canadian-born Jew who struggles with the dissolution of his marriage to his non-Jewish wife and his struggles as a father to two young sons. The play begins with Nathan on a personal mission to discover the facts that surround the massacre. Along the way he is confronted by a flurry of different characters—some notable and others less so—who challenge, provoke, attack, and question everything Nathan knows and believes. The play oscillates between eyewitness testimonies and Nathan's own real, and surreal, experiences.

Sherman's play explores not only a single massacre but also Nathan's conflicted feelings about the State of Israel itself. On the one hand, he is grateful for a state that has harbored his persecuted people; on the other, he has great difficulty understanding how Israel has treated the Palestinian people and why violence has permeated the complicated history of that land. He must contend with how some Israelis and some North American Jews have completely contradictory views of the same events, how some find ways to justify the violent acts of some extremists, and how people in the diaspora are entrenched in their views. Despite his desire to remain a somewhat neutral questioner of the events of the massacre, Nathan is told he is either a self-hating Jew or a delusional person who is less interested in the facts of the case than in his own feelings of guilt over his association with Israel. Nathan is repeatedly confronted for his self-imposed inquiry. Even the real-life community leaders and scholars who appear in the play— Noam Chomsky, Edward Said, Hanan Ashrawi, Cynthia Ozick, and A.M. Rosenthal—attack his motives for the search. Nathan also suffers from his mother's disapproval for marrying a woman she did not approve of, his wife's anger that he does not spend enough time with the children, and his Jewish employers who detest his critical views regarding Israel. The play digs deeper and deeper into facts, counter-facts, arguments, rebuttals, testimonies, conflicts, and debates surrounding the Arab-Israeli conflict. Nathan, who never visited Israel before the events of the play, finally visits Israel and is put on trial by the very judges who presided over the inquiry into Goldstein's actions. Nathan tells the judges,

> I fear that/ if the Jewish state/ and the Jewish people/ continue to act as we do/ we will disappear as surely/ as the Palestinian people/ whose homes we have taken/ whose families we have dispersed/ whose dignity we have denied/ whose dreams we have ended. (Sherman 2006, 356)

The judges retort that, since Nathan does not live in Israel, his concerns are of no value to those who do live there. The play ends with the judges deciding that Goldstein committed a murderous act and that future acts like his should be prevented.

Sherman's *Reading Hebron* is a long, complicated, and compelling look at how a Jew living in the diaspora tries to cope with the actions of a Jewish state that, in theory, represents him. He wrestles with a long and conflicted history that he is associated with yet is so distant from. He tries to reckon the varying and contradictory histories and accounts that constitute a long and violent century, and to make sense of the seemingly incomprehensible horrors that take place, perpetrated by people representing all sides of the conflict. Plays like *Reading Hebron* leave many more questions than answers, but in doing so they attempt to bring understanding to events that are so horrifically incomprehensible that the only recourse is to ask why they occurred and how they can be avoided in the future.

Another play that deals directly with the costs of war survivors living in diaspora is Heather Raffo's *Noura*. Her first play *9 Parts of Desire* (2002) was a one-woman show that dramatizes the experiences of nine Iraqi and Iraqi American women who contend with the fallout from the First Gulf War and with life in the aftermath of the American invasion of Iraq. She followed the success of *9 Parts of Desire* by writing the libretto for the opera *Fallujah* (2012), with music by Tobin Stokes. *Fallujah* followed the story of American veteran Christian Ellis, who suffered from PTSD from his tour of duty in Iraq. Her play *Noura* (2018) is a rumination on a Christian Iraqi family that has fled Iraq to live in the United States yet are haunted by the memories of their displacement and the rise of the so-called Islamic State in Iraq.

Noura/Nora is a Christian Iraqi American architect from Mosul, Iraq, who lives in New York City with her husband Tareq/Tim, a former surgeon from Baghdad. They have a child named Yazen/Alex, who is eleven years old and very Americanized. Their colleague Rafa'a, Noura's childhood friend from Mosul, is a Muslim American OBGYN. Maryam is a young physicist from Mosul in her twenties. The play takes place during Christmas Eve and Christmas Day at Noura's home in New York City.

The fact that the characters have both Arabic and "American" names is a display of the dichotomy many Middle Eastern Americans live with. Many in this community have their birth names, and the names that are either given or chosen in order to "fit in" with American society. Noura says they changed their names to make them pronounceable and relatable, though she prefers her real name "Noura." Tareq wants to have another child, a daughter, with Noura. Noura instead wants to sponsor an Iraqi orphan from Mosul who was raised in her ancestral church there. Tareq tells her they cannot support every Iraqi refugee, and Noura reminds him that they, too, are refugees. When Maryam arrives unexpectedly, she tells Noura she has an internship with an American weapons contractor with the hopes of a future hire by the US Department of Defense after graduation. She is also visibly pregnant but is without a husband or boyfriend. Noura tries to convince her that having a child will not protect her from her loneliness, but Maryam tells her that everyone she knows is a refugee, or dead, reminding Noura that she wouldn't survive a day in Mosul after Isis has destroyed it. Noura fears that Tareq will not accept Maryam in their house as an unmarried, pregnant woman, yet Rafa'a reminds Noura that she, too, has passed judgment on her. Noura feels the weight of the loss of Mosul, as does Rafa'a. Noura reminds him that her grandfathers carved half the city of Mosul, which was destroyed by the Isis forces. Noura blames Rafa'a for not admitting that there was a genocide in Mosul carried out by Iraqis, but Rafa'a tries to convince her that nowhere is safe anymore for them as Christian Iraqis. New York, she says, may be the only place they can still celebrate Christmas together in peace.

Rafa'a admits he only loved one woman, Noura, yet he could never speak of his feelings for her. The next morning, as the television blares the latest Isis atrocities in Iraq, Noura becomes upset and agitated. She asks why no one defended one another or spoke out when the war crimes were committed. She laments spending a month preparing a Christmas dinner when no one will arrive to celebrate with them. Tareq is grateful for his new life in America, even though he can never practice surgery again because of his shaking hands, a product of his own post-traumatic stress disorder. He asks her what is wrong with being safe and having a place where they can forget their painful past, but Noura tells him she does not want to forget.

When Maryam and Rafa'a finally arrive for dinner, they have an awkward meeting. When Rafa'a asks why she left Iraq, Maryam tells him that the neighbors burned the convent and killed the head mother. As Noura suspected, Tareq is not pleased with Maryam and with supporting an Iraqi woman who is unmarried and pregnant and who wishes to work for defense contractors that had a hand in destroying his homeland. Maryam replies that everywhere she goes, she's a scandal. Unlike Rafa'a, Noura feels a kinship with Maryam since they survived the war in Iraq together. Maryam tries to convince Tareq that Isis is also comprised of Iraqis, no matter how much he and others want to deny it. Noura loses her composure at dinner and divulges the truths no one was willing to admit. After everyone leaves, Tareq tells Noura he no longer wants to support Maryam, who he deems a profligate woman. Tareq and Noura also have their difficulties, wrapped up in notions of shame and sexual desire. Noura realizes that Tareq has also seen her as too free with her sexuality and chastity, and that he does not think she is honorable. Tareq tells her he is tired of feeling ashamed of being Arab in America. The day he changed his name, he says, was the day that Iraq could finally be behind him. The play climaxes when the audience discovers that Maryam is Noura and Tareq's child, who she had when they were young and unmarried. She gave the child to the orphanage rather than bring shame on Tareq and his family. Noura sees millions of people fleeing Iraq with nothing, leaving behind ancient libraries and languages. It is no wonder they are drowning, she says, because the responsibility of being erased is simply too much to bear. Noura wants to tell Yazen about Maryam; she wants to return to Iraq and help rebuild it, but she also knows she cannot do so. Noura's inability to let go and hold on to her homeland at the same time is a condition so many Middle Eastern American immigrants feel being torn away from their countries and forced to make a new life in America. The wounds of their past are still a part of them, while they are expected to restart and rebuild in a new land without any of the hallmarks of home. Tareq, Noura, Rafa'a, and Maryam are victims of a painful history that is scarred with war, displacement, and cultural loss. The Iraq they knew will never be the same after their communities were uprooted and destroyed. Now, they must contend with a new life in a new land and try to heal the wounds that they carry with them every day.

Raffo's play grapples with the horrific rise of Isis in Iraq, and the aftermath of the horrendous atrocities they committed there and throughout the Middle East. She also focuses on the Iraqi Christian community, one with a 2,000-year history, which, according to Aid to the Church in Need (ACN), has, "within a generation, declined 90 percent to below 250,000. Some reports suggest that the actual figure may be lower than 120,000" (Pontifex 2020). The play *Noura* gives insight to those who survived the scourge of Isis yet are left with unseen trauma that affects their lives in the diaspora.

Turkish American writer, actor, and musician Melis Aker has written several plays including *Manar*, *330 Pegasus: A Love Letter*, *Azul Otra Vez* ["*Blue Revisited*"], *Scraps and Things*, *When My Mama Was a Hittite*, and *Dragonflies*. Her plays deal with many issues facing the Turkish American community living in exile including internet radicalization of youth, Turkish American alienation, and cultural, familial, and immigrant identity. Her play *Dragonflies*, which she subtitles "a memory play," takes place from 2005 to 2018 in Brooklyn, and in several undefined locales that include a group therapy session, cyber space, and what she calls a "liminal memory

Figure 2 *Manar* by Melis Aker, LaGuardia Performing Arts Center, 2017. Michelle Tailor (Leslie), Freddie Stevenson (Henry), Layla Wolfgang (Najla), and Tom Waal-and (Benji). Directed by Isabelle Kettle. Photograph by Juan Zapata.

space." The four characters of the play include Lale, a female Turkish girl who we see from eight to thirteen years old; Selma, her mother with a slight Turkish accent; her father Henry; and Najla, a Syrian tutor and friend (Figure 2).

Young Lale presses her mother to tell her what an alien is, and if Tarik was one because he went away. Her mother, Selma, does not want to hear about Tarik prompting Lale to leave to be with her father. In a flashback to 2005 in the Financial District in New York, Selma is watching a video of Osama Bin Laden's speeches. Henry is horrified that Lale would watch such barbarity, especially since she is pregnant with a child who he wants to call Lale, the Turkish word for tulip. A flash forward to the same apartment in 2018 shows a thirteen-year-old Lale reminding Henry that it is Tarik's birthday, and we learn that Lale has never met Tarik before. Meanwhile, in Bay Ridge, Brooklyn, Lale and her tutor Najla discuss Tarik, and how he has been gone for thirteen years with "no trace." Lale discovers her mother Selma (now wearing a hijab) watching more violent videos online. Lale was a successful journalist back in Turkey, but she was forced into political exile. Selma believes she sees Tarik as an Isis executioner in an online video, something Henry vehemently denies. After a violent confrontation, Selma tells Henry she is leaving and taking Lale with her. Later we see Selma and Lale reminiscing about Tarik as they flip through old photos of him giving

Lale a dragonfly for a present. When Henry discovers Lale is watching the execution videos and believing her mother about Tarik being an Isis executioner, he demands that she move in with him. Lale refuses. Henry refuses to believe his son is a terrorist. Selma joins a group therapy session for mothers of sons who fight with Isis. She tells the group that she used to teach her son Turkish, but she would not risk the same with her daughter because she is so afraid of her daughter's involvement with the region. Lale begins dressing in Tarik's old clothes and cuts her hair short. She tells Najla, who is troubled by her behavior, that she does it to get into Tarik's character. In a strange turn, Lale, dressed as Tarik, speaks to the audience in Tarik's persona while sending an email to Selma. In the following scene, we find it was Lale that sent the email disguised as Tarik, with Najla's help. Lale's identity crisis spirals until she alienates Najla and her mother Selma. Najla decides to leave New York for Dearborn because in Dearborn she will not be surrounded by what she calls "neoliberal *fucks*" who pretend she is just like them, when she is not. Lale and Selma reconnect, deciding they will visit Turkey someday together, and they sing the Turkish song "Uzun İnce Bir Yoldayim" ("I'm On a Long and Narrow Road"). They reconcile, learning that they need one another more than they ever thought they might.

Aker's play *Dragonflies* is a deep exploration of the fraught time period between the events of 9/11 and, like Raffo's *Noura*, also explores the rise of Isis throughout the Middle East. Thousands of young people from Europe and North America traveled to Syria and Iraq to fight with the group, and some became proselytizers and executioners for the cause. This led to a crisis in families whose children were lured into terrorism by online materials that promised them a life of acceptance, a life of traditional values, and a place where they would find themselves within a twisted interpretation of the Islamic faith. In *Dragonflies*, Henry and Selma's relationship began well but, gradually, the tensions between her Turkishness and his Americanness tore them apart, especially when Selma suspected their son had left to fight with the jihadist army. Lale, the Middle Eastern American child stuck between them, must negotiate how to live her life as a bicultural girl who also must contend with living in her brother's shadow. By cutting her hair, donning his clothing, and sending emails in his name, Lale attempts to recreate a person she never really knew, and a person who joined a group that has caused such human catastrophe. Lale's relationship with Najla, a Syrian refugee who also cannot find acceptance in America, brings her closer to her understanding of what it means to grow up Middle Eastern in America where one is never fully accepted, and where one must move from place to place to finally land in a spot where there is some sense of belonging. Selma, Najla, and Lale are contending with the forces that shaped them, exiled them from their homelands and their families, and made them the rich and complicated women they are.

Iranian American playwright Farhad Ayeesh's play *Suitcase*, translated by Iranian American playwright, actress, and director Bella Warda, is a nonlinear play that also dramatizes the plight of the immigrant. Set in a waiting room that is more like purgatory, the play features characters carrying suitcases they never release. Archetypal characters with names like "Psychiatrist," "Tailor's Wife," "Civil Engineer," "Military Man," and "Military Man's Wife" wander on stage, looking at each other in horror. The characters move in "false and exaggerated" ways and are directed to act non-realistically. At one point, the Psychiatrist cries out asking if anyone knows where they are.

The play has strange and circular dialogues that mirror the characters' lives in the diaspora. The Military Man's son is accused of odd behavior due to a lack of love and the neglect of his sexuality. The characters break into short poetic speeches and live in a state of self-contempt and loathing. The Man says they are helpless, they always have been, and they will always stay that way. Suddenly, a wedding breaks out, and the Girl and Tailor's son marry. They all begin to dance but trip over the suitcases strewn across the stage. The Psychiatrist asks if they are all dreaming. The Military Man tells of a man who placed his wife in a suitcase. When she died, he went mad because they were in love. At the end a large group enters, the door slams, and a man with a violin—an artist—plays a melody. The unifying element of the artist attempting to make order in the chaos of the room full of immigrants is akin to what Ayeesh is attempting with the play itself. What stands out is that these immigrants are disjointed, discombobulated, and caught in a state of utter turmoil. Ayeesh is attempting, through absurdism and dissonance, to capture the ruptured lives immigrants experience attempting to transit from their homelands to their newly adopted homes, wherever they may be.

Laila Farah's solo performances include *Shaping the World with Our Hands* and *Living in the Hyphen-Nation*. Farah, an associate professor of women's and gender studies at DePaul University, merges her critical theory and her personal experiences to create works that examine her diasporic understanding of living as a woman who was born in the United States, but raised in the Middle East. Her works focus on the depiction of Arab women's lives, their multiple and complex identities, and she challenges the racial constructions ascribed to Arabs in the Western media. "I map the routes many women, as described in their localities, choose or are forced to take in a global context," she writes. She performs as a "bicultural, biracial, bilingual woman" using what she terms "auto-ethnographic diasporic performance" (Farah 2005, 317). She states that she employs this reflexive, auto-ethnographic perspective using moderation, and positions herself as American Lebanese rather than Lebanese American in order to draw her US audiences into a liminal space that appears less "foreign" to them: "As a diasporic subject, I utilize my hybridity to expand audience understanding, foster further exploration, and dispel negative stereotypes" (ibid., 318). Her performance text for *Living in the Hyphen-Nation* includes "Sheherazade Don't Need No Visa," "Stars and Stripes Forever," "Adolescence in 'Absentia,'" and "Resisting Arrest: Arresting Resistance." She utilizes four axes of analysis for her diasporic performance—reflexivity, agency, political dissent, and activism—and believes her work is both pedagogical and coalition building in nature (ibid., 318–19).

The first section titled "Sheherazade Don't Need No Visa" explores checkpoints Farah has traversed both during the Lebanese Civil War and in US airports. In both spaces she is a woman being scrutinized by men with weapons who wield power over her ability to cross from one border to another. Syrian soldiers occupying Beirut, Christian Phalangist officers controlling the infamous "Green Line" during the Civil War, and US immigration officers at Logan Airport all demand papers, answers about where she has been and who she has been with, and about her political affiliations. She recalls having to cross the US-Mexican border, being evacuated on an American Marine helicopter during the evacuation of Beirut in 1984, and even having to answer post-performance questions about her sexual orientation. With each of these "colonizing frameworks" she becomes more and more aggravated and annoyed, finally shouting "KHALAS . . . ENOUGH." During the section titled "Stars and Stripes Forever: Sheherazade's Sequel," she examines institutional racism against racialized "Others" which is found in government-sanctioned policies that target Arabs and Arab Americans entering the United States. She asks, "Does America prefer order over justice?" (ibid., 326). The constant categories, stereotypes, and lists that either keep people in or keep people out leave her with the desire to either act out or internalize her anger after constant harassment by passport control officers who create lists that alienate passengers with exotic sounding names. She recounts Arab and Iranian passengers being interrogated, made late for their flights, having their luggage rummaged through, and being detained: "You think about where this places you on the hyphen this time . . . where does this experience fit in the schema of alienations . . . of hypen-nations . . . of 'One nation under God, indivisible, with liberty and justice for all'" (ibid., 328–9).

Her "Adolescence in 'Absentia'" monologue focuses on the years she spent in Beirut during the Lebanese Civil War and the Israeli invasion of Beirut in 1982. She recounts her apartment building rocking with each bomb landing, of glass flying, and panic-stricken people rushing into hallways for supposed protection. She tells of buildings torn in half, body parts jutting from smoldering rubble, and the survivors' shattered lives. She connects this to the countless wars and destruction in New York, Kandahar, Ramallah, Baghdad. A last image: suntanning on the beach when jets drop bombs, obliterating soldiers: "Smoke and dust swirl and spiral as metal and rock and bones fall onto my towel on the cement below" (ibid., 333). Her last section, "Resisting Arrest: Arresting Resistance," focuses on the notorious Karakol Hbeesh, Al-Khayam, and Abu Ghraib prisons where people were tortured and raped. She tells of how resistance is impossible under the cruelty of torture and how there is no accountability and no possibility for justice. She cites the Geneva Conventions, the UN Convention against Torture, and Amnesty International, and how nothing seems to stop the proliferation of torture in all the wars, including those carried out by the United States. "It wouldn't be so bad if the U.S. government hadn't been holding up a higher moral code and a superior sense of democratic process and justice for the Iraqi people. In our quest for accountability," she asks, "how arresting will our RESISTANCE be?" (ibid., 341). Farah connects the brutality of multiple sites of conflict, attempting to create an act of political resistance and dissent. Her work attempts to understand the transnational diasporic subject through performance-centered research, and to bring humanity to our understanding of the suffering of people who must traverse borders and survive countless wars.

Keeping Tradition Alive: *TRAYF, A People: A Mosaic Play*, and *Detour Guide*

Lindsay Joelle's play *TRAYF* explores the experiences of two Chabad (Lubavitcher) Chasidic Jews living in Brooklyn in 1991. The Jews of the Orthodox order, known as the Haredim, follow strict piety, "fastidious, retro attire" of Poland, Ukraine, and the Carpathian regions of Hungary and Slovakia, religious dietary restrictions, and specifically prescribed Sabbath rituals. This group also primarily speaks Yiddish at home and in their daily communications, and they live in clustered communities. Their traditionally large families are composed of arranged marriages for their eligible children. The Chabad-Lubavitcher Hasidic community, however, "missionizes energetically within the wider Jewish population, taking their inspiration from their late leader, 'the Rebbe,' Menachem Mendel Schneerson (1902-94)" (Lederhendler 2017, 267–8). The Rebbe (also known as "the Lubavitcher Rebbe") is viewed as the seventh and last leader of the Hasidic Chabad-Lubavitch movement (Dine 2017, 776). As the Messiah (or Moschiach), and his followers, "went about singing in public places, 'We want the Messiah now,' in the hope that God would reveal to the Rebbe his true identity as the hoped-for redeemer, to the consternation of most of the other Hasidim and traditional Orthodox Rabbis" (Jacobs 2003). Chabad sponsors soup kitchens, charities, orphanages, and rehab centers around the world and Schneerson was awarded the Congressional Gold Medal for acts of charity. In order to "bring the messiah," the Chabad conducts significant outreach among unaffiliated and nonobservant Jews with the hopes of increasing their numbers and to bring more Jews into Orthodox practice (ibid., 776). One way this outreach occurs is through what is called "Mitzvah Tanks," or recreational vehicles that are "mobile temples" in a secular world.

> In much the same way that bloodmobiles roll into a shopping mall and offer to check people's blood pressure, Mitzvah tanks carry the good news about Jewish observance, and the Jewish soul, in college campuses and selected sites in midtown Manhattan. They approach (some would say "accost") men on 53rd Street and ask them, point-blank but politely, if they are Jewish. Say "No" and the Lubavitchers quickly move on. However, say "Yes" and the next question will invariably be, "Have you put on tefillin today?" And pretty soon the man, reluctant or not, finds himself inside the tank, winding leather straps around his arms and reciting the ancient blessings. (Pinsker 2000)

A Mitzvah is considered both a precept (or commandment) and as a good deed done for religious duty. Some contest the fact that mitzvot are meant to be "good deeds"; rather they are considered the 613 mitzvot derived from the Hebrew Bible. Therefore, a "Mitzvah tank" is a vehicle that provides spiritual outreach, beneficial acts, and an opportunity for Jews to "tip the universal scale of justice toward good" (Joelle 2019, 11).

The two protagonists in *TRAYF* (which is a Yiddish word for things not in accordance with Jewish dietary laws) are Zalmy and Shmuel, nineteen-year-old males from the Crown Heights neighborhood in Brooklyn, New York. They are dressed in the traditional black fedora with large brim turned down in the front. They also wear yarmulkes, beards with no sidecurls, white button-down shirts, tzitzit (or tassels) worn long, black suits, and black shoes. Their white RV displays a painted sign stating, "Mitzvahs on the Spot for People on the Go." Zalmy (the navigator) and Shmuel (the driver) are good hearted, fun loving young men who are as confused by secular culture and music as they are about dating and women. In the tank they listen to many Jewish artists including Mordechai Ben David, Avraham Fried, Shlomo Carlebach, and the Miami Boys Choir.

They attempt to find fellow Jews by asking, "Excuse me, are you Jewish?" but find little success until they meet a record producer named Jonathan. Shmuel believes that Jonathan is a goy, or non-Jewish person, but Zalmy is convinced he is a Yid, or a person of Eastern European Jewry. Jonathan tells them that his father's biological parents were Jewish, but his mother is Catholic. This poses an immediate problem since Jewish identity is based on matriliny, or the tracing of descent through the mother's line of a family. When Jonathan has difficulty articulating what makes a Jewish person Jewish, Shmuel is even more suspect of Jonathan's connection to Judaism. Shmuel tells him that it does not matter what a person eats or how they pray but that one is a Jew if they have a Jewish soul, and has a mother who is a Jew. Shmuel tells Jonathan plainly that he is not a Jew.

Meanwhile, Zalmy and Shmuel's families are trying to set them up with potential wives. Naturally, they are nervous about speaking to women since they have not had interactions with women outside of their own family. The things they hear about what occurs on a wedding night are equally bizarre, and their knowledge of sexuality is hilariously incorrect. The fact that Jonathan has had multiple sexual partners is both astonishing and bewildering to both of them (Figure 3).

Zalmy and Jonathan's friendship grows, eclipsing Shmuel's connection with his best friend. Jonathan becomes absolutely committed to living his life as a Hasidic Chabad-Lubavitcher, learning prayers, dressing in the traditional ways, and eschewing much of his previous life to the chagrin of his girlfriend, Leah, a Jewish woman who is tired of Jonathan's religious appropriation, making everything kosher, and unscrewing all the light bulbs

Figure 3 *TRAYF* by Lindsay Joelle, Theater J, 2018. Tyler Herman (Zalmy) and Josh Adams (Shmuel). Directed by Derek Goldman. Photograph by Teresa Wood.

in their apartment on Fridays. Leah, whose grandparents were Holocaust survivors, and who is atheistic, says she had to endure the embarrassment of growing up Jewish, which included attending over a hundred bar mitzvahs, wearing hand-me-down clothing from her cousins, and attending Hebrew school. She wants Shmuel to stop his mission converting Jonathan because she believes Jonathan is diving into his Jewishness as a way of grieving his father's loss. Gradually, both Leah and Shmuel realize they have been replaced as Zalmy and Jonathan have grown closer. Shmuel discovers that Zalmy is creating secular music mix tapes and attending "scandalous" Broadway plays like *Fiddler on the Roof*. As Jonathan goes "all in," Zalmy's faith waivers. He quits the tank. Eventually, Zalmy and Shmuel reconnect, and their friendship survives the test of secular ideology into their lives. The play ends happily with the two men listening contently to the Miami Boys Choir.

Joelle's lighthearted play takes audiences into a very traditional society and, by doing so, exposes them to a subculture that is rarely seen or understood. While confronting serious issues such as Jewish identity and intra-faith conflict, the play also provides a humorous portrait of two young men navigating a confusing world together. It is rare to encounter characters like Zalmy and Shmuel on American stages. To see this subculture with all its humor, love of Yiddish language and music, and the desire for the spreading of mitzvahs, is a fascinating glimpse into a world that further expands our understanding of yet another minority community living and thriving in the United States.

L M Feldman's play *A People: A Mosaic Play* is subtitled "For Anyone Who Comes From a Long Line of Someones" (Feldman 2019, 1). Featuring a cast of six to ten actors meant to play over fifty characters; the playwright states that the production should feel like an experience, or special event, to the audience. The play contains Jewish poems, prayers, songs, and music. The script is nonlinear and reads more like a musical score than a playscript. Audience interaction is part of the experience of the play. The archetypal characters are from all walks of Jewish life—Klezmer ensembles, Yeshiva Teachers, Hassids, Yiddishkeits, and Rabbis; however, there are also famous personages such as Martin Buber, Anne Frank, Abraham Koralnik, and even Moses. Characters marry, dance, debate the Torah, discuss the stages of womanhood, philosophize, and sing strains of Bob Dylan songs. Feldman attempts to create a massive tapestry of Jewish/Yiddish life, tying together previous generations with current generations as a celebration of all that these people have endured over the millennia. The characters also debate what makes one Jewish and whether trauma is a defining identity. They also fight over the status of Israel, and whether there should be a two-state solution. This debate comes down to an existential fear of loss and why some Jews struggle to be so observant while others are comfortable foregoing traditions and cultural norms.

The second half of the play begins after the Yiddish world dissolves (ibid., 57). Suddenly talk shifts to refugees, the building of walls, Islamophobia, human rights, and Christmas. Many of the characters talk about the work that it takes to be Jewish, to study Torah, and to live a traditional life in order to retain the bonds with their faith and their people. Rituals permeate the play, providing guideposts to usher the characters along through their journey in the diaspora far from their homeland(s). Feldman's play encapsulates so much of the Jewish experience that it demands a cast of diverse Jewish characters that can bring to light the complexity of this culture. Plays like *A People* are extremely ambitious, yet deeply moving. They are an attempt to reclaim, in drama, what might have been lost in faith.

Karim Nagi's tour de force, *Detour Guide*, is described as a "One Act Musical" in which Nagi performs as a solo performer. Nagi, a multi-instrumentalist performing and teaching artist, was born in Egypt to a

Cairine father and an Alexandrine mother who later immigrated to the United States when Nagi was a child. He has led the Sharq Arabic Music Ensemble since 1999 and has taught at major educational institutions across the United States as a drum and dance teacher. His expertise is in Arab hand percussion, music ensemble performance, and Arab folk dance. He has created several solo live performances including *Arabized*, *Arabiqa*, *Turbo Tabla*, and *Detour Guide*.

The characters in the play—Guide, Tony Dabeek, Sheikha Iman, Hani, Bashir, Marwa, and Amu Rezq—are all played by Nagi, who also sings, dances, and plays all the instruments during the performance including the tabla, bendir drum, finger cymbals, and buzuq. Nagi acts as a guide, but rather one who is going to provide a different tour of the Middle East. The new alternative trip around the Arab world he promises is one that will refute stereotypes, defy audience expectations, and inform audiences of what the actual lives of Arabs consist of, rather than the perverted and distorted view that has been handed down to Americans from the media. As someone who is representing what he calls "The Ministry of Detourism," he says he has experience in the region, and he has studied his own psyche. He explains his life journey that took him from birth in Egypt to adolescence in the United States where he had an unpronounceable foreign name and a love for heavy metal, mix tapes, and music. His love for music changed upon returning to Egypt and discovering the tabla/derbeke/dumbek drum that is central to so much of Middle Eastern music. He says that discovery of Arab music "re-rooted" and "rerouted" him. Instead of visiting well-traveled tourist sites, he visited the places where people lived and worked, and learned their music, songs, and dances instead. During the "detour" he explains dancing a zikr at a saint's street celebration, learning how to dabke dance from a Levantine Arab friend named Tony, understanding envy from a religious woman (sheikha), learning how to dance from the Nayli women of Algeria, the music of Saudi Arabian drumming teams, and the tarab songs of Syria. In each instance, he demonstrates his embodied knowledge of the music and dance of the region, and by doing so, he introduces audiences to Arab culture.

As Nagi inhabits the various characters, he tells us about the lives of Arabs living in the Middle East and in the diaspora. He recounts his Egyptian friend, Bashir, who immigrated to America but returned after two years to start his own "Tuktuk" business (the tuktuk is an automotive rickshaw). Bashir's Syrian girlfriend, Marwa, was a great musician forced to leave her musical instruments behind in Syria during the war and now works in a kitchen dreaming of playing her beloved instruments by using kitchen utensils instead. He also inhabits the character of Amu Rezq and performs a "raqs assaya" (cane dance) for the audience while wearing a galabayya and kufiyya.

Nagi provides maps and graphs that demonstrate Arab American census statistics and Syrian refugee numbers. His approach is multifaceted; he entertains, he instructs, he confronts, and he elicits empathy for those that are deemed by some Americans as too Muslim to travel and too Arab to be trusted. The alternative view of the Middle East exposes audiences to the pernicious nature of Orientalism, how Hollywood has distorted the culture's view of Middle Easterners, and how those distortions lead to realistic consequences. He likens the Hollywood racist portrayals of Middle Easterners to blackface, and he asks why Middle Easterners are not expected to feel offense at ugly images of racist and ethnic stereotyping. The images are seductive and dangerous, he says, and yet they are leading to anti-Arab, anti-Muslim violence. Nagi concludes his performance by playing a rhythm from each of the twenty-two nations that comprise the so-called Arab world. His virtuosic display highlights the similarities and the intricate differences between these rhythms. This dizzying display of cultural knowledge provides audiences with a musical, and cultural, tour of the region. Nagi humanizes the dehumanized and, in the process, he entertains and instructs.

Searching for Roots: *Baba* and *(dis)Place[d]*

Egyptian American playwright Denmo Ibrahim's 2014 play *Baba* is a solo performance that is based on a true story involving an Egyptian American man named Mohammed who is desperately attempting to take his daughter for a trip to Egypt to visit his homeland. Ibrahim is the founding artistic director of Mugwumpin, a performance group based in San Francisco, and she is also the playwright of *Ecstasy: A Water Fable*. The first act of *Baba* is set in 1983, where Mohammed is stuck in endless lines at governmental offices trying to get his five-year-old daughter's passport. He tries to keep from utter boredom by telling jokes, speaking to other people in line, and entertaining his young daughter. Repeatedly he is rebuffed by the officials for not having the proper documentation. He tries to understand the American system, but the entire bureaucracy confuses and eludes him. He even breaks out into a hilarious rap song about how red tape defines the

American system. He also muses on how he tried to "wash away the brown" by changing his accent but it was not successful. Even his name "Mohammed Abdullah Yusuf Omar Ahmed Tarik Karim" must be shortened simply to "Moe." Monologues flash back to how Mohammad came to America, first found work, he and his wife went from eating traditional Egyptian meals to eating American food and McDonald's happy meals. He remembers how he and his wife met, married, had their daughter Layla, and how their marriage deteriorated after his wife endured several miscarriages. After the marriage dissolved, Mohammed wanted custody of his daughter. The audience learns that he is in the airport because he decided to kidnap Layla and take her back to his native Egypt. The second act shows Layla is seen three decades later traveling to Egypt to see her father. Her mother has become an assimilated American while her father returned to Egypt and to reclaim his original nationhood. Layla, on the other hand, is a hybrid of two worlds who does not speak any Arabic since her parents only spoke English with her. She is a first-generation Arab American who is expected to have a completely different set of behavioral norms from the other girls around her regarding dating, sex, drugs, and religion. She returns to Egypt to meet her father and her family, both of whom she had lost touch with over the years. She arrives at the gate calling out her father's name with the sound of the Islamic call to prayer in the background.

According to Hala Sayed, Ibrahim "used the transformative power of her body and relied upon gesture and movement to perform a play that covers thirty years and two continents and tells the story of both love and forgiveness between an American-born daughter and the memory of her estranged Egyptian immigrant father who failed to adjust to the New York City life" (Sayed 2016, 22). A play like *Baba* is a Middle Eastern American woman's attempt to bridge the gap she felt between her and her immigrant father, as well as a show that demonstrates her own longing for connection to her parents' homeland. By physically embodying her father herself, Ibrahim creates a psychic and physical connection with her father, and her cultural background. Playing both the father Mohammed and the daughter Layla allows Ibrahim to fully embrace the parts of herself that desired this connection, and to find an empathetic link to the man who would stop at nothing to have his daughter in his life.

Debórah Eliezer is a writer, performer, playwright, and co-artistic director of foolsFURY, a San Francisco-based performance ensemble. Her play *(dis)Place[d]* is a one-woman performance about an Arab Jewish woman whose father hails from an ancient Jewish community in Iraq. The play is a daughter's reflection on her Iraqi-Jewish father's life as he deteriorates with dementia in a nursing home. There is also a nonhuman character, simply titled "Land," that sings a song of the Tigris and Euphrates in Arabic. We learn that the father has two names: "Edward" (his given name) and "Uri" (his "underground" name). In flashbacks we meet a younger Edward living in Baghdad as a boy, with a beautiful and peaceful life. In 1941 Hitler tried to influence Iraq and pro-Nazis took over. Then "the Farhoud," or pogrom, against Iraqi Jews took place. Edward recounts how, in the Jewish Quarter, there were hangings, shootings, and murders of Jews. In forward flashes we see The Daughter living in America, sharing a contemporary life with her friends who have little understanding of The Daughter's history, culture, or memory. The Daughter tells her friends that her father was an Israeli spy, one who even carried cyanide in his sock. She reminds them that Jews had an ancient, 2,500-year history in Iraq, but that there are no more Jews there now. Edward and his family survive the horrors of the Farhoud, where he eventually fought to escape Iraq in order to arrive at the newly established Israeli State. The character "Land" tells Edward that he may eventually avoid the map, but the map will always find him. Gradually, The Daughter realizes the painful, complicated, and disparate life her father lived—wondering about how he chanted in the synagogue, how he spoke Arabic and Hebrew, and how he might have killed other people as a spy. She tells him that each part of her knowing him complicates the person she believes herself to be. In another flashback, the Iraqi Jews struggle with the fact that the Iraq they knew was changing, and that they gradually realize that they must leave. One of them, Abu Hajjar, says that in the future Palestinian Arabs and Jews might live in peace, God willing.

The final push factor for the Jews in Iraq came with the 1948 Arab-Israeli War. Young Edward realizes that the Jews must immigrate to Palestine or die in Iraq. Aba recounts how, once again, Jews were being stabbed to death and buried in mass graves and how suddenly the Jews there realized that Iraq was no longer their home. Edward becomes a member of the Haganah—a Jewish paramilitary group in Mandatory Palestine between 1920 and 1948. Edward's repeated saying was, "We were Israel before Israel." The Daughter tells her friends that she wants to write a play that will shed light on Iraqi-Jewish history, but her friends find the notion ridiculous. In trying to understand who she really is, "Land" tells her that the Middle East is a long story of people being displaced from their homelands. Finally, The Daughter realizes that she is not one thing—she is a mixture of all the various influences and histories that make her who she is now.

Eliezer attempts to reconstruct her father's Iraqi-Jewish-Israeli history as he himself is losing that history to his dementia. As another Middle Eastern American of Arab Jewish parentage, the protagonist watches helplessly as her father's mind deteriorates. In *(dis)Place[d]* Eliezer captures that liminal state where Middle Eastern Americans live their lives in America, while knowing their parents lived long and eventful lives filled with tragedy, displacement, war, and loss. Her desperation to understand her father's history before he is gone forever is captured in flashbacks and flashforwards that contrast her peaceful, comfortable life in America with the turbulent and violent life he lived in Iraq after the pogroms, in Palestine as a soldier, in Israel after statehood, and as an immigrant to America. In this deeply personal play, Eliezer reclaims her history and creates a loving tribute to her dying father in the process.

Diaspora and Its Discontents: *Stunning*, *Deep Cut*, and *The Man in the Sukkah*

Of course, there are those diaspora plays that highlight the negative cultural aspects of certain Middle Eastern American communities. In plays like David Adjmi's *Stunning* and Karim Alrawi's *Deep Cut*, the negative social constructs some diasporic Middle Eastern American subjects endure are exposed for dramatic purpose. These plays highlight the traditional norms and overbearing patriarchy that can be found in some Middle Eastern American communities. Specifically, they focus on how females are directly affected when they grow up in conservative communities that have overwhelming expectations that are brought to bear on young women. In plays like these that explore the discontent suffered by women in these communities, the constricting religious and filial expectations are examined and dramatized in order to highlight the complicated negotiation women face living in religiously conservative cultures.

Playwright David Adjmi was raised in the close-knit Syrian Jewish community in the Midwood section of Brooklyn where he attended the local yeshiva. Adjmi, who calls himself "a gay, eccentric, arty person," felt "Other within this Other" growing up there (Cote 2009). The Syrian Jewish community of Midwood, with an estimated population of 75,000 people, is considered the largest Syrian Jewish community in the world (Myers 1992). This diasporic community is dominated by Orthodox Sephardic Jews, most of whom emigrated from Syria. The community there was once dominated by Ashkenazi Jews, but as they steadily moved to Long Island and New Jersey, the Sephardim became the prevailing population (Friedman 2010). This group speak English colored by Arabic expressions, and they consume Arabic food such as kibbe and saubousac. In 1992 the Assad government in Syria lifted a travel ban imposed on Syria's Jews to allow them to immigrate. Since that time the Midwood community has gradually embraced the Sephardic community and integrated them into their fold.

The play *Stunning* is the story of two couples living in Midwood. Adjmi writes the neighborhood is a "very affluent, largely Jewish area; one that exerts a centripetal force on the people who live there" (5). The main couple in the play are the Schwecky family—Lily, a sixteen-year-old bride, and Ike, her mid-forties husband. Lily's sister Shelly is married to JoJo, a thirty-something entrepreneur who sells JoJo Jeans. The other pivotal character is Blanche Nesbitt, a forty-something African American woman who is employed as the Schwecky's housekeeper. From the beginning we see that Lily and Shelly are at the mercy of their husbands, who are the only ones working outside the home. The young women are preoccupied by fashion, popular culture, and community gossip. By contrast, the older men are obsessed with work and money. Lily and Ike's home is comprised of an all-white minimalism with reflective surfaces. Blanche tells Lily that despite holding a PhD in semiotics, she has taken the housekeeping job to pay off student loans. Blanche also tells Lily she doesn't look Jewish, but rather Middle Eastern, which Lily discards as the result of overtanning on vacation in Aruba. Lily tells Blanche she's white, demonstrating that she does not fully understand her own ethnic background.

During the play we learn of Ike and Jojo's boorish behavior with one another and their dominating patriarchal views of their wives. With Blanche's help Lily gradually realizes how trapped she is in a marriage she was destined for since the age of twelve, and how she might have feelings for Blanche. As Lily and Blanche grow closer to one another, Ike feels more threatened. Through her affair with Blanche, Lily realizes her Sephardic roots, her sexual desire, and how her family and community have cornered her into a loveless marriage where her primary function is to procreate and raise her children. When Lily gives Blanche $8,000 to pay off her student loans, and when Blanche makes it clear that she will not run away with Lily, the truth about Blanche's history is exposed by Ike. The play then takes a dark turn where Lily remains with Ike and, after being attacked by Ike and almost drowned in a bucket of white paint, Blanche realizes she has no outlet other than suicide.

Adjmi's play does not deeply explore the diasporic condition of these Syrian Jewish characters, but he does touch upon the notions of whiteness, Jewishness, and Middle Eastern heritage that serve as a backdrop for the play. He adds what he calls "Syrian-American Terms" throughout their dialogue, using words like "dibeh" (slang for idiot), "ibe" (a comment on shameful behavior), "shoof/shoofie" (a command to look somewhere), among others. The main theme is the crushing patriarchy in this community where some young girls are married and are expected to produce large families without question. Lily's awakening due to Blanche's tutelage and love opens her eyes to a wider world that she has never experienced. Unlike other plays that celebrate minority Middle Eastern communities, a play like *Stunning* takes a critical view of this small, tight-knit Syrian Jewish community, telling a disturbing tale about the negative aspects that circumscribe women's lives there.

Playwright and novelist Karim Alrawi's play *Deep Cut* begins in a pleasant holiday home on an island of the Pacific Northwest. Jennifer, an English woman, is engaged to Andrew, an American academic. Their friend, Bertrand, is a wise-cracking multilingual professor who banters endlessly with his friends. A young doctor named Michael Chan arrives to work with his professor, Andrew. Chan was a doctor in China during the Tiananmen Square protests where he cared for the wounded. When he was pressed by authorities to give names of those he treated he refused, and he was later mercilessly tortured by Chinese government officials. Andrew's daughter, Farah, is the child of Andrew's first marriage to his Sudanese wife, Nadia, who he met living in Egypt. After Nadia's death, Andrew and Farah moved to the United States and settled in Washington State.

The play centers on a moral argument about when it is necessary for one to intervene while living in a foreign country and witnessing an unethical act. As the play unfolds, the audience discovers that Andrew paid for a clitoridectomy for his then servant's daughter. Farah, haunted by nightmares about the girl being circumcised, reveals that she, too, had been partially circumcised as a girl at her mother's directive. This revelation leads to a conflict between the characters where they debate the merits of intervening in another culture's practices versus remaining passive out of respect for that culture. Andrew believes it is not the role of outsiders to intervene in other cultural practices, be they torture of doctors by Chinese officials, or circumcisions by traditional practitioners. For Farah and Michael, Andrew's silence is assent; yet for Andrew remaining silent is one way of extending cultural respect. Farah confronts Andrew, blaming him for his passivity in the face of the trauma she endured in the decades since the clitoridectomy. Meanwhile, Michael cannot tolerate Andrew's belief that he would have no right to stop Michael's torture had he seen it take place while in China. The final reckoning outside under the tree where Nadia is buried is one of deep anger and forgiveness. Farah and Michael find solace only after they enter the sound and swim with the Orcas under the moonlight.

Alrawi's play confronts the trauma of second-generation Middle Eastern Americans coping with the suffering they endured living in a place where ancient traditions dominate daily existence. Farah and Michael's abuse overseas complicates their attempts at creating a normal life in America. For Michael, Andrew's belief in a hands-off approach is a matter of ethical malfeasance. Farah believes Andrew's actions were a fundamental betrayal of the father-daughter's sacred bond. Where Andrew believes that American interference overseas has led to too much war, colonialism, and oppression, Michael and Farah see a perfidy of basic humanity. What began as an enjoyable social gathering descends into an evening of uncovering past sins, exposing terrible deeds, and discovering truths that were meant to be buried forever. Alrawi forces audiences to confront the complicated moral dilemmas they most likely would rather not think about. However, a play like *Deep Cut* asks how far any of us would go if faced with the same complicated moral conundrums faced by his protagonists.

Deborah Yarchun's drama *The Man in the Sukkah* takes place in the year 2000 during the last three days of Sukkot (Festival of Shelters or Tabernacles). Sukkot is one of three biblically based pilgrimage holidays as thanksgiving for the fruit harvest. The play is set in Greenwood, South Carolina, on a once-thriving slave plantation in a place known as "Jew's Land" where dandelion weeds and trees infested with laurel wilt cover the land. The four characters Aviva (14), Elaine (39), Harris (40), and Nate (36) are interconnected through their family history and Jewish traditions. A sukkah, or hand-built hut with three walls, stands in the backyard of the Harris home with a menorah, a Kiddush cup, and other Jewish ceremonial items dangling from the ceiling. Aviva has planted herself in the sukkah with only a blanket and candy. Elaine and Harris, her new foster parents, are having a very difficult time adjusting to Aviva's anger toward them. Elaine is haunted by dreams of her father, who was interned as a boy in the Buchenwald Concentration Camp; however, now she has nightmares of her brother being interned there and being executed by a guard. Her father had achromatopsia, which made it possible to see the red in the Nazi guards' armbands. Her father's death anniversary coincides with Sukkot for the first time in twenty years, and the trees named after her missing brother Nate are diseased with laurel wilt. Elaine collects broken birds, while Harris (who is color-blind) finds this habit disturbing. Aviva tells Elaine and Harris there is a man in the sukkah, who turns out to be the long-lost Nate. Harris believes Nate killed Elaine's father, and was responsible for a little girl's disappearance in the community. Elaine has sublimated her trauma, which appears only when she recalls her past and leaves dark red bloody crescent-shaped marks in her skin from her fingernails.

Meanwhile, Nate and Harris begin a dangerous relationship, cutting dead trees with axes in the forest together, while Elaine attempts to grow closer to Aviva through old Hebrew songs and reciting family names pulled from the Tzedakah box. Elaine views parenting Aviva as a test of her faith while Harris views Nate's presence as a test of his fatherhood. As Nate and Aviva conspire to run away together, Elaine evicts Nate from her home. Harris, discovering Nate's plan, takes him to the woods with an axe for a final reckoning. Aviva runs away but is found by Elaine. They share a last song together and let a red-winged blackbird fly from its cage. After a violent fight, Nate refuses to kill Harris. Nate flees and never returns. The final image is of Aviva, Elaine, and Harris finally sitting together in the sukkah with a vibrant sunrise washing over them.

Yarchun's play, set on a piece of land that had been inhabited by Jews after the Revolutionary War, by white slave owners on plantations where Black slaves were incarcerated there, and a land soaked with blood from the Civil War, creates a haunted landscape for all of these characters embodying their own traumas. The time—Sukkot—which coincides with the anniversary of the death of a Holocaust survivor, creates the backdrop that sets the menacing tone for characters trapped in a desperate struggle for the present. Elaine's post-trauma as a daughter of a survivor of Buchenwald Camp and Aviva's trauma as a young Jewish girl desperately trying to find her place in the world intersect at the place where Harris is struggling with his test of fatherhood. Yarchun's drama ties together ancient names of lost souls, haunting Hebrew songs, a recollection of the wandering Jews searching for the Promised Land, and the hope for a better future in the diaspora for a new family. With a deep pathos and understanding for all her characters, Yarchun creates a world where healing can finally replace the suffering that has crippled her characters' lives. The play ends with a beautiful sunrise and a family finally reconciling their troubled past. This metaphor of new beginnings provides a hopeful future for a community that is dealing with the horrific history of the Holocaust, and the inevitable loss of the survivors of that unimaginable event.

Diaspora plays contend with the notion that Middle Eastern Americans are inextricably tied to their countries of origin, yet they are expected to eschew their connection to these places in order to be fully accepted in their new homelands. These plays address the manner by which American theatre and Hollywood tend to Orientalize actors and Middle Eastern cultures, how Middle Eastern Americans contend with the aftermath of catastrophic events like the European Holocaust, the Islamic Revolution in Iran, the persecution of religious minorities in Iraq, and the uprisings of the so-called Arab Spring. These works take a searing look at the state of those in the diaspora, contending with momentous events that preceded them and attempting to create a better and more hopeful future going forward.

CHAPTER 5
PLAYS SET IN THE HOMELAND

Many Middle Eastern American plays and musicals are set in the homeland. This dramaturgy is the desire to recreate the homeland they left, or the homeland from which their ancestors emigrated. Some take place in the distant past while others are dealing with issues that are currently relevant. Regardless of the setting, the characters are in that place and the action is rooted specifically within a time period the playwright wishes to explore. This reimagining of a lost homeland or of a homeland that is being destroyed, occupied, or under siege is an attempt by these playwrights to reclaim a lost history or heritage. These plays are also usually political since they attempt to address issues including colonialism, occupation, genocide, and life under dictatorships.

Plays Exploring the Refugee Crisis: *Urge for Going* and *Not My Revolution*

Mona Mansour's *Urge for Going* is part of "The Vagrant Trilogy" she wrote which also includes the plays *The Hour of Feeling* and *The Vagrant*. While many writers have approached the situation of Palestinians living in Palestine, few have dramatized the situation of millions of Palestinians living in refugee camps scattered throughout the Middle East. These permanent residences in exile began following the suppression of the Arab uprisings of 1936–9 but were hastened by the founding of the State of Israel in 1948, and with the subsequent wars between Israelis and Palestinians. According to BBC News, the Palestinians comprise "one of the biggest displaced populations in the world" (Asser 2010). The resulting Israeli contention that all refugees should relinquish the right of return has only aggravated an already desperate situation. According to the United Nations Relief and Works Agency (UNRWA), there were 475,075 Palestinian refugees living in 12 camps in Lebanon as of 2019. Palestinians in Lebanon are denied the right to work in certain professions, are unable to claim the same rights as other foreigners living and working in Lebanon, and often live in abject poverty (unrwa.org). According to *Al Jazeera*, "Today, Palestinians in Lebanon continue to suffer from draconian measures which the Lebanese state claims are there to prevent them from becoming permanent guests" (aljazeera.com 2009). To make matters worse, there have been massacres of these refugees in their Lebanese camps such as the Sabra and Shatila massacre in 1982, the massacre of civilians during the Black September war in 1970, the deaths during the Nahr al-Bared Camp conflict in 2007, and the suicide attack on the Burj el-Barajneh camp in 2015 to name only a few (Figure 4).

The main character in *Urge for Going*, Jamila, is a seventeen-year-old Palestinian girl who dreams of a life far from the squalor of the Palestinian refugee camp she inhabits. She looks up to her father, Adham, who left Palestine to pursue his studies as a young man in England. Her mother Abir and her uncles Ghassan and Hamzi are all doing their best living under the most difficult circumstances. Jamila's brother, Jul, who was beaten by Lebanese soldiers, and who is mentally handicapped because of it, is her only confidant. They are living in limbo since they cannot fully integrate into the Lebanese state as citizens, and they cannot return to Palestine.

Figure 4 *Urge for Going* by Mona Mansour, Golden Thread Productions, 2013. Terry Lamb (Adham), Camila Betancourt Ascencio (Jamila), and Tara Blau (Abir). Directed by Evren Odcikin. Photograph by David Allen Studio.

The play opens with Palestinians themselves debating how the crisis began with each citing historical facts to prove their positions. *Urge for Going* also focuses on the urge to flee the camps for a better life elsewhere. This urge to leave is strong, given that life in the refugee camp is untenable: from lack of sanitation and electricity to beatings from Lebanese soldiers that have left family members physically and mentally injured. The only clear way out for this family is through academic opportunity, yet even Jamila knows that no matter how much one masters their intellect, without innate talent she will not succeed. For Jamila's father, Adham, the opportunity to escape came when he was invited to London in 1967 to lecture on Wordsworth's "Lines Composed a Few Miles above Tintern Abbey, On Revisiting the Banks of the Wye During a Tour. July 13, 1798." Although the lecture's reception grants Adham a fellowship to study in London, the defeat of the Arab armies in 1967 forces his return to a homeland that is ultimately lost, leaving him and his wife as refugees in neighboring Lebanon. For his young daughter, Jamila, who was born in the camps, however, the opportunity arrives thirty-six years later when she tests for her baccalaureate. She passes and, unlike her father who returned with the hopes that someday his Palestinian homeland might be liberated, and he might be allowed to return, she decides to leave the camp and forge a better life elsewhere. The play ends with Jul and Jamila reciting statistics about the painful situation Palestinian refugees face. Therefore, the family in Mansour's drama, like many Palestinian families living as refugees since 1948 and 1967, have a Hobson's choice: either stay put in their refugee camps or rely on the hope that a better life exists elsewhere. Mansour allows audiences to take a moment to empathize with those Palestinians who are living in the ongoing purgatory known as exile.

Elizabeth Huffman's play *Not My Revolution* deals specifically with the Syrian Civil War through the eyes of a displaced woman who, in her own way, finds a deep connection with France's Marie Antoinette. Huffman, a Syrian American writer and performer, plays all of the characters in this monodrama which begins with Displaced Woman in the lobby of the theatre wearing tattered burlap clothing and asking audience members where she can find refuge in multiple languages: Arabic, English, and French. The setting is comprised of a small wooden table, two wooden chairs, a platform, a folding chair, an old used card table, and a hard box. She tells the audience she is not a beggar, but rather an educated woman who was once living like a queen but is now left to roam the world pleading for food and money.

The opening scene is set in what Huffman calls "A Five Star Ghetto in Istanbul" with a small bed, her children's picture, and a table with a teacup and a saucer. She is visibly upset by a verbal assault she suffered on the street outside and she performs a small ritual with her scarf, lantern, thermos, towel, and lotion. As she prays, she hears Marie Antoinette's voice overhead. She is interrupted by rats that run through the shelter and over her feet. She tells the audience she is not afraid to die, only to die without honor. The Displaced Woman living in her rodent-infested shelter is meant to mirror the horrid conditions Marie Antoinette experienced in prison while awaiting her execution. Both women lived lives of luxury before their respective revolutions. The Displaced Woman was married in Syria to a man named Shadi, and together they were successful art dealers under the Assad regime. They lived well and had two children named Rami and Nina. They vacationed in Europe and the United Arab Emirates, and she lived like royalty with servants, despite her mother-in-law's constant verbal abuse.

The Displaced Woman tells of how she and her husband were caught up in the Syrian street protests that preceded the war and, when violence broke out, her husband was killed. A young protester named Adila reminds the woman that people are suffering, living on less than two dollars a day, and that they are demanding the fall of the regime and the release of tortured political prisoners. The Displaced Woman and Adila are captured by government forces and taken to prison. Huffman's script then alternates between the actual words of Antoinette and The Displaced Woman's monologues.

After being released, The Displaced Woman is given money and told she must leave Syria immediately. She is forced to leave without her children; all she can take with her are some jewels, clothes, her passport, a picture of her children, and her mother's teacup and saucer. She is taken to Beirut and then smuggled to Turkey. Her plans to escape to Europe are thwarted when she is robbed and forced to go to a refugee camp where she lives in squalor with no privacy, with disease, and little food or clean water. She meets a motherless child and considers taking care of him as her own but realizes she can barely care for herself. She discovers that she is living in the same lawless and brutal situation Antoinette found herself under the Reign of Terror in France. She feels guilt over her lost children and for leaving the child in the camp, but she resolves to start a school for the children in the camp, making a contribution with the little time she has left. The play ends with captions that contain statistics of those killed during the Reign of

Terror, those killed during the Syrian Civil War, and the number of people forcibly displaced from their countries due to wars and famine.

Huffman's drama connects two completely different women from two disparate eras yet finds the brutal commonalities between them. By highlighting the plight of the Syrian people who have suffered in a horrific civil war, Huffman attempts to humanize refugees and she also humanizes the Syrian people suffering from almost a decade of war. Few American plays have dealt with this topic. Huffman's play reminds viewers that the refugees we see on the news suffering in squalid camps throughout the Middle East, the Aegean, and Europe came from all walks of life. Huffman confronts her audience from the moment they enter the theatre when audience members think they are dealing with a beggar from the streets, to the end of the play where we see a single refugee woman who resolves to make the world better despite living in conditions few could ever imagine. Huffman asks audiences to make an empathetic connection with those who are living in the most difficult conditions imaginable at home and abroad.

Plays of the Holocaust and Plays Set in Israel and Palestine: *The Zionists*, *Abraham's Daughters*, and *Food and Fadwa*

Zohar Tirosh-Polk's play *The Zionists* is set in 1930s–1940s Warsaw, Poland, Palestine, and Israel; 2006 in Jerusalem; and 2007–8 Jerusalem, Tel Aviv, and New York City. The play centers around the Goldenberg family living in Tel Aviv, their relatives in Poland living under Nazi persecution, and contemporary Jewish settlers in the West Bank. The trans-generational trauma is first experienced in Poland during the pogroms, then in Israel during the early days of the founding of the Israeli State, then later during the war in Lebanon, and finally in the present day. The female protagonists— Sonya in the past and Sheila in the present—are the ones that carry the brunt of the family's pain. Sonya Eylon (née Goldenberg) opens the play with a letter she is writing to her Tateh explaining why she is leaving Poland. In it, she explains what it means to be a Jew and a Zionist. She reasons that "the way I see it, being a Jew means one *must* also be a Zionist. It is the same thing" (Tirosh-Polk 2018, 84; emphasis in original). In her mind, the Mashiach has arrived in the form of Theodor Herzl, the father of contemporary Zionism. Sonya leaves Poland for the land of Israel, leaving behind her brothers Morris and Shemel (who is crippled). She arrives in Israel and begins working at a kibbutz where "everything is shared," even her husband Menachem. She says the Arabs make them feel unwelcomed, and the British make their lives miserable. Back in Poland, Morris and Shemel are in the Warsaw Ghetto, and the Nazi purge is underway. Morris tries to convince his crippled brother that it is better that he, not the Nazis, kill him. He gives him a poison pill and tells him to swallow it. When Morris comes to Israel he is changed, unable to find his way in the new land, and unable to relate to the new Israelis he meets. Sonya must contend with his news that none of their family survived the Holocaust. Morris, unable to find his place in the new Jewish state, leaves Israel permanently for Argentina.

Sheila, Sonya's daughter, an ex-teacher turned painter, is racked with anxiety. Her daughter Dory and son Boaz are both serving their compulsory military duty in the Israeli Defense Forces. Her husband, Avi, is a psychologist but all his training cannot help his wife who obsessively carries their son Asaf's ashes in a box. Asaf was killed in the Israeli-Lebanese war, and Boaz is accused of murdering a Palestinian villager. Dory hates the occupation and her brother's part in it, but Boaz contends he rightfully killed the Palestinian man. After a trial, Boaz is acquitted of the murder. Dory has lost patience with the Israeli State's reasoning for the occupation and for the wars it has waged, especially with using the Holocaust as a justification.

> DORY: All I'm saying is that if I hear one more person bring up the Holocaust as an excuse I'll explode, that's all!
> BOAZ: It's not an excuse. It happened.
> DORY: Exactly, happened, past tense, it's over. Did you hear about Burg's book *The Holocaust is Over; We Must Rise From Its Ashes*?
> BOAZ: Well, you know, some people say that a trauma like that would take decades—
> DORY: It's been decades, it's fucking time they put it/
> AVI: centuries to heal.
> DORY: Sorry, I don't have centuries. I want to live my life. (ibid., 21)

After his acquittal, Boaz decides to visit the settlements in the West Bank where he befriends another Israeli Defense Forces (IDF) ex-soldier named Yoram, a Russian-Moroccan-Jew who served in the same unit. Yoram has no sympathy for the Palestinians. He tells Boaz, "I would kill one every day if they let us. I have no problem just (*he motions*) taking one out" (ibid., 32). Boaz decides to leave the army and live with his friend Yoram in the settlements. Yoram says the settlements are home, far from Tel Aviv and "all the sinners." We find later that the band we have seen throughout the play called *The Zionists* is one that includes Yoram and Boaz wearing yarmulkes and carrying guns. They scream "I'm HERE" over and over during their rock songs.

Sheila, meanwhile, presents a lecture about flowers found in the area, to the Bereaved Families Circle which is a group of Palestinian and Israeli, Jewish and Arab bereaved mothers, fathers, sisters, brothers, children, and grandchildren. She speaks about her loss of Asaf, her grief and inability to paint, and her gradual healing which allows her to pick up her brush and paint again. She tells them, "It took me a long time to understand that we are all bereaved. I realized that if I could find the courage to join this Circle, maybe together we could transcend something, the pain, the perpetual pain" (ibid., 83). Dory leaves Israel to live in New York City with her husband Dan. In her final speech, she explains how she envisions her "New Altneuland":

> DORY: Maybe there will be bridges instead of walls
> Maybe we'll learn to forgive
> Maybe there will be no more fighting
> Maybe we'll learn to share.
> Maybe there will be— (ibid., 270)

Her writing is interrupted by the cry of her baby at the end of the play.

Tirosh-Polk's play attempts to bridge the divide between the Holocaust, the establishment of the State of Israel, and the tragedies of the occupation. By rooting the play in the condition of Jews being murdered by the Nazis in Poland, she provides the psychological motivation for the Zionist claim to Palestine, but she also contrasts the Zionist ideal of "A land without people for a people without a land," with the crushing weight of the realities of the creation of a state at the cost of lives from all parts of the region. Sonya represents the Aliyah, or immigration of the Jews to Israel, while Sheila is meant to be the Sabra, or the Jew born in Israel. The contrast between them is stark; Sonya believes that there is little time for grief and tears when one is fighting to establish a state in a place where everyone is hostile. Sonya is devastated by her son's loss in Lebanon, her other son's actions in the West Bank, and her daughter's lack of faith in the Zionist project altogether. The three generations of women contend with their own sense of grief and loss, and the Zionist ideal means different things to each of them. What is clear is that they have all suffered and that the future that Boaz and Yoram believe in—the settlement of the West Bank—is the new Zionist ideal.

The titular Zionists of the play are now the militant, metal-rock loving, gun-toting soldiers who believe that the settlement of Judea and Samaria is their new birthright no matter the cost. For Sheila and Dory, however, the cost of losing family is too high a price to pay for Sonya's vision of a homeland.

Emma Goldman-Sherman's play *Abraham's Daughters* is set in Jerusalem, Tel Aviv, and Nablus in 1993. The play revolves around Abraham Abramowitz, a seventy-year-old Jewish American man from Queens who fought for the United States in the Second World War, then for the Haganah during the 1948 war. His forty-year-old daughter Maxine and her eighteen-year-old daughter Racie all live in Long Island, New York. The other characters are Huda, a 44-year-old Palestinian Muslim woman, and her 19-year-old daughter Amel. The play opens during the first Palestinian intifada with a horrific scene of Abraham bleeding and dying on the ground surrounded by Maxine, Racie, Huda, and Amel. His bloody kufiyah is handled with care as the characters reveal their histories.

The story flashes back to earlier that summer when Abraham, Maxine, and Racie are burying Abraham's wife Sarah, while Huda is simultaneously burying her mother, Haajar, with her daughter Amal by her side. Their normal Tel Aviv day is interrupted by Huda, who arrives at their door with a request to meet with Abraham. Huda tells Maxine that she is Abraham's illegitimate daughter when he was younger and loved her mother Haajar. Maxine is completely opposed to Abraham meeting Huda. Huda's family were displaced from their home in Jerusalem and eventually ended up in a refugee camp in Nablus. Huda tells Maxine that it was not strange to grow up without a father, but rather to grow up without a country. When Racie is taken aback by the militaristic feel she gets walking in the streets of Tel Aviv, Maxine tells her that everyone must defend themselves because they are surrounded by Arabs. Racie does not want to live in a world filled with guns and does not feel safer in Israel because of them. Abraham starts the play with fierce pride for Israel because he first arrived in 1946 and fought in the 1948 Arab-Israeli War. Abraham believes that, despite spending his entire life in America, he fought for Israel and it is his land which he won. For her part, Racie is more interested in the freedom in Israel and for the ability to live her life openly as an outed lesbian.

Abraham admits to Maxine and Racie he did once have a love affair with a Palestinian woman named Haajar Barakat, and that it was possible that Huda is his daughter. Abraham, who keeps referring to himself as "Father of Nations," is very welcoming when Huda arrives, leaving Maxine to deal with her anger and fear about the woman who claims to be her stepsister. Huda recounts the sorrowful story of when her family was forced from their home in Jerusalem only to find themselves in a refugee camp in Beirut, then to Damascus, Amman, and finally to another refugee camp in Nablus where every day is worse than the day before. Amel, who like Racie, is a peace maker; she believes Israelis and Palestinians must recognize and live in peace with one another. They eat dinner together and Huda invites Abraham, Maxine, and Racy to her home in Nablus the following day.

Arriving in Nablus, Maxine is shaken by the experience of having to travel through an Israeli checkpoint. They arrive during "Closure" or the Palestinian protests that shuts down their towns in opposition to the Israeli occupation. When Huda tells Abraham of her five sons, he is initially excited to meet his grandchildren; however, he learns that all five have been killed by Israeli forces at different times in their young lives. Racie and Amel form a fast friendship while Abraham and Maxine learn more about Amel's difficult life in the refugee camp. Abraham wishes for peace, and Huda feels reborn now that she has found her father. Dancing with her father, Huda feels a great release, but it is short lived. When Israeli soldiers fight with Palestinian children in the camp, Abraham tries to get between them and stop the violence. He is shot dead. The women gather around him, comforting him in his final moments. *Abraham's Daughters* retells the biblical story of Abraham and his two wives Hagar and Sarah, set in a contemporary Israeli and Palestinian setting. It is only in later age, when Abraham returns to Israel and discovers he is the father of a Palestinian woman living under occupation, that he understands the true nature of the occupation and how it has severely curtailed the lives of Palestinians living in refugee camps. All the characters in *Abraham's Daughters* are protagonists, but they are victims of a history that left the Israeli people victorious occupiers, and Palestinian people as the occupied living on their own land.

The play *Food and Fadwa* by Lameece Issaq and Jacob Kader is also set in Palestine during the occupation. The pall of occupation weighs heavily on the characters, who reside in the Israeli-occupied West Bank. The two "sites" the play inhabits—Bethlehem and New York City—represent the ancestral, and the adopted, homeland of the characters. Within the dynamic of the play, occupation in Palestine equals stagnation and death, while exile in New York offers the promise of fame, fortune, and escape.

As with other Middle Eastern American plays, food plays a central role in Issaq and Kader's drama. Along with the Arabic language, the foods prepared by Arabs are another hallmark of what defines Arab culture. Issaq and Kader center their protagonist's life on her love of cooking, eating, and serving food. Fadwa's only escape is her imaginary cooking program, in which she makes a range of Arabic dishes from Baba Ghanoush to Tabbouli. Her loving descriptions of the foods, and her brief explanations about how to prepare them, bring levity to a story that, despite its comedic moments, has all the weight of a classic drama. For Fadwa, food is everything: "No food, no respect. Bad food, bad reputation. You will be the laughingstock of Bethlehem. It is vicious" (Issaq and Kader 2014, 143). Food also has negative powers as well. For Fadwa, the food she prepares takes on the mood she finds herself feeling. All of this makes her relationship with her cousin Hayat more complicated since she not only stole her lover Youssif away from her but has also perverted traditional Arabic recipes in order to create "fusion" cuisine. Hayat has made a fortune with her New York restaurant, her cuisine, and her cookbooks. For Fadwa, Hayat's perversion of traditional Arab dishes is offensive—and her taking Youssif away from her is repugnant. Like Palestine and New York, Fadwa and Hayat are opposites of one another—the old world and the new world, the rural and the cosmopolitan, the traditional and the contemporary—and there is little common ground between them. It is not only food that separates them but also the fundamental question of which life is best for the ailing Baba. For Fadwa, uprooting Baba and taking him to New York is like uprooting an ancient olive tree from the earth.

The dichotomy of rootedness versus exile is a major theme of the play. For many Middle Easterners, leaving and starting a new life overseas was the only option worth considering. However, for those Middle Easterners who stayed behind, there is great pride in remaining in the face of the difficulties of life in countries scarred by perpetual wars and occupations. For, if food is the cultural backdrop for the play, occupation becomes the political one. The checkpoints, summary searches, and seizures, as well as the "separation wall," all create a sense of imprisonment for the characters. In the play, the characters mock the separation wall with a humor that is part cynicism, part absurdism, and mostly anger. The wall, which is three times longer and 14 feet higher than the Berlin Wall, is called a "separation fence" by Israel and an "apartheid wall" by some Palestinians. Like the occupation itself, the wall becomes both a source of division and frustration between Palestinians and Israelis. The situation turns even darker when the characters are confronted with a curfew that traps them in untenable conditions and leads to Baba's disappearance.

Perhaps the greatest indignity that Fadwa and her family must endure is the loss of their precious olive groves. Olives are considered one of the most important symbols of Palestinian culture, and the decimation of many olive groves during the Israeli-Palestinian conflict has been a great issue of contention, especially with Israeli settlers living on the West Bank. The olive tree is a metaphor in the play for both the Faranesh family and the Palestinian people. Baba tells the story of Adam and Eve's expulsion from the Garden of Eden, and how the Archangel Gabriel gifted Adam with an olive tree, instructing him to plant and harvest it as a panacea for all afflictions. Baba, whose actual name is Zein, spent his life as an olive farmer, creating olive oil. For Baba, the olive tree is blessed. He tells Fadwa, "To appreciate God's great bounty, simply look, Fadwa, at the blessed olive tree. Its very branches a symbol for peace, its fruit a holy gift" (ibid., 182). During the curfew, the characters turn to olive oil for survival, since they have no more water available to them. Baba's entire existence is tied to the olive groves; when they are destroyed, so is he. Baba's death beneath an olive tree is a fitting end to his life—he was born beneath an olive tree and he died beneath one as well. Everything changes by play's end—Baba has died, Emir and Dalal leave with Youssif and Hayat to New York City to start a new restaurant together, and Fadwa remains in Palestine with her old aunt Samia. The olive saplings that are left for Fadwa are a promise for a new future. Fadwa, like many Palestinians who refuse to leave no matter how difficult life becomes, embodies the Arabic ideal of sumūd, a state of perseverance and hanging on no matter how difficult the situation becomes.

Food and Fadwa is yet another attempt by Palestinian Americans to remember a fragmented, occupied, and disappearing Palestine. The play highlights the horrors of the occupation, how it damages Palestinian lives, and how the very hallmarks of Palestine such as the olive trees are being uprooted and destroyed. The play also dramatizes the fracture between Palestinians living in Palestine and Palestinians who immigrated to the United States. The rift between Fadwa and Hayat is one born of diaspora— the betrayal one commits by leaving home and not staying to fight for the future of the land. This is an attempt to bridge the gap between the world that was left behind by past generations, and the guilt felt by those born in diaspora who feel a connection with the land but cannot do anything tangible to reclaim their lost heritage. Plays like *Food and Fadwa* are valuable reminders of the painfully difficult negotiations that are inherent to the Palestinian diaspora who are gradually witnessing the loss of their potential state while the world looks on with apathy.

Plays and Musicals About the Troubled Homeland: *Pera Palas*, *The Band's Visit*, and *We Live in Cairo*

Turkish American playwright Sinan Ünel's time-shifting drama *Pera Palas* is divided into three overlapping time frames: 1918–24, 1952–3, and 1994. Ünel has written many plays that examine Turkish history including *The Cry of the Reed* and *Chatal*, but *Pera Palas* is, in his words, "a love letter to Istanbul" (Fletcher 2011). This sprawling, multigenerational play examines Turkey in three of its most volatile periods: the decline of the Ottoman Empire leading to the rise of Ataturk, the year 1952 which marked the time that Turkey abandoned Ataturk's neutralist policies and joined NATO, and 1994 and the rise of political Islam. The characters in each period are linked in interesting and necessary ways, and the view of Turkey by outsiders (the English and the Americans in this case) provides a fascinating deconstruction of Orientalist views in this period. The play has twenty-five characters played by ten different actors. The setting is Istanbul's Pera Palace Hotel, which was founded in 1892 servicing clients on the famed Orient Express. It stood next to the Grand Rue, a main street with embassies, restaurants, and clubs. Over time the hotel was a hub for writers, diplomats, businessmen, émigrés, and other prominent figures in Istanbul.

> The Pera Palace was meant to be the last whisper of the Occident on the way to the Orient, the grandest Western-style hotel in the seat of the world's greatest Islamic empire. Like Istanbul itself, the hotel was Europeans' first major port of call when they went east into a traveler's fantasy of sultans, harems, and dervishes. (King 2014, 4)

The main character in the first storyline is Evelyn Crawley, a 28-year-old English writer, invited to stay in a harem by a 15-year-old girl named Melek. Melek's father, Ali Riza Efendi, is a member of the ruling elite. Melek is going to be married to a man she has never met, which outrages Evelyn, who believes that the world of the harem and the patriarchal system that would have young girls married off in an arranged manner is an affront to her sensibilities. Another important character is the young female slave/ odalisque, Bedia, who is seen as an older woman in the 1952–3 period, and who is also Orhan's mother. The second story focuses on a teacher named Kathy Miller who is visiting Istanbul with her sister Anne. Anne is married to a small-minded, boorish American named Joe. Kathy falls in love with Orhan Bayraktar, a dashing and progressive young Turkish man. The last story revolves around a Turkish-born man named Murat Bayraktar, who returns to Istanbul with his lover Brian. Murat has been estranged from his father Orhan, his mother Kathy, and his sister Sema. Murat does not want to contact his family, but Brian arranges a meeting that goes terribly wrong.

Utilizing the Pera Palace as its backdrop, Ünel takes audiences into worlds that are either unseen or have been grossly Orientalized in the past. He also lets us see the world through the eyes of the British and the Americans who arrive with wide-eyed optimism and interest, but inevitably bring their Western values into a society that does not desire them nor respects them. Following the Orientalist trope of the unchanging East, Brian sees Istanbul as a city frozen in time, whereas Murat must remind him of the multiple bridges over the Bosphorus and the ubiquitous presence of American chains like McDonald's. Likewise, Evelyn's outrage over Melek's marriage to a man she has not met is another trope Ünel confronts in the play. Evelyn covets her freedom and independence and cannot accept the notion that a man can have multiple wives; other women like Ayse, Ali Riza Efendi's third wife, cannot see why a woman would not want a husband and children. Evelyn tells Melek she must demand her rights instead of remaining a prisoner in a gilded cage. Likewise, Sir Robert Cave, a man from the English Embassy, views the Turks as primitives who cannot understand Westerners. In another contradiction, Evelyn berates Ali Riza Bey for allowing England to divide his land after the end of the First World War, accusing him of being a puppet for foreign powers. Evelyn steals Melek away from her husband and tyrannical mother-in-law, but Melek realizes that Evelyn's dream, like the dream of the English who desperately attempted to keep Turkey in the mode of European culture and ethics, is not one that she can abide. Ali Riza Efend's wife, Neyme, pleads with her husband to let Melek leave her marriage. He finally concedes. When the sultan abdicates and the British arrive, Ali Riza Efend hangs himself. As Neyime, Melek, and her half-brother Cavid prepare to leave for France, to exile, at England's behest, Bedia begs to be taken with them and is rejected. In France they are lost and Melek dies, Neyime marries a wealthy French diplomat, and an older Cavid returns to Istanbul as a poor, homeless man only to be taken in by his old friend Bedia.

Another theme the play explores is the cross-cultural relationships of Kathy and Orhan, and Murat and Brian. In both instances, the cultural expectations placed on Orhan and Murat are overwhelming, and their relationships with those outside of Turkish culture and the Islamic faith are severely tested by those around them. For Kathy, a young schoolteacher in her twenties in the 1950s, the romance with Orhan was invigorating and new. As time went on, she and Orhan grew further apart, whether it was his cruelty to their maid, his rejection of his son's homosexuality, or his disappointment at being rejected by an American firm for being Turkish. The relationship is permanently damaged when Orhan physically attacks Kathy. Orhan becomes a metaphor for Turkey itself; as the country declines, so Orhan declines and becomes a shadow of himself filled with guilt, regret, and remorse. After the Older Orhan and Murat have a fight that exposes the guilt and recrimination of their past, they are left on the Bosphorus Ferry together, looking out onto the shore. Orhan tells his son, "[O]nce you assimilate the ideas of another country, once you understand the essence, you have no alternative but to be alienated from your own" (Ünel 2015, 111). The play ends with all three storylines concluding not with hope but with a kind of heartbreak and a look toward "the frightening, unfamiliar future" (ibid., 120).

Pera Palas exemplifies a diasporic Middle Eastern American play. Here we have a playwright who was born to Turkish immigrant parents in San Francisco and moved back to Turkey with his parents, only to return to the United States for college. His plays are informed by the immigrant experience to and from America, and his characters are deeply rooted in the history, culture, and complicated politics of the region. A play like *Pera Palas* is epic in scope and character because the country it dramatizes is equally so. So much has transpired in Turkey in the past century that it would be nearly impossible to encapsulate all of it in a play; however, *Pera Palas* attempts just that—to bring the hopes, glories, and fears of the Turkish people to the stage from its zenith as the Ottoman Empire, to its rise as a secular republic, to a nation facing the choice between embracing Europe or becoming embroiled once more by coups and possible dictatorships. The characters in *Pera Palas* are as rich and diverse as Turkey itself; and the play leaves us feeling the deep love for the country and the deep sadness that it faces. An older Orhan says, "We did not become the people we thought we would become." Murat replies, "Your sadness is a gift. Soon you will be free. You'll overcome destiny. You'll make your own future" (ibid., 111). For the people living in Turkey, one wonders which of these characters' predictions will ultimately come true.

The most renowned musical in this entire genre is *The Band's Visit* with music and lyrics by David Yazbek and book by Itamar Moses, based on the film of the same name by Eran Kolirin. The musical swept the 2018 Tony Awards with wins for best musical, best book of a musical, best original score, best leading actor in a musical (Tony Shalhoub), best leading actress in a musical (Katrina Lenk), best featured actor in a musical (Ari'el Stachel), best lighting design of a musical (Tyler Micoleau), best direction of a musical (David Cromer), best orchestrations (Jamshied Sharifi), and best sound design in a musical (Kai Harada).

The musical follows the same plot as the film. A group of Egyptian musicians from the Alexandria Ceremonial Police Orchestra mistakenly arrive in the Israeli town of Bet Hatikvah instead of Petah Tikvah and find themselves stranded there for a night. During that time they meet the eclectic townspeople including Dina, a café owner; Itzik and Iris, two parents of a baby; Papi, an employee at Dina's café; Avrum, Iris's widower father; Zegler, Papi's friend; Anna, Zegler's girlfriend; Julia, Anna's cousin; Sammy, a married man; and a young man known simply as Telephone Guy, who waits for his lover to call him on a pay phone in the town square. In the band, Tewfiq is the main conductor and Simon is a musician and clarinetist who also writes concertos.

The musical combines Arab and Israeli musical styles with an attempt to dramatize the romantic feel of the overall place and to connect the two peoples. Unlike other plays in the Israeli-Arab conflict genre, this play displays a genial relation between the two cultures rooted primarily in the peace that has existed between Israel and Egypt since the 1979 Egypt-Israel Peace Treaty. Although the musical is primarily in English, there are Arabic translations provided by Mouna R'miki and Hebrew translations by playwright Zohar Tirosh-Polk. Music is the language that most connects these characters, and Yazbek and Moses find multiple connections through the musical idiom. For instance, Dina and Tewfiq find a common appreciation of Egyptian musical and film stars Om Kalthoum and Omar Sharif in the song "Omar Sharif." The town of Bet Hatikvah is presented as a boring backwater where nothing happens. The band's arrival brings an air of romance, adventure, and musical collaboration to the otherwise dull setting. The main relationship that the musical focuses upon is Dina, lovelorn café owner spurned by Sammy, and Tewfiq, a man who lost his wife and son in the past. Other relationships include the strained marriage between Itzik and Iris, the youthful and troubled romance between Papi and Julia, and a less turbulent pairing of Zelger and Anna. Ultimately, it is Haled and Dina who connect romantically before the band leaves the next day and plays for the opening of the Arab Culture Center in Petah Tikvah.

The musical presents a vision of a Middle East that is more interconnected than divided. Because the Egyptians and Israelis in the musical are free to travel back and forth and to have artistic collaborations, the small town of Bet Hatikvah becomes a microcosm for how Arabs and Israelis can not only coexist but also find deeper connections with one another that transcend the vitriolic history that often divided these people. The musical tends to romanticize the relations between the characters in its attempt to create this fictional utopia, but in doing so it provides a vision of the Middle East that rests more on the similarities in food, music, and culture. The fact that a musical with Middle Eastern motifs and a Middle Eastern American creative team and cast could not only find a large audience but also win so many important awards demonstrates that the American theatre establishment is becoming open to these voices, and that the elusive peace that may not exist in the Middle East might be found instead on American stages.

Patrick and Daniel Lazour's musical *We Live in Cairo* is set in Egypt in 2010–13 in the years leading up to the downfall of the Hosni Mubarak regime through the Mohammad Morsi presidency, and ending with the Abdel Fattah El-Sisi regime. The musical follows six young Cairenes who are desperate for a better life than the ones that previous generations had endured under the Mubarak regime for three decades. As part of the so-called Arab Spring, the Egyptian revolution that centered in Tahrir Square was considered one of the most vibrant and possible for real, lasting change. The play opens with the actors singing a song that repeats the lyric, "I was one person / Who had an idea / Who made it words / And someone heard / Someone heard" (Lazour 2019, 4). The story focuses on revolutionary years and dramatizes the overwhelming hope the young had in the heady days of Tahrir Square; it ends with how that hope was dashed as a military regime came to power once more.

The characters, of very different social and religious classes, are a tech-savvy, hip, and aspirational group who truly believe that change is possible. Fadwa Bassiouny is a passionate young woman who is often arrested and detained by government forces. Karim Farouk is a young gay street artist and political cartoonist. Layla Hakim is a Muslim photographer who is interested in using her art to further her revolutionary aims. Hany and Amir Salib are brothers from a Christian family. Amir plays guitar and is in an on-again-off-again relationship with Layla. Hassan Ahmed is a young man who is from a Muslim family who are supporters of the Muslim Brotherhood. The young people coalesce around a series of murders of young student activists by police forces, especially that of real-life student Khaled Mohamed Said. Said was brutally killed by authorities, and his murder led to protests that sparked the Egyptian revolution that ultimately brought down the Mubarak regime. The group start a Facebook group titled "We are All Khaled Said," which garners thousands of followers. Tweets are then projected that take the audience through the various events that followed including the protests in Shubra and Aswan, the explosion at the Al-Qiddisayn Church, the torture and deaths of Maryam and Martina Fekry and Sayyid Bilal, and the immolation of Abdu Abdel-Monaim Kamal. The musical utilizes these real-life events to give motivation for the young protagonists and their desire for freedom.

Screaming "HORREYA! HORREYA!" (Freedom! Freedom!) they gather in Tahrir Square and endure multiple attacks and assaults by government forces, yet they emerge victorious. As the months pass, the Supreme Council of the Armed Forces takes over which sets up an election that puts the Muslim Brotherhood in power. Once this occurs, the group begins splitting along ideological lines. Fadwa, Hassan, Layla, Amir, and Hany are all dejected by the Muslim Brotherhood victory. Fadwa is completely against the newly elected government while Hany believes that the first free and fair election results should stand no matter who is elected. For his part Hassan supports Morsi's victory, which alienates him from the group. Karim and Hassan's gradually developing relationship is severely tested, and Hany decides to apply to study abroad in America. The group splinters much as Egyptian society has following the contentious events that ultimately put a military dictator in power. Two years later, Amir is killed in a protest, and Fadwa and Hany are arrested for protesting. Layla is left singing the lyrics "We still have our hands, / We still have our name, / We still have our past, / And time sprawling in front of us. / We're not surviving, / We're living here" (ibid., 138).

We Live in Cairo is an attempt to portray the hopes, aspirations, and struggles of the youth of Egypt trapped in a difficult choice between life under a dictatorial regime and change that threatens to tear their society apart. The rise of El-Sisi's government and the brutal crackdowns on dissent that followed are events that may be distant to many in the United States, but for Middle Eastern Americans it is both personal and real. Like Jonathan Larson's *Rent* before it, a musical like *We Live in Cairo* is a testament to the will of the youth who are not content to remain silent when they see injustice and death all around them. *We Live in Cairo* is a theatrical memorial to those who spoke out, protested, and were ultimately disappointed by the failure of the so-called Arab Spring. Despite that failure, as the final lyrics of the musical sing out, "We remain in a city of the sky, / We remain a river to the sea, / We remain in light, / We remain in light" (ibid., 138). The hopeful song promises a better future for Egypt's youth.

As these plays and musicals demonstrate, Middle Eastern American playwrights, composers, and lyricists recreate homeland on American stages in various ways. For some, they are reflections of the lives they and their families lived overseas, while for others, these plays and musicals are recounting historical tragedies that occurred in the past. There is a deep concern for the plight of displaced persons, of those living in refugee camps, and those suffering under unjust and corrupt regimes. However, there are also plays and musicals that celebrate the similarities in the Middle Eastern culture through music, dance, and theatre itself. All these works are rich explorations into a world that few know or understand outside of the news coverage seen on the internet or cable news. For the playwrights and composers in this genre, life in the Middle East is not abstract—it is a very real part of their everyday existence.

CHAPTER 6
CONFLICT PLAYS

This chapter is labeled "Conflict Plays" because they deal directly with many of the major wars and conflicts that have taken place in the Middle East. The largest body of this work focuses on the Palestinian-Israeli conflict, which has been a part of the region from the late nineteenth century to the current day. In play after play, these conflicts serve as the often-tragic backdrop to the wars that plague this part of the world and, most importantly, how these wars are devastating the lives of those who live there. Other conflict plays deal with issues like civil war, the ongoing refugee crisis, life under dictatorships, and foreign involvement in the Middle East.

The Palestinian-Israeli Conflict: *The River and the Sea*, *Facts*, *Martyr's Street*, and *Wrestling Jerusalem*

As the previous chapters demonstrated, there are tens of plays written about Israel and Palestine by both Arab American and Jewish American playwrights. Like the conflict itself, it takes up much of the time and attention of those who have ties to this holy land. Other Middle Eastern American and Canadian playwrights who are not mentioned elsewhere in this book but have contributed to this genre include Soha Al Jurf (*Pressing Beyond in Between*), Martin Cohen (*Checkpoint*), Peter-Adrian Cohen (*To Pay the Price*), Hanna Eady (*Sahmatah*, cowritten with Ed Mast), Jonathan Garfinkel (*House of Many Tongues*), Emma Goldman-Sherman (*Abraham's Daughters*), Natasha Greenblatt (*Two Birds One Stone*), Nathalie Handal (*Between Our Lips*), Israel Horovitz (*What Strong Fences Make*), Ismail Khalidi (*Tennis in Nablus*), Jamil Khoury (*Precious Stones*), Mike Leigh (*Two Thousand Years*), Stephen Orlov (*Sperm Count*), and Martin Sherman (*Onassis*) to name only a few.

These plays are most often set in Palestine or Israel, though some take place in the diaspora of the United States or Canada. Unlike the plays included in the previous chapters, these plays are pointedly about the conflict itself, as opposed to being family dramas that are set in Israel or Palestine. Almost all these works focus on the human tragedy of the conflict, which is not to say there is not an abundance of humor in them as well. The stories deal with connections between Palestinians and Israelis, how those connections are tested and frayed, and how these most often end with a tragedy or clash that leaves both sides longing for a resolution. In the most optimistic plays, characters vow to create a solution that is mutually beneficial for everyone involved. These plays are mostly an attempt by these playwrights to re-humanize the Arab/Israeli other, despite containing characters who sometimes act out of their worst, rather than their best, instincts and intentions. These conflict plays offer audiences a glimpse into a world as it might be, rather than the world as it is. In play after play there are characters dealing with the vestiges of wars waged by those who have little concern for the civilians caught in the crossfire. However, these are works of deep empathy and understanding, not propagandistic plays that support one side or the other. Of course, they all have a definite political point of view but, overall, they are promoting peace and not a continual war.

There are contentious issues that should be addressed in the production of such plays. In the coedited anthology titled *Inside/Outside: Six Plays from Palestine and the Diaspora*, editors Naomi Wallace and Ismail Khalidi discuss the "uphill battle" Palestinian plays face in order to get produced in American theatre. They contend that Palestinian playwrights are culturally delegitimized and derailed by the Palestinian-Israeli conflict which always privileges the Israeli perspective. They also believe there are various levels of censorship, intimidation, and misinformation that bias an open discussion about the conflict in the media and theatre (Wallace and Khalidi 2015, xi). They dismiss the idea that both sides of the conflict must be presented in anthologies, festivals, and other theatrical events in a "balanced" manner; this means that any issue Palestinian plays present must be answered by an Israeli play and that it deprives these plays the right to be judged on their merits. Palestinian plays are part of "the long struggle of Palestinians and other oppressed and marginalized people who insist that they do not need permission to narrate their own stories, their own history, and their own visions of a future" (ibid., xii). In the edited volume *Six Plays of the Israeli-Palestinian Conflict*, coeditor Jamil Khoury writes, "Many theatres are also reluctant to produce Israeli Jewish playwrights who question and challenge dominant narratives about Israel and its future—and still, some have confused this patriotism for 'disloyalty,' even 'treason.' Not only do such allegations sabotage artistic freedom, they impede the robust dialogue we now so desperately need" (Khoury, Najjar, and Pond 2018, 3). In his edited volume *Modern Jewish Plays*, Jason Sherman writes about how the Canadian theatre is too concerned with losing subscribers, having controversial productions, or reinventing musicals. According to Sherman, plays about the Palestinian-Israeli conflict are rarely, if ever, produced in Canada because they are too controversial and require daring and courageous artists who are not willing to take a chance on plays that might challenge their audiences (Sherman 2006, 363–6).

Danny Bryck's play *The River and the Sea* is a documentary theatre piece that was created after Bryck's own travel to Israel and Palestine in 2012 and 2013, where he interviewed those he met. On his website, he asks the provocative question, "When everyone tells a different story, how do we tell the truth?" (Goldberg 2014). Bryck interviewed many people from a soldier in Tel Aviv to a mother from Gaza, a Holocaust survivor, and a Sudanese refugee. The play was developed through donations and a two-year residency Bryck had at New Repertory Theatre in Watertown, Massachusetts. The play takes place at various locations in Israel and the occupied Palestinian territories in December 2012 through March 2013. In the script Bryck states that most of the text was taken verbatim from his transcribed recordings of interviews and other personal interactions he had with people living there, and some were translated from Hebrew and Arabic. He changed the names of those interviewed and, in a few cases, he composited several people into singular characters. Bryck writes that all the characters should be played by five actors except for the character David, who should be played by the same actor. "Actors should speak and move with energy and momentum, and avoid the trap of portraying these people as if they live in constant pain, self-pity or defeat," his playwright's note concludes (Bryck 2016, 2).

The characters include David, a twenty-something Jewish American writer on a birthright trip to Israel; Anat, a twenty-year-old conservative IDF soldier; Nitzan, an Israeli tour guide; Ismail, a Palestinian professor and citizen of Israel; and Mark, a middle-aged conservative Jewish American settler. David begins with a monologue explaining that he is going on his birthright trip and that his mother and father are frightened for him. He tells them he must see the land, Jerusalem, the wall, and what lies between the river and the sea. The play then shifts to interviews with the various people David meets on his journey. David explains that following his birthright trip he extended his visa so he could travel around and meet people living through the conflict. He claims he's an artist and writer who wanted to have a dialogue with people on both sides. The Palestinian professor, Ismail, tells him the situation is extremely complicated and there are scores of different religions and ethnicities that make up what are commonly known as "Israelis" and "Palestinians."

David meets a dizzying array of people from all over the area. The dialogues with the various people reveal the fears, trepidations, and historical injuries that have come to define the Arab-Israel conflict over the past century. Despite David's desire to remain neutral in his understanding of the conflict, he realizes his position as a Jew automatically places him on one side of the issue. When David tells Najla he is trying not to take sides, she responds that when one refuses to take a side, they are already taking a side. Another person David talks to tells him he is still young and naive, and that as a Jew he only has one place to be, which is Israel. The Israelis recount the horrors of the Holocaust, the wars they fought with Arab forces in 1948, the fears they have of Arabs attacking them with suicide bombs, and the lack of democracy among the Arabs and Palestinians. From the Palestinians he interviews there are tragic stories of occupation, curfews, shootings, bombings, lack of food and water, and tales of death at the hands of the IDF. Despite David's desire to interview as many people as possible, he is constantly met with notions that challenge everything he thought he knew about the place. A Palestinian woman, Najla, tells him he is not the first person to attempt to find themselves through the suffering of others in the region, and that he is ultimately there only to make himself feel better. Similarly, Anat, an Israeli, tells David that Palestinians understand only violence, not negotiation. David comes to realize that his desire to remain unbiased and somewhat journalistic in his approach is not accepted by all of those he interviews. David's desperate desire to understand the conflict is stifled by the fact that each story he hears contradicts the one that came before. A Palestinian man named Ismail tells him that if Palestinians get their own state, they may end up behaving just as the Israelis did when they were occupiers. In this character's view, oppression is human nature.

David has three monologues in the play: at the beginning, midway through, and at the end. In the first monologue we hear about the young man who always heard stories about "life," "hope," and Jerusalem; in the second monologue we hear about a dream David has about home and homelessness; and the third is about not knowing what to do with stories and experiences he has heard. David is left in a liminal state between the past he's inherited and the present he is left to contend with.

The play had a staged reading on March 24, 2014, at the New Repertory Theatre, directed by Megan Sandberg-Zakian. Jill Goldberg of *Tikkun Daily* wrote,

> It's not common to have the opportunity to know so many sides of the same story, and to really reckon with the painful contradictions implicit to Israel/Palestine. By being open to the process of unlearning as much as learning, Bryck has created a work that will undoubtedly provide a worthwhile challenge to both our intellect and our hearts, asking us to hear not only the stories we already know, but to pay attention to the ones that make us uncomfortable or disoriented. Surely this work has the capacity to push audience members to make room for empathy, and to allow their definitions of their own identities to evolve and shift in order to begin to accept the multiplicity of identities and stories that share the very small piece of land that is Israel/Palestine. (Goldberg 2014)

The River and the Sea provides important narratives about the conflict because it employs a polyvocal approach that allows all sides to have a voice. Unlike traditional plays that are the invention of a single playwright, Bryck decides on a documentary theatre format that creates a space for actual voices to be heard. In doing so Bryck grows as an artist and allows the audience to experience such growth for themselves. As reviews of this reading attest, this style of dramaturgy is a forum for empathy building in a conflict that requires such empathy now more than ever.

Arthur Milner's play *Facts* is a three-character play that takes place in an Israeli Army facility in the West Bank. Though the play is written in English, the playwright states that the characters would be speaking in Arabic or Hebrew. Based on the 1992 killing of Doctor Albert Glock, an American archaeologist from Birzeit University, the play is the interrogation of a young West Bank settler named Danny Rakoff by two characters: Khalid Yassin, a police inspector with the Palestinian Authority, and Yossi HaCohen, an Israeli police detective. Khalid arrives late to the interrogation after being stopped at a checkpoint. Khalid explains how he, a Palestinian official, must drive from checkpoint to checkpoint being searched by Israeli soldiers. Khalid tells Yossi he refuses to accept checkpoints as normal, and Yossi replies that he should hold on to his resentment and let it eat away at him. Yossi, who is fifteen years older than Khalid, seems to think that the anger makes for better police work. They also disagree on the need for "facts" in investigations:

> YOSSI: Europeans are a modern people. They appreciate facts, but they know their limitations. Americans worship facts, like peasants. They idolize facts. We're supposed to be Judeo-Christian but Americans are peasants. Well, half are peasants, who don't accept facts. And then there are the artists who transcend facts. (Milner 2012, 42)

This tenet will be severely tested in the play as they encounter the young Israeli settler accused of murdering an American archaeologist named Gordon Philips. Philips was a fundamentalist Christian who came to the Holy Land to walk in the footsteps of Jesus, but later had a conversion to science. Philips, however, concluded that Israelites were never in Egypt, and never ruled the Kingdom of Israel. Khalid believes that Danny, a fundamentalist Zionist settler, may have killed Philips because of this conclusion. Yossi asks Khalid to be "the good cop" because he hates the settlers and wants to punish Danny.

When interrogated by Khalid, Danny refuses to speak Arabic and rejects Khalid's authority as a police officer, telling Khalid that Arabs don't tell Jews what to do in Israel. Yossi demands that Danny treat Khalid with respect, even threatening him with physical violence. Danny flaunts the fact that he has a weapon, and the men make him surrender it. Danny believes archaeologists desecrate sacred soil with their work. While Khalid and Yossi try to get Danny to confess by telling him that the entire history of the Kingdom of Israel has no factual basis in history, Danny refuses Yossi's claim to Judaism.

> YOSSI: (furious) You know what, Danny? You don't get to decide who is a Jew. I'm a Jew. I am a descendant of Jews. My mother was Jewish and her mother before her and her mother before her. And I'm circumcised. So even in your archaic, tribal bullshit rules, I get to be a Jew. (ibid., 91)

For Danny, there is no debate; God granted the Jews the land of Israel and God commanded them to keep it. He believes Israelis are their own worst enemy because they want to trade land for peace. Danny knows, however, that time and Israeli law are on his side; for every ten settlements established and one evacuated, nine remain intact. The men realize they cannot implicate Danny in the murder, so they let him go. Khalid tells Yossi members of his family were killed by the zealotry of Dr. Baruch Goldstein, who in 1994, entered the Cave of the Patriarchs and massacred 29 Palestinian Muslim worshippers, wounding 125 others. Khalid tells Yossi there is no real justice when a Palestinian can be arrested by the Israelis, held in jail for years without trial, and then have their home destroyed by bulldozers. Danny returns for his gun and tells Yossi that he ultimately won and spits on Yossi. Yossi lifts the gun and fires it toward Danny, just missing him. Danny takes the gun and leaves.

Milner's *Facts* pairs a Palestinian and Israeli in a fight for justice in a place where justice is questionable. The settler movement that Milner criticizes in plays like *Facts* dramatizes the notion that many Israelis cannot abide some settlers' zealotry and zeal for taking the entire West Bank and driving Palestinians out of their ancestral homes. Danny is a symbol of those who have decided that Zionism lost its way and must be reclaimed by any means possible, even if that entails the death of Palestinians living on the land. Yossi, who wishes to find a way toward peace, is seen as a weak and cowardly Jew who has sold Israel out. Khalid is seen as an interloper on the land who has no authority and no place there in the future. Danny, for all of his vitriol and hatred, is winning the war through building settlements, encouraging an armed struggle against the Palestinians, and ultimately deciding that he and his fellow settlers will take the land since the government does not have the will to do so. A play like *Facts* awakens audiences to the harsh reality on the ground in the West Bank—a place where compromise becomes less possible, and the land is forever contested.

Misha Shulman's *Martyrs Street* continues Shulman's exploration of the Israeli-Palestinian conflict found in his other plays *The Fist*, *Desert Sunrise*, and *Apricots*. *Martyrs* Street is centered on two disparate families—one Israeli and one Palestinian—and set in Hebron on Martyrs Street/al-Shuhada Street. The set consists of the Palestinian home of Noor and her daughter Aisha, and the other half of the stage is the home of Dvorah and Eilyahu. Both homes are in danger. Noor's home is set to be demolished by the Israeli government because her son, Nimer, is a Hamas operative who has been accused of violence against Israelis. Dvorah's home is also to be demolished by the Israeli government because it is an illegal settlement. Therefore, both families face the destruction of their homes, but for vastly different reasons.

The play opens with a meeting between Nimer and Tsadok, Dvorah's cousin and the leader of a messianic Jewish settler group called "The Hand of God." They conspire to help one another achieve their goals, despite being on the complete opposite ends of the political spectrum and vowed enemies of one another. Tsadok needs a bomb to set off in Jerusalem in order to begin the apocalypse he believes will return the Messiah; Nimer wants the bombing to occur in order to destroy a number of people he considers enemies, and to get money from Tsadok for his mother to purchase another home. In order to ensure that Tsadok keeps his end of the deal, Nimer keeps his grandfather's tzitzit and yarmulke as collateral. At the same time, Noor's friend Salim informs her of the government's plan to demolish her home which she and her dead husband spent their life savings building. Salim urges her to move to Jerusalem with his assistance, but Noor, a university sociology professor, does not want to leave Hebron. Noor's daughter, Aisha, disapproves of Noor even being alone with Salim because her brother Nimer says it is against Islam for a single woman to be alone with another man.

Shulman creates a dramatic narrative about two extremists—Nimer and Tsadok—to dramatize the tensions in a city like Hebron that is continually marred by violence. The loss of homes for both the Palestinian residents and the Israeli settlers creates the circumstances that then propel the characters in the play to act out malevolently. The civilians like Noor and Aisha are trapped by the machinations of a war that has little regard for their civilian lives. Aisha's school teaches her about Palestinian martyrs who have committed atrocities which Noor disapproves of. Aisha retorts that there is no way to coexist with settlers who attack and debase Palestinians on a daily basis. Another character, Mashiach, is a young man whose family was forcefully ejected from the Israeli settlements in Gaza. He comes to Eliyahu, Dvorah, and Tsadok for community and they prey upon him, convincing him to become the suicide bomber who will attack Jerusalem. When Nimer tries to persuade his mother to take the money he received in exchange for building a suicide vest for Tsadok, she refuses it as blood money and chastises Nimer for his radical ideas.

Dvorah and Noor begin a strange relationship as they pass one another's homes on Martyr's Street. They are entirely suspicious of each other, yet they see their shared humanity, especially as women and mothers. In a simultaneous scene, we see Nimer confront Noor and Salim, and Dvorah and Tsadok confront Eliyahu. Salim and Eliyahu desperately try to convince the younger men in their lives not to commit acts of violence in the name of their respective ideologies, but they are both unwilling to listen. Dvorah and Tsadok give Mashiach their blessing to conduct the bombing, and Aisha decides to leave her mother to live with Nimer. In a final epilogue,

Dvorah convinces Noor not to go to Jerusalem that night and to tell Salim not to meet her at the square where the bombing is to occur. An explosion is heard in the distance.

Shulman's play attempts to humanize even the most radical among the combatants in the Israeli-Palestinian conflict by portraying those the Israelis believe are the extremists—Hamas—and those the Palestinians view as the extremists—the Israeli settlers. In doing so, and by setting the play in the most contentious city, Hebron, and on the most contentious street, Martyr's Street, the play dramatizes the lives of those who are quite literally living at the center of the conflict. Shulman was born and raised in Jerusalem and spent his professional life working in North America. The play is based on Shulman's own visit to Hebron, and therefore is both an insider and outsider's view of the way Palestinians and Israelis are sometimes working to destroy one another. Shulman says,

> I have [also] used my plays as platforms for creating dialogue, and deepening the understanding of what is going on in that part of the world. For Theater for the New City's production of *Martyr's Street* last year we brought in experts from around the U.S. and Israel/ Palestine for a series of talkbacks. That type of activity, as well as intention around a production, give it what I'd call an overtly political ring. (Bagatourian and Shulman 2016)

Therefore, like other plays in this genre, despite dramatizing extreme views and dark subject matter, the play's ultimate function according to the playwright is about dialogue and understanding. By setting the play in the epicenter of the West Bank, Shulman places his audience in the uncomfortable position of confronting uneasy truths about the conflict.

Aaron Davidman's solo performance titled *Wrestling Jerusalem* is an exploration of a Jewish man's connection to his religion and Israel. Like Danny Bryck's *The River and the Sea*, and British playwright David Hare's *Via Dolorosa*, Davidman makes a journey to Israel and Palestine in order to understand why the situation is so intractable. However, Davidman comes to this experience asking where he, as a Jew, fits within it. By embodying seventeen different characters—Arab and Jewish—he takes audiences on both a personal and theatrical journey into his struggle with understanding this conflict through the embodied experiences of the Israelis and Palestinians he meets. In the synopsis for the play it states, "Davidman finds both entrenched isolation and shared humanity in the shifting moral compasses and competing narratives of all his characters" (wrestlingjerusalem.com). Originally produced as a minimalist one-person show for theatre directed by Michael John Garcés, the play was later directed by Dylan Kussman for film.

Davidman performs his script with accurate accents, singing, and dancing interspersed throughout the performance. The play opens with a litany of "ifs" regarding the political events that have shaped the conflict for the past century. Davidman lists the endless wars, peace accords, murders, assassinations, peace processes, and political maneuvers that have occurred only to find himself in a crescendo that results in his falling into a heap onto the floor. His main metaphor is that of the Kabbalistic story of creation, the encapsulation of good into vessels that could not hold, the disbursement of that good all over the world, and the necessary quest to gather all the sparks of goodness once again. He then discusses his childhood in Yiddish Brooklyn and his attendance of Camp Kinderland where he was taught the values of freedom, equality, and justice for all. He first traveled to Israel as a young man to learn the Torah, but in doing so he realized the political situation in the country and questioned why Israel was so deeply troubled. He travels through checkpoints to the West Bank, visits Israeli Army officials, speaks to pro-peace activists, psychologists, coffee shop owners, West Bank settlers, Arab farmers, rabbis, traumatized civilians escaping to the Dead Sea, and he prays at the Western Wall. The stories he relays are filled with grief, trauma, war, occupation, and death. This is not to say there are not humorous moments but, overall, the feeling is one of immense melancholy over people fighting and dying over the land. Davidman's performance is a tour de force both as a masterwork of a trained actor and as a work of documentary theatre chronicling the Israeli-Palestinian conflict. Like others before him, he leaves with more questions than answers.

Plays of the Armenian Genocide: *March!* and *Night Over Erzinga*

Plays and films about the Armenian Genocide are chronicles of the 1915–16 events that caused the death of 1.5 million Armenians out of an estimated population of 2.5 million. The issue is contested by Turkey; the Turkish government and many intellectuals there refute that genocide ever occurred. Films like Garin Hovannisian and Alec Mouhibian's *1915*, Atom Egoyan's *Ararat*, and Terry George's *The Promise* dramatize the events, yet several important dramas written for the stage have continued to tell the story that remains cataclysmic to the Armenian community to this day. Some could argue that these plays are European American and not Middle Eastern American dramas. However, many Armenian plays are staged at prominent Middle Eastern American theatre companies and Armenians were, and still are, living in countries that are technically in the Middle East. Therefore, these plays have been widely accepted as Middle Eastern American dramas. Bianca Bagatourian and Adriana Sevahn Nichols both consider their works as those categorizable in this genre as well.

Bianca Bagatourian's play *March!* is based on 800 hours of Armenian Genocide oral history. There are only four named characters in the play: Man (labeled as "persistent"), Alin (an orphan), Lusine (labeled as "chatty"), and Anahid, who is silent. Because the play does not follow a traditional linear play structure, the dialogues are quick exchanges made up of actual survivor testimonies. In each testament, we hear gripping and horrifying stories of genocide: a boy bayoneted and dying after eight hours of torture, men dismembered, women buried alive, and entire families executed. The operative word in the play is "memory" and the characters state that, with the passing of time, these memories will fade away. The man says, "But forgetting will turn us into a blank page. We will become invisible. We will disappear from all history. And that's the way it was planned" (Bagatourian 2010). Bagatourian states that she doesn't only write Armenian stories, but rather stories that focus on human rights and social justice: "You know, it's interesting, as a writer of Armenian heritage, it is almost impossible to ignore the Armenian genocide in my work. And the fact that Turkey is still denying that it happened, pushes it to the front of the mind." Regarding her play *March!* she says that it "looks at genocide through the prism of memory and how it can live on to destroy generation after generation" (Bagatourian and Shulman 2016).

Armenian American playwright Adriana Sevahn Nichols's play *Night Over Erzinga* follows four generations of Armenians who were victims of the Armenian Genocide and its horrific aftermath. The expansive drama spans the lives of the Armenians living in Armenia before the genocide, their children who were sent to America for safety, and their grandchildren's children who struggled with the trauma they witnessed their parents enduring. The play was a commission by the Lark/Golden Thread Productions/Silk Road Rising Middle East America Playwrights Fellowship, but gradually it became a way for the playwright to delve deeper into her own personal history, and the history of her people who were decimated by the events of the Armenian Genocide.

The play flashes back and forth from life in Armenia in the 1910s to life in America in the 1960s. The first act deals primarily with Alice, an Armenian woman, and Ardavazt, her Armenian husband, dealing with their families' haunted past with the Armenian Genocide. Their daughter, Ava, cannot understand why her mother is so disturbed and why she must be committed to a mental hospital where she is regularly given electroshock therapy. Although Ardavazt was sent to America before the horrors of the genocide, Alice endured horrific trauma during the genocide before being sent to America to marry Ardavazt. The play flashes back to Alice as a young girl in 1914 living a bucolic life with her parents in the Armenian village of Erzinga. This changes when Turkish soldiers arrive and demand that all Armenian boys, including Aram, Ardavazt's father, must join the military. Aram sends Ardavazt to live with his family in America to keep him safe from the oncoming violence, giving him a pocket watch to remember him by. Alice, on the other hand, is left to suffer the carnage of her family's slaughter in her village. She is rescued by a Turkish couple who take pity on her and ensure she can leave for America. In a flash forward, Ava, their daughter, becomes the singer that Alice only dreamed of being. She meets and marries Bienvenido Raymundo (Benny), a Dominican man, and they have a daughter named Estrella. Ava and Benny's marriage ends with Benny's infidelity, and Ava and her father Ardavazt finally reconciling after years of conflict. In ghostly hauntings, Ava realizes the horrors her mother endured, watching her little sister being raped and her entire family slaughtered around her, and that her father's family was eradicated in their village of Erzinga. Ava realizes that the mother she thought was so cold and distant and the father who was so strict and cruel were once young people who suffered unspeakable horrors. Her epiphany is discovering that they both deserve immense empathy and forgiveness (Figure 5).

Sevahn Nichols, who identifies as Armenian, Dominican, and Basque, tells of her upbringing by a single mother, and being a descendant of Armenian Genocide survivors: "As the granddaughter of Armenian genocide survivors, I was being asked to write something on behalf of healing, repair, restoration—and reminded that I carried a responsibility as an artist to give something on behalf of all who perished and on behalf of all who survived" (Sevahn Nichols 2015). In 2015 she traveled to Yerevan, Armenia, for a performance of *Night Over Erzinga* at the Yerevan State Youth Theater for the commemoration of the one-hundred-year anniversary of the genocide. During that visit, she toured the ancestral villages of Armenians in Turkey

Figure 5 *Night Over Erzinga* by Adriana Sevahn Nichols, Silk Road Rising, 2012. From left: Nicholas Gamboa (Bienvenido), Rom Barkhordar (Older Ardavazt), Sandra Delgado (Ava), Carolyn Hoerdemann (Ardavazt's mother), and Levi Holloway (Younger Ardavazt). Directed by Lisa Portes. Photograph by Michael Brosilow.

and paid tribute at the Armenian Genocide Memorial. After watching the production, which was translated into Armenian, she concluded, "I am no longer the playwright. I am a granddaughter watching my family story. I am home" (ibid.). Sharing the many upheavals and dislocations of Armenian history during the modern age, the theatre continues to play an important cultural role both in the communities of the diaspora and in the homeland. Armenian American writers in the diaspora gained renewed interest in their culture and ethnicity in the 1960s along with other hyphenated groups. The noted Armenian American theatre scholar Nishan Parlakian writes,

> For Armenians, this new ethnic elan allowed them to focus their attention on matters that were often on their minds and often repressed as they made their way in America. The most serious of these was their concern with the genocide perpetrated against the Armenian race in Turkey and the need for justice in an international context. Surely the Armenian sentiment was no less serious than that of African Americans who in their own way had suffered genocide two centuries before. (Parlakian 2004, 16)

Like the Holocaust plays written by Jewish American playwrights, the plays *March!* and *Night Over Erzinga* are attempts by Armenian Americans to reconstitute a history that has been erased or denied even in the United States. In addition to being well-written and moving dramas, these plays serve as reminders of an event that remains seminal to the Armenian American experience.

Civil War Plays: *Scorched*, *Game of Patience*, and *Smail*

Wajdi Mouawad's searing drama *Scorched* is the story of two Québecois-Canadians who were born in North America being forced to travel back to the ancestral homeland to uncover their mysterious roots following their Lebanese mother's death. Her cryptic final will states that one of the siblings, Janine, must find her father, and the other sibling, Simon, must find his brother if they wish to bury their mother properly. Once they deliver the letters to her attorney Alfonse Lebel, they will receive a third letter, and a stone can finally be placed on her grave.

This is the same filial and psychological terrain Mouawad had explored in a previous play, *Tideline*, where a son named Wilfrid is expected to take his father's corpse back to Lebanon for burial. Mouawad, who was born to a Lebanese Christian family in Lebanon in 1968, witnessed the horrific massacre of Palestinian children on a bus in 1975 which sparked the bloody civil war there. His family emigrated to France after four years of living through the war. He was later an exile in Canada where he enrolled in the École Nationale de Théâtre in Montreal. Mouawad believes that he became a writer because of his war experiences. His plays *Alphonse* (1996), *Tideline* (1999), *Scorched* (2003), *Forests* (2006), *Seuls* (2008), and *Ciels* (2009) are all deep explorations of Mouawad's history, understanding of his past, and grappling with the present. "Theater is a way of filling up our days," he said. "When children are born, they are filled with a kind of goodwill. Then their conviction that the world is enchanted is shattered. Every time I try to glue it back together the result is a play" (Daydé 2013, 39).

Scorched layers generations of women and their painful and complicated journeys from adolescence to adulthood. Nawal, a young girl growing up in a very traditional village, falls in love with, and is impregnated by, a man from another religion for whom she is forbidden to love. After he is killed in the fighting, she is forced by her mother to give the baby away. That baby is taken to an orphanage, and Nawal pines for him in her adulthood. After meeting a woman named Sawda, she decides to find her child. After believing the child is killed, she realizes she can no longer stand by and watch the slaughter taking place all around her. Nawal assassinates a military leader and Sawda sacrifices herself in a suicide bombing. After the assassination, Nawal is imprisoned and put under the torture of an infamous soldier who repeatedly rapes her. She gives birth to twins in prison, but they are taken by an old man to be dumped in a river. He secretly raises the children himself, and when Nawal is finally released from prison, the children are given back to her. She immigrates to Canada to raise the children, but she is forever cold and distant. One day she falls silent and later dies. The children are left to travel back to her homeland and take a harrowing journey that leads them to the horrific discovery that their father was the notorious rapist named Nihad Harmanni, and he is also their brother. After they face the monstrosity that is their birthright, they return, give the letters to Nihad (the father and the son) which explains his origins, and bury their mother. The final letter they are given is one that explains her love for them and that there are truths that can only be revealed after they are discovered.

Janine and Simon's return to their ancestral homeland is akin to the journeys many Middle Eastern Americans face when traveling back to their homelands which were ravaged by war. Traveling back entails visiting people and places scarred by generations of trauma inflicted by war, occupation, and dictatorship. This journey "home" is further complicated by the inability to speak the language, to understand the customs, and to make sense of the often-confusing history that comprises their histories. In addition, many of the relatives they meet carry the scars of decades of historical trauma that predate their parents' departure from the homeland. Although Mouawad's plays read like contemporary retellings of Greek tragedies, they are metaphors for the painful disconnection many living in diaspora feel from their parents' lives. Mouawad says, "In all my plays, there is the story of someone who discovers his origins are different than what he thinks, and he tries to get back to those origins" (Morrow 2008). It could be said that many Middle Eastern American plays in this genre are attempting the same feat. *Scorched* is a play about civil war, how it tears at the fabric of society, and how it leaves generational scars that require great healing.

Lebanese Canadian playwright Abla Farhoud's play *Game of Patience* is a diaspora play that deals with Lebanese Canadian immigrants who fled the war in Lebanon yet remain disturbed even in their distance from the conflict. In the preface Farhoud writes, "I offer this play to all who have lost their child, their country, their dreams, their taste of life. I offer these words to all those forgotten and all who are trying to forget . . . to everyone who, every day, every moment, confronts the silence of death" (Farhoud 1994, 41). The protagonist, a forty-year-old novelist and playwright named Monique/Kaokab, immigrated to North America when she was nine years old. Her cousin, Mariam, also forty, has moved to Canada after suffering the loss of her daughter, Samira, during the Lebanese Civil War. Mariam's fifteen-year-old daughter, Samira, appears as a ghost who haunts the play. Monique/Kaokab is struggling to write while Mariam has given up the will to live, grappling with the notion that her daughter's death is somehow her fault. Mariam is lost—she is an immigrant in a new country where she does not speak the language, she is separated from her husband, she has small children to care for, and she cannot forget the horrors of her past. Monique/ Kaokab has succeeded as a writer in her new homeland, but she believes her writing lacks authenticity.

> MONIQUE/KAOKAB: I've written the surface of things. To please, to rock people to sleep. I've written to put myself to sleep, to forget. I have written pushing my memory back inside, deep in my stomach. I borrowed a language and I lent my soul. I have lived between the heartbreak of remembering and the heartbreak of forgetting. (Farhoud and MacDougall 1994, 58)

Monique/Kaokab tried to return to her homeland of Lebanon but found she had forgotten much of her native language, the customs, and the names of those left behind. Mariam is upset with Monique/Kaokab for lamenting her comfortable life in diaspora while her fellow Lebanese are dying in a civil war. However, even living in the diaspora, Monique/Kaokab is tortured with thoughts of her fellow Lebanese suffering in war. When she cannot write, she plays solitaire to pass the time. "In solitaire," she says, "you have what is hidden and what is given, what you have to grasp immediately and what takes more patience" (ibid., 70). Mariam urges Monique/Kaokab to tell Samira's story so her memory can live on. After much indecision, she decides to attempt to tell the girl's story. "Pain is everywhere," she writes in the play, "but so is life, it's irrepressible, here, there, everywhere . . . despite the odds" (ibid., 81).

Abla Farhoud's play is a deep autobiographical rendering of the life of a Middle Eastern American woman who is struggling with her own immigrant past, her cousin's painful immigrant present, and the death of an innocent child they both loved dearly. The play highlights the grief many immigrants carry having to flee their beloved homelands due to war, famine, and other factors that made living there untenable. The Lebanese Civil War claimed an estimated 150,000 lives and left the entire nation ruined. The Lebanese diaspora, like other Middle Eastern diasporas, can be found across the world. The survivors of that war grapple with the deaths that occurred and with the fact that many dead were unaccounted for and forgotten after the war ended.

Another play set in the homeland is *Smail* by Tariq Hamami, a play based on a true story. The play is set in Algiers, Algeria, in 1990, 1994, and 2014. Ismail Said is a 36-year-old male living in Algiers who goes by the shortened name Smail. Smail is first seen in a dark interrogation room in Algeria in 1994. He is being interrogated by an Algerian government agent named Rifat. Smail has been arrested because he is suspected to be a member of the Islamic Salvation Front, a radical Islamist group that is against the government of President Liamine Zeroual, who succeeded President Ali Kafi.

Hamami attempts to take audiences into the horror of the civilians trapped between a government that is aggressively committed to wiping out Islamist terror and Islamist groups that wish to overthrow a government they deem dictatorial and fascist. Smail suffers from epilepsy, a condition that the people around him erroneously consider contagious. He also grows a beard to cover the cuts on his face he has suffered from his seizures, a beard that many mistake for his allegiance to Islamist groups. Rifat is intent on making Smail confess to being a member of the Islamic Salvation Front, and on making him turn over the names of others he believes are also affiliated with the group. Smail insists he is innocent, but Rifat tortures him physically and emotionally, continually clicking a light on and off attempting to trigger another seizure.

In his cell Smail imagines he is visited by loved ones including his girlfriend Saida. She urges him to stay strong and not submit to the government's brutal tactics. She also reminds him that the nation is fighting the terrorists in order to retain their democracy; yet Smail reminds her that the Islamic Party won the election and was overthrown by the government. This debate over the character and soul of Algeria itself is one that Hamami contends with as he takes audiences into the darkest period of contemporary Algerian history. Smail wants nothing to do with politics and believes he is cursed because of his epilepsy. In flashbacks we see Smail and his family together in their courtyard. His sisters Raniya and Amani are hopeful that President Benjedid will hold elections and that Algeria might have a better, more democratic, future. Amira, his mother, brings an empty birdcage home: a symbol of the imprisoned Algerian people and the empty cage that has become their country. Their brother, Farrad, moved to the United States and is free from the turmoil that has embroiled his homeland. Amani wants to vote Benjedid out of office, but Smail reminds her that he will still be president no matter the results. Raniya wants to vote for the Islamists since Algeria is a Muslim country. Smail wants neither Benjedid nor the Islamists, but rather a Muslim leader with a non-Muslim government. The play captures how even the closest families are torn apart by politics.

Audiences discover that Rifat has withheld Smail's medication and he lies, telling Smail that his family has not come to visit him. Rifat tells Smail that twenty-seven people were massacred by the Islamists outside the military base, which makes discovering their confederates an even more urgent task. Rifat also tells Smail he knows Raniya voted for the Islamists and that there is nothing he can hide from the government. When Rifat tells Smail he is a good Muslim because he is trying to rid the world of terrorists, Smail tells him Muslims do not torture, threaten, or murder others. Despite Rifat's treacherous ways, Smail tells him he will pray for him because every Algerian needs a prayer. Finally, Rifat tells Smail that it was Saida who turned him in. When Smail has a hallucination that his mother has visited him in jail, she begs him to confess and come home. She tells him that nothing is right in Algeria, and that the factions that are fighting are nothing more than bullies who are hurting the children around them. She begs him to be a moral person who stays alive, no matter what he tells Rifat. When he refuses, she tells him to be like his father who fought the French during the Algerian War of Independence.

In another flashback, Smail sees his sisters Raniya and Amani becoming more Islamicized by wearing hijabs and he worries for them. Amani says men have been abducted by soldiers simply for looking like Islamists. She urges him to shave his beard to reduce his guilt by association. Smail tells them that praying too much will get them arrested by the military, and not praying enough will get them taken by the Islamists. He believes everyone says that they are fighting for the Algerian nation, but none are fighting for the Algerian people. Smail realizes the reason he and others like Saida are taken, tortured, and killed is because all that is left to take from the people now is their happiness. He swears that no matter what his torturers do to him, they cannot have his happiness. Rifat tells Smail that the people cannot see that the government is like a parent taking care of all the responsibilities of the country for the children that are its citizens. Rifat believes he is not an extremist because he is fighting on the side of right, yet Smail reminds him that both sides believe they are right and that is the very thing tearing the country apart. When Rifat threatens to arrest and torture Smail's mother, he suffers a massive epileptic seizure and dies. The final scene takes place in 2014 in the family's courtyard. Rifat arrives and approaches Smail's mother Amira telling her to sign a paper that exonerates the government for the death of her son in return for a monetary payment. He tells her President Bouteflika wants closure. She refuses to sign. She says her country is lost and will be lost forever and that when arrogant men take over, it is the good men who die.

Hamami's play dramatizes a horrific and painful moment in Algerian history. Smail is just one man caught up in an escalating situation where a fearful government becomes tyrannical in their attempt to destroy what they considered a radical fundamental Islamist uprising. The play is set in his ancestral homeland of Algeria, yet it provides a chilling portrait of what can happen when societies are consumed with fear and loathing, and the extreme measures they can take in order to restore order. Bouteflika's presidency, which lasted from 1999 to his resignation in 2019, was a controversial tenure that was gradually diminished with the Arab Spring uprisings that began in 2011. Hamami's play is a testament to the more than 200,000 lives that were lost during the Algerian Civil War. It is also a testament to the survivors who refused to allow the successive governments the immunity against prosecution they desired by compensating families in return for forgiving the war crimes that were committed. Plays like *Smail* remind us that peace is extremely fragile and that individual liberties can be stripped away in periods of fear and nationalism.

The conflict plays written by Middle Eastern Americans are sometimes derived from their own painful experiences growing up in the various Middle Eastern conflicts, or they are by those in the diaspora who are speaking out against the inhumanity of genocides, wars, dictatorships, and civil conflicts tearing apart their ancestral homelands. These plays demonstrate that while leaders are busy making speeches and attacking their enemies, it is the people on the ground that are being destroyed. These plays chronicle events like the Armenian Genocide at the start of the twentieth century, the ongoing Palestinian-Israeli conflict, and the various civil wars that continue to decimate Middle Eastern nations. Where no physical monuments stand to chronicle the human toll of these events, these plays are testaments to the lives that have been lost so that audiences never forget the human toll of war.

CHAPTER 7
THE CURRENT STATE OF MIDDLE
EASTERN AMERICAN THEATRE

Middle Eastern American theatre is undergoing a renaissance with more plays, more companies devoted to producing these plays, and more theatre artists working professionally than in previous generations. In 2018, a Middle Eastern American theatre steering committee was formed consisting of Shoresh Alaudini, Andrea Assaf, Debórah Eliezer, Leila Buck, Catherine Coray, Yussef El Guindi, Nora El Samahy, Tracy Cameron Francis, Kathryn Haddad, Pia Haddad, Denmo Ibrahim, Taous Claire Khazem, Jamil Khoury, Kate Moore Heaney, Torange Yeghiazarian, Michael Malek Najjar, and Evren Odcikin. The purpose of this steering committee is to address these works, find solutions for how to amplify these voices, increase access to resources, and impact and expand how stories from and about these communities are told on US stages. The group had their first convening in November 2019 at the Golden Thread Productions in San Francisco. After many discussions and votes, the name MENA Theatre Makers Alliance, or MENATMA, was adopted by the members of this group.

Some of the major issues explored at the convening were the following: coalition building and networking, MENA in the academy, artistic and administrative mentorship, naming and defining the MENA coalition, and strategies for getting more MENA plays on US stages. By examining other successful theatre coalitions such as the Black Theatre Association, Consortium of Asian American Theaters and Artists (CAATA), and the Latinx Theatre Commons, there was a desire to learn from other theatre artist groups that are dealing with similar issues. These companies have different organizational structures, nonprofit statuses, meeting schedules, and connections with various theatres and academic journals. Another important aspect explored was how Middle Eastern American plays were being taught, produced, and integrated into American educational institutions. In this session, plans were discussed regarding building relationships with play selection committees, creating new syllabi, and casting issues for MENA plays in predominantly non-MENA student groups. Artistic and administrative mentorship was also a major concern that required discussion. The various approaches proposed were informal and formal mentorships, transnational and multigenerational mentorships, mentorship surrounding civic engagement and philanthropy in the MENA community, and consultancy as mentorship. As far as strategies for having more MENA plays on US stages, several questions were asked: How can cultural consulting assist more theatres producing more MENA plays? How can there be a better balance between more opportunities for MENA actors and more opportunities for MENA playwrights for productions? How can more MENA artists find leadership roles in American theatres nationwide? Also, how can MENA artists educate theatre critics about the plays and inform them about their cultural specificity?

After a year of virtual meetings with the members from across the country leading up to the convening, this in-person gathering was the first major opportunity for MENA artists to gather, discuss important issues, and create action plans for moving forward. As with the theatre communities, it is difficult to have so many varied communities under one umbrella and to find policies that can serve them all. Another difficulty is how to define the various groups that are working in the American theatre and how these groups overlap. For instance, the CAATA is primarily for Asian American theatre, but since the Middle East is technically located in Southwest Asia, there may be overlap between those who identify as Middle Eastern and those who identify as Asian American.

Concurrently, Theatre Communications Group (TCG) added a "Middle Eastern Artists' Initiative" to their "networks of Theatres of Color" which includes the Black Theatre Commons, the Consortium for Asian American Theatre Artists, Indigenous Direction, and the Latinx Theatre Commons. TCG states that their Equity, Diversity and Inclusion Initiative (EDII) is meant to "transform the national theatre field into a more equitable, inclusive and diverse community" (tcg.org). Programs include the EDI Institute, Legacy Leaders of Color Video Project, and different ways of supporting coalition building.

These various convenings, coalition-building efforts, and networks are meant to transform an American theatre landscape that has excluded and/ or omitted minority and marginalized voices for much of its history. The formation of steering committees and the inclusion of Middle Eastern American artists herald a new period of growth in this genre. In the past, disparate groups representing this community were working separately on similar goals but gaining little traction in the larger theatre community. Now, as Middle Eastern American artists realize their similarities are greater than their differences, there is an opportunity to find common purpose going forward. This can only benefit the American theatre because it is a reflection of the diversity of the nation presented on its stages. In the coming decades, the hope is that all groups of color find their place at the table, rather than accepting leftovers from the banquet. Many challenges remain, but Middle Eastern American theatre has finally reached the point where it is gaining recognition, including more communities, and becoming more accepted as a legitimate genre of theatre in the Americas.

CHAPTER 8
CRITICAL PERSPECTIVES

This book concludes with several critical perspectives about Middle Eastern American theatre by important figures who have worked to define the genre in the past few decades. Where the previous chapters focused primarily on playwrights, the first critical perspective is an interview with four of the leading directors working in this genre: Kareem Fahmy, Evren Odcikin, Megan Sandberg-Zakian, and Pirronne Yousefzadeh. These directors are of Middle Eastern descent themselves, and their work in the group Maia Directors is focused on bringing more stories and artists from the Middle East, North Africa, and South Asia to the stage and screen "with respect for the multiplicity of cultures, languages, and religions of these regions" (maiadirectors.com). These directors also exemplify the polycultural nature of the Middle Eastern American community, and they are also leading figures in the American theatre. The direction of these plays is just as important as their dramaturgy, since directors are part of the creative process that shapes representation. Therefore, a discussion with these directors about their work allows a deeper understanding of how these plays are translated onto the stage.

The second critical perspective is an extended interview with Golden Thread Productions founding artistic director Torange Yeghiazarian and Silk Road Rising co-founder and co-executive artistic director Jamil Khoury. Yeghiazarian is one of the longest-tenured artistic directors of a Middle Eastern theatre. Her company, which celebrated its twentieth year of productions in 2016, continues to produce plays by Middle Eastern American artists. Yeghiazarian also writes about theatre in her ancestral homeland of Iran from the perspective of her Iranian Armenian heritage. She has been deeply involved in the American theatre for decades and is able to provide a valuable overview of how this kind of theatre has evolved over the past decades, with a unique view regarding the Bay Area theatre scene. She is also a playwright and director, so she brings a unique perspective as one who both produces these plays and writes and directs them herself. Jamil Khoury, another playwright/artistic director, provides his perspective on Silk Road Rising, a company he and his husband Malik Gillani founded in 2002 (originally as Silk Road Theatre Project) as "an intentional and creative response to the terrorist attacks of September 11, 2001" (silkroadrising.org). Their mandate covers the entire Silk Road region, the historical network of trade routes that stretch from China to Syria. Therefore, they produce plays by writers from backgrounds such as East Asian, South Asian, and Middle Eastern countries. Their core values, which they list as "Discovery, Pluralism, and Empathy," guide their choice of plays, and their history of play productions reflects those values. In this extended interview, Yeghiazarian and Khoury share their views on Middle Eastern American theatre, their personal histories writing and producing these works, and how these works manifest and are perceived in the wider American theatre landscape.

By including the voices of these six individuals who have shaped Middle Eastern Theatre artistic production for the past decades, we arrive at a more critical perspective about this genre; how it has developed, the challenges faced by its artists, and how the American theatre has both supported and hindered the production and proliferation of these plays. These artists, revered by their artistic community, and sometimes criticized by their respective audiences and communities, are on the front line of artistic creation. Their companies have shaped, and will continue to shape, this genre for the foreseeable future.

"THEATRE THAT DISRUPTS OUR UNCONSCIOUS BIAS WITH HUMOR AND JOY": AN INTERVIEW WITH MAIA DIRECTORS KAREEM FAHMY, EVREN ODCIKIN, MEGAN SANDBERG-ZAKIAN, AND PIRRONNE YOUSEFZADEH

Author's Note: The directors' names are initialized below—Kareem Fahmy (KF), Evren Odcikin (EO), Megan Sandberg-Zakian (MSZ), and Pirronne Yousefzadeh (PY). When the directors answered as a group, I have written the abbreviation "MAIA." Also, MENA refers to Middle East/North African, while MENASA refers to Middle East/North African/South Asian.

MMN: How do you self-identify? In your own words, what is your personal relation to the Middle East?

KF: I identify mainly as "Middle Eastern," but will sometimes use the term "Arab." I'll often say "Middle Eastern American" or "Arab American" but this is actually a bit of a lie as I'm not an American citizen. I was born and raised in Canada, a child of immigrants from Egypt. My parents came to Canada in the late 1960s. I visited Egypt many times as a child (the vast majority of my family is there), and more recently as an adult. I feel a strong kinship to my Egyptian heritage.

EO: If we are going with a full-list, I'm an immigrant, Middle Eastern, Turkish-American, Muslim, queer artist. Depending on the day and the task at hand, different identifiers will take more space in my psyche.

PY: I identify as Middle Eastern, Iranian American, a Jew, and a child of immigrants.

MSZ: I identify as a queer woman. My mother is Armenian, and my father is Jewish. I identify as Middle Eastern, mixed-heritage, and American.

MMN: What do you consider to be a "Middle Eastern American Play"? What defines a play of this genre for you?

MAIA: The plays that we are interested in are created by artists that self-identify as part of the Middle Eastern American community and portray people and cultures of the Middle East and its diaspora in a nuanced way.

MMN: Which plays have you directed that you would characterize as "Middle Eastern American"?

EO: My work has always focused on the story of the outsider—narratives about and from those that have been traditionally excluded from mainstream storytelling. And because of my background and my deep involvement with Golden Thread Productions as an artist and producer, a large portion of my work specifically focused on Middle Eastern American work. I have directed numerous plays by Yussef El Guindi, Mona Mansour, and Jonas Hassen Khemiri, as well as developing work with such writers as Melis Aker, Hannah Khalil, Ken Kaissar, Saïd Sayrafiezadeh, and Betty Shamieh. I've also had the honor of working with non-Middle Eastern writers such as Kevin Artigue, Gabriel Jason Dean, and Guillermo Calderón on pieces that pertain to Middle Eastern and Middle Eastern American identities.

KF: I have directed, created, and written a number of plays that fit that category. The most notable example is the play *This Time*, which I co-created with playwright Sevan K. Greene. It tells the story of how my paternal grandmother fled Egypt and came to Canada because she was having an affair with a Canadian professor. It received a world premiere in New York in 2016. More recently I wrote and directed *The Triumphant*, which is based on interviews I conducted with gay men in Egypt. It was developed and presented at Target Margin Theatre in Brooklyn in June of 2018. My play *Pareidolia* is about an Egyptian-American artist who enters into a mysterious online relationship. I also created the first-ever English-language adaptation of Alaa Al Aswany's bestselling novel *The Yacoubian Building*.

MMN: Maia Directors is committed to MENASA works. In your opinion, what differentiates Middle Eastern/North African plays from South Asian plays?

MAIA: We had extensive conversations before deciding to include South Asia in the scope of the Maia Directors mission, since none of our co-founders is of South Asian descent. This was in response to our recognition that South Asian artists are often cast as Middle Eastern characters, and vice versa. We wanted to make sure that if our Middle Eastern artist community is benefiting from the talents of South Asian artists, we are committed to supporting those artists and their stories as well. With this decision, we are purposefully putting ourselves in the middle of a complex conversation. In agreeing to this larger umbrella, we strive to honor the difference among all of the cultures represented while highlighting the commonalities. The question of differentiating between plays from MENA versus South Asian communities is a difficult one as the sample size of produced plays by MENASA writers in the United States is not large enough to be representative of the full diversity of voices, aesthetic, and traditions from these regions. We were specifically founded with the intention of championing more artists and stories to counteract this. It will be exciting to see what kind of conversation is possible about this in ten to twenty years once we've seen many more MENASA plays on US stages.

MMN: On the Maia Directors website it states: "We believe that increasing the visibility of MENASA stories is critical to deepening our national empathy." Why, in your opinion, does our national empathy require deepening? How do MENA plays contribute to this deepening?

MAIA: As we've seen over and over again, othering and dehumanizing is the first step towards some of the darkest chapters of history—in this country and around the world. We're living in an era where immigrant communities of all backgrounds are actively vilified by the highest seats of our government, and it is our imperative as artists to counteract that. Specifically, MENA communities represent only around 3 percent of the total US population and 20 percent of those are clustered in the larger metropolitan area of only four cities (Los Angeles, Detroit, Chicago, and New York). There are large swaths of the country where it would be totally possible, if not likely, that an average citizen has never met a MENA person. Although TV, film, and pop culture representations of MENA culture and peoples are getting better, there is still a very narrow perspective that is usually highlighted based in a fundamental lack of understanding of MENA culture and history nationwide. Any opportunities to put American audiences in dialogue with MENA stories is essential in fostering a deeper understanding.

MMN: Also, on the Maia Directors website it states: "We believe in the importance of centering the voices of artists who identify as part of the MENASA-American community in telling these stories. We believe that the American theatre must reject cultural conflation and lift up the complicated and intersectional reality of MENASA communities. We believe that our work in the American theatre is part of a larger movement towards inclusion and equity." Why is it necessary to center the voices of MENA artists? Why is cultural conflation something that must be rejected? What are some of the intersectional realities of MENA theatre that you are particularly interested in exploring in your work?

EO: This feels obvious to those of us that come from these communities, but this is something that we continually have to advocate for in mainstream spaces. Not all MENASA artists are the same—our lived experiences are unique and touch upon wildly divergent histories, cultures, languages, and religions. No single artist or play speaks for all of us, and we must continue to push for more inclusion to help create a more rounded and complex representation of our communities. It's also worth noting that just because a play is set in or deals with MENASA regions or cultures, it doesn't mean that it serves these communities. Maia Directors strongly advocates for work generated by MENASA artists because we know that the most impactful, nuanced, and accurate work representing our communities is created by people from those communities. Although it can come with good intentions, American theatre's benevolent approach to helping "others" through the authorship of white artists can be profoundly dehumanizing and damaging. This is not to say that artists cannot work outside of their culture, but we believe that it is essential for MENASA artists to be empowered as decision-makers at the center of these projects and processes.

MMN: What do you believe having a personal connection to the Middle East brings to your work on MENA plays that, perhaps, a non-MENA director might not bring to the work?

MSZ: There's an incredible diversity of experiences in the region. I think that having a personal connection to the region actually more finely attunes me to the need to get very granular and specific in the research I do and the questions I ask. Although I have some degree of lived cultural knowledge of the region, it's knowledge that is very specific to me. I know that variations in religion, language, and geography—which might seem unremarkable to a white American—are hugely significant and would drastically affect how characters move, speak, and relate to one another.

PY: Though I haven't spent time in the Middle East, my time in America as a third culture kid and child of immigrants has made me very aware of my identity and the specificity of my family's culture. Having had personal experiences of microaggressions, cultural conflations, and cultural erasure, accuracy, and specificity in the work I do are of the utmost importance; I want MENA artists, stories, and audiences to be seen and heard with respect and pride. My identity and experiences have made me more attuned to creating a process where no one person is a sole cultural ambassador because of the multiplicity of viewpoints, experiences, and expertise represented in the rehearsal room. It is through that rich exchange that the work can be specific, and demonstrate respect and appreciation for languages, cultural traditions, and rituals.

KF: The key thing that my Middle Eastern upbringing allows me to bring to my directing work on a MENA play is a lived cultural knowledge. While I think a director of any race or background can (and should!) tackle any play, I feel we are still early in building a canon of new Middle Eastern American work, and representations of our community that have been put on stage up to now have too often been lacking in nuance and specificity.

EO: It took me a long time to articulate the ways in which my identity and heritage impacts my work in other ways than just content. I grew up in a country filled with contradictions—ancient and new, East and West, masculine and feminine—and I am drawn to works that have those conflicting ideas at their core, and tonally, stylistically, and structurally center dissonance. My lack of interest in subtlety that is endemic in American theatre is also deeply rooted in my heritage. I come from a family and a culture where people say what they mean—usually loudly and with passion. I feel more at home in plays that do that as well. I also find that I am drawn to unexpected metaphor. Satire and camp have always been key parts of Turkish artmaking especially in the ways that artists speak to power. So, it's not surprising that I love camp, caricature, big visual and sonic ideas that have deep political meaning and can speak to difficult truths.

MMN: What directorial choices do you find you must make when directing a MENA play that are specific to this genre? In other words, what makes preparation for a MENA play different than preparations for directing a play by Eugene O'Neill, Arthur Miller, or Tennessee Williams, for instance?

EO: First off, I wish American artistic leaders would consider that a MENA director like me might be an option for an O'Neill, Miller, or Williams. But if I were at some point able to direct an American classic, I am sure I'd be approaching it with a slightly different lens. A director has to always think of their audience, but when dealing with MENA work, I think the question of audience's perspective and preconceived biases come earlier into my process. Along with the research that goes into any works that deal with oft-ignored stories, I also think deeply about the ways in which the creative teams' intentions may be co-opted and misunderstood. This usually means that MENA works I direct will be more colorful and more direct. I find that I spend more time to find and highlight the joy and laughter in MENA works.

KF: Preparation and research is a vital part of the directing process for any play. It's up to the director to understand the world that the writer is trying to create, and that takes a knowledge of context and history. The great American canon of theatre (O'Neill, Miller, and Williams are great examples) has a long and celebrated production history so much can be gleaned from how other directors have interpreted the work in the past, and how your own interpretation will be in conversation with those that have come before. In working on a MENA play, a director is usually tackling a first production, or possibly a second or third. Very few MENA plays have been canonized or have received multiple productions. The choices a director makes—staging, design, structure—can become part of the very fabric of the play.

PY: I find that my preparation varies because the plays themselves are so singular and varied in terms of tone, style, narrative, and aesthetic. The key difference is that in working on a MENA play, I am not inheriting a set of assumptions about how the play must be performed in the way I am when working on a piece of the American theatrical canon. I find this liberating, and in lieu of researching an extensive production history, I immerse myself in research on the play's circumstances. I think the other key aspect is that when working on a MENA play, I am more consciously aware of the political act and activism my job requires. What unconscious bias can I disrupt? How can my work on this play allow for a MENA audience member to feel seen, heard, and understood? These questions are fundamentally a part of my process, because of my vested interest in ensuring that we accurately represent our communities and our stories.

MMN: Are there particular MENA playwrights that you collaborate with often? If so, why do you feel artistically compelled to work on their plays?

EO: Three playwrights come to mind, and I think it's worth noting how different their works are. Mona Mansour has become a key collaborator and is part of the reason why I have a career in the American theatre. I love how actor-friendly her plays are, and that she brings an undeniable complexity to her characters and their political and personal relationships to their culture. She creates with great generosity and is one of the most giving collaborators I've ever worked with. Yussef El Guindi has been an important part of my growth as a director. His plays are difficult—and purposefully so. He writes anger rooted in injustice like no one else I've ever read. And he does it with humor, sharp wit, and brave honesty. Any time I feel like I need to be braver as an artist, I think of his *Language Rooms* and the difficult and personal conversations he put in that play. Lastly, Jonas Hassen Khemiri is someone I need to mention. He is the master of unreliable narratives and creating flawed young men whose complexity and jagged edges make it impossible for the audience to look away. His hip-hop poetic sensibility and bold theatrical vision are a great match for my strengths as a director—and his plays have been some of the most satisfying artistic experiences of my career to date.

KF: I've had an excellent working relationship with the Pakistani-American playwright Rohina Malik, who does not identify as MENA, but is a devout Muslim and writes passionately about the Muslim-American experience. We've had a very fruitful collaboration as I'm able to draw from my own Muslim upbringing to translate her work for non-Muslim audiences. I take the responsibility of putting Muslim characters on stage very seriously. Rohina and I have developed a great dialogue about why it's important to be doing this kind of work in today's American theatre.

MSZ: I've gotten to workshop and brainstorm a lot with MENA writers, but have never gotten to direct a MENA play in production! I'm looking forward to this changing as more and more of these plays make it to full production. Recently I've been workshopping a new play by one of my theatre heroes, Eric Bogosian, based on his book *Operation Nemesis*—which is really exciting and has been the first time I've worked with an Armenian writer. It is an extraordinary experience to have so many very specific things from my family and personal history—food, language, gesture—echoed on the page and in the rehearsal room.

PY: One of my closest collaborations is with Ramiz Monsef, and for several years, we have been developing his play *3 Farids*, a clown show about Middle

Eastern representation in Hollywood. I love working on comedy and clown, particularly, but my appreciation for Ramiz and his work is much deeper than that. In ways that are buoyant and joyous, Ramiz has crafted a subversive narrative, where the Middle Eastern men at the center of the story are also the play world's moral compass. So often, in mainstream entertainment, Middle Eastern characters are rendered without basic morality or decency, and/or those same characters rely on white characters in the story to "save" them. In this play, the Farids are the heroes of their own story, and this is the kind of theatre I want to be a part of: theatre that disrupts our unconscious bias with humor and joy, and gives Middle Eastern characters a sense of agency and fullness as three-dimensional human beings.

"BE A PART OF CHANGING THE AMERICAN NARRATIVE ABOUT THE MIDDLE EAST": AN INTERVIEW WITH GOLDEN THREAD PRODUCTIONS EXECUTIVE ARTISTIC DIRECTOR TORANGE YEGHIAZARIAN AND SILK ROAD RISING CO-FOUNDER AND CO-EXECUTIVE ARTISTIC DIRECTOR JAMIL KHOURY

MMN: How do you personally identify as a Middle Eastern American, and what is your relation to that term?

TY: I identify as Iranian American, and Middle Eastern to me is an umbrella term that includes that, and I would say I mostly identify as an immigrant woman. That's, I think, the thing that informs my perspective.

JK: And I identify as a mixed-heritage Arab American and a queer feminist Arab American. Middle Eastern American becomes useful when talking about our theater movement, and, in the case of Silk Road Rising, when talking about the "heritage communities" that we focus on—East Asian, South Asian, and Middle Eastern North African.

MMN: Jamil, you talk about polyculturalism as an idea. How do we bring polyculturalism into the conversation when someone is not born from two parents who are from the Middle East, for instance?

JK: I am the product of a polycultural marriage and the union of two cultural communities. I'm part Arab and part Slavic, and both backgrounds inform my worldview. Arguably I'm more attached to my Arab heritage, as it was my father who was the immigrant. He immigrated from Syria in the early 1950s whereas my mother was born in Chicago of Polish and Slovak heritage. I also have an actual lived relationship with Syria and with the Arab world that I don't yet have with Poland and Slovakia. So that immigrant piece of me, that consciousness about being the son of an immigrant, has always been central to who I am. And to how I understand my Americanness, and whatever sense of belonging and affinity and hyphenated existence I may feel at a given time.

TY: So, fundamental to why we started Golden Thread and why we chose to go with the term "Middle Eastern American" is this idea of a pluralistic society, a pluralistic background. From my perspective, nobody's really pure, nobody's one thing; we all have many layers to our identity. As someone who's from a mixed marriage, someone who's an immigrant, who's, you know, displaced and "othered" on multiple levels . . . pluralism is, I think, central to the idea of who I am and how I bring people together and what Golden Thread is. So, we are a company made up of many mixed people.

JK: And I think the polycultural model, or the pluralistic model, is ultimately more useful for us than the multicultural model, in that it's about cultural interchange and relationships between communities. It's about the intersections and the overlap. And although I often say that we were born of a multicultural politic, we quickly migrated to a polycultural aesthetic, because multiculturalism all too often silos communities and polices identities and doesn't necessarily acknowledge the fact that we all inhabit and embody multiple identities at any given time.

MMN: So, is it inherently problematic to say someone is, say, Iranian American or Arab American, when people obviously have such plurality in their lives and in their backgrounds? And if we do try to create these definitions, then is that really for our consumption, or is that to help those outside of our groups understand better our connection to a Persian culture, for instance?

TY: I don't know what you mean by problematic. I mean, I think people self-identify, and people arrive at that self-identification wherever they are. So, if someone defines themselves as Iranian American, that's where they are, that's how they define themselves. I think for me what's difficult is when people argue racial purity or cultural exclusiveness. Those conversations become difficult, those conversation and that mindset ignore our very mixed and very long history of shared cultures in the Middle East. That's again one of the reasons why Golden Thread has such a broad and inclusive definition of the Middle East is that we are not one thing. And the Middle East over the many centuries, over the millennia, has been inhabited by people of many different cultures, and all of those races and ethnicities have left an impact there. And we are the product of that history. So, I think for me what's exciting is to dive into that mix and see what we come up with, as opposed to try to, you know, pull out exclusive threads out of it.

JK: And I think that complexity and the fact so many of us have assimilated this idea, usually for historical reasons, that we don't like each other or that we're somehow adversaries, be that Arabs and Israelis or Turks and Kurds or Sunnis and Shi'ites. And that isn't to deny some very painful history of course. But Middle Eastern American theatre gives us an opportunity to move beyond so many of the narratives that either divide us or pit us against each other and to focus instead on that which unites us, the cultural experiences that we share, without homogenizing or hegemonizing us. Without denying our specificities. And I think there are so many cultural traditions and ideas and practices and expectations that so many of us who fall under this complicated, messy rubric called "Middle Eastern" can identify with or attach to.

I do want to say something else about Arab American for me, and why I call myself Arab American as opposed to Polish American. For me, it's largely a political choice, and it's a political choice that I made at a very young age. I know that there was, and is, prejudice against Slavic peoples and that it was much more pronounced in earlier generations, directed at earlier waves of immigrants, than it is today. But my entire life I have been hugely aware of anti-Arab sentiment in this country, and hostility and stereotyping and scapegoating. And so it was always important for me politically to align myself with Arabs and Arab Americans because of anti-Arab racism and stigma. And also, in part, because when I self-identify as Arab American and people respond with "Oh, but you don't look Arab," whatever "look Arab" may mean, I'm also doing the work of refuting or somehow challenging perceptions of who is and isn't an Arab, or what "Arab" even means.

So, I think when the Polish Independence Day Parade passes through downtown Chicago, where I live, and I catch pieces of it, I feel very proud, you know, I feel very happy for all the Polish people waving flags, that kind of thing. But I also feel a little removed. So there's this sense of, Yeah! I'm part of them and they're part of me and we share something, and I'm happy that Poland is quote, unquote "free," however we want to define "free," but it is different. And so many of the Slavic immigrants, so many of my relatives on my mom's side, really became white Americans, they assimilated into a version of "whiteness," whereas with my Arab side that was never really the case, it wasn't even a possibility or an option for many.

MMN: What then do we do with people who are Middle Eastern but perhaps don't fit within the boundaries of a map, for instance. What if somebody who's Afghani says I'm Middle Eastern, or if somebody who's Pakistani, or North Africa of course becomes its own conversation, what does Middle

Eastern then mean if it's based first of all on a colonial representation of what this region is, and second of all when even maps are excluding certain countries and peoples from this definition.

TY: Jamil and I have come up with a definition of a broad and inclusive Middle East, basically not defined by geography or politics, language or religion, but by a broad cultural brushstroke. So we have that definition on our websites.

JK: You know, and, if an Afghan person or a Central Asian person or a South Asian Muslim, a Pakistani, chooses to identify as Middle Eastern, that's great. You know, I'm not going to police or contest how someone self-identifies. It could be that they self-identify as South Asian and Middle Eastern or that somehow Islam connects them to the Middle East, or Eastern Christianity, that expatriate experiences in the Arabian Gulf connect them to the Middle East, you know, they feel an attachment culturally or religiously or professionally or linguistically. I do like the term "Southwest Asian," and I will sometimes identify as Southwest Asian, but it oftentimes creates confusion and some people think I'm saying I'm from the Philippines, which becomes all the more confusing. So I've learned that Southeast Asian has real meaning for people; it has a particular geographic resonance, whereas Southwest Asian. . . . Herein lies the debate: I mean, yes, we're calling ourselves a MENA movement, yes, we absolutely need to embrace the acronym MENA, we've kind of figured that out. But it would be nice if, at some point, a term like "Southwest Asian" or "West Asian," particularly within our broader conversations about Asian Americans and Asian-ness, could be more readily recognized and embraced.

MMN: One of the questions about our coalition's name, for instance, is the addition of the word "American." So for instance Middle East North African American, and then the problematics of North African American as a term, for instance, where, in truth, people from North Africa are technically African American, but they do not fit within the box of the American ethno-racial construction. So, what are the inherent pitfalls of us identifying with this notion of Middle Eastern American or Middle Eastern North African American?

TY: I wanted to go back to the previous question and share just the fundamental philosophy of inclusiveness. There's, in the politics of identity in the United States, in the process of claiming one's identity, what has happened is that people have in fact isolated themselves more. This is something Jamil touched on briefly. In our work at Golden Thread Productions, and I imagine also at Silk Road Rising, our philosophy is a philosophy of inclusiveness. It's basically widening the embrace as much as possible because, at the end of the day, we have more in common than we don't. So just going back to the Middle East, the term "Middle East" and how we identify it or how we describe it, at Golden Thread, we have produced plays that deal with Andalucía, with Bosnia, with Sicily. We include the Caucasus, you know, Azerbaijan, Armenia, so it's a very wide net. And part of that is that, through sharing these stories, we can broaden peoples' idea of what this culture is, right? And its historic heritage and wealth and how it has impacted the world, right? So, if anyone contacts Golden Thread and says, "I self-identify as Middle Eastern," I don't even ask them where they're from. I say, "Come on in." And then, just to touch on the American side of it, it's interesting. In describing Golden Thread from the very beginning, we had really taken care to talk about the Middle East and how we define the Middle East and what it means. And for years we had debated using the term. It wasn't until when we started doing our strategic planning back in 2013 that it occurred to us that we were actually an American company. So, we had talked about being Middle Eastern American and Middle Eastern American theater and we were part of Middle East America new plays initiative and all of that. But we had taken that for granted, and I personally hadn't thought about what that means. And it was in 2013 in those conversations that we, that I, realized we are an American company with a focus on the Middle East, and that is inherently a very different perspective than a company in any of the countries of the Middle East producing, even with a similar philosophy to ours. So, for me that was very revealing, and it was very interesting to think about, well, what does it mean to be American? What does it mean to be Middle Eastern American? And I think that, I don't know, shifted something in me personally.

MMN: What, then, is a Middle Eastern American play?

JK: We are committed to producing playwrights of Middle Eastern backgrounds who create protagonists or central characters of Middle Eastern backgrounds. We call it "the playwright-protagonist imperative," or alignment. Now, I'm not going to argue that that's the only definition of, or the sole definition of, a Middle Eastern American play, but that is how we decided to tell Middle Eastern American stories. I want to add that the American piece of that is huge, and that we cannot disentangle our American-ness from our Middle Eastern-ness. Nor can we deny the fact that we're speaking to mostly non-Middle Eastern American audiences, who bring their own impressions and perceptions and understandings to the table, either of our part of the world or the cultures emanating from our part of the world. And with that comes a certain set of aesthetic choices and political responsibilities. So we are—and I don't mean this in a propagandistic way or an ideological way—but we carry this constant awareness that we're creating art against a backdrop of stereotypes and animus directed at all things "Middle Eastern." I think we also have a lot to say about what it means to be an American. I mean, in many respects, that's been the central question for Silk Road Rising from the beginning. After all, 9/11 was our company's moment of conception. Our American-ness was being questioned and challenged in profoundly disturbing ways. Middle Eastern Americans were basically exiled from the American story. And so we set out to reclaim and reassert *our* American stories, on our terms. And to create spaces where we could define ourselves.

MMN: Torange, is the playwright-protagonist model something Golden Thread Productions also adheres to?

TY: At Golden Thread, we produce plays about any topic written by playwrights of Middle Eastern heritage, and then plays written by anyone about the Middle East. So we have an "about from, or about" mission. And that's informed by an emphasis on dialogue and bringing diverse artists together to the table. Having said that, I would say historically, over the past twenty plus years, we have produced 90 percent plays by playwrights of Middle Eastern heritage. Mostly in the ReOrient Festival, sometimes about maybe, I don't know, [one] third or half of the short plays are by playwrights not of Middle Eastern heritage. Because it was initially just a philosophical thing, but then it became really important during the war years, the Iraq war, and then to create space for Americans who were also exploring alternatives to what the government was, the official narrative in the media, and the official narrative that the government was doing. And so, in a way, we were kind of a rare space for those perspectives.

MMN: I think what's unique about both of you is that, not only are you artistic directors but you're also playwrights who've written plays in this genre. In thinking about plays like *444 Days* or *Mosque Alert* what, to you, was necessary in writing those plays, and how did those plays then become Middle Eastern American plays?

TY: I mean, I don't set out to write a Middle Eastern American play. I think I do by virtue of who I am, but in the case of *444 Days* it was my . . . what I needed to say was that, here are two countries that are behaving like belligerent teenagers, instead of adults, and I wanted to convey that through a love story, or a love story gone bad, basically, which is in many ways what I feel has happened between the US and Iran. So more than anything it was political intrigue à la—I don't know—romance kind of play. I think what makes it Middle Eastern American is that it . . . it very directly depicts the relationship between the US and a country in the Middle East. It's different from some of the other Middle Eastern American plays in that it's not the perspective of a Middle Eastern American character. The lead characters—one is American, the other one is Iranian from Iran—are not Middle Eastern American, per se.

JK: I think that in the case of *Mosque Alert*, what makes it a Middle Eastern American play—first of all—six of the eleven characters are Arab Americans, Egyptian and Syrian—essentially, it's a play about Islamophobia. And Islam, you know, gets wrongly conflated as this Middle Eastern religion that is somehow monolithic, and that all Muslims are tied to that part of the world, even though geographically it might extend from Nigeria to China, but who has time to parse that out? I tend to think that all Middle Eastern Americans, or at least most Middle Eastern Americans—including those of us who are not Muslim—are affected by Islamophobia and the egregious assumptions it propagates. So, this was a play that was not written in a conventional style, in that we invited participants, virtually and in-person, to contribute to the crafting of the narrative, and to contribute insights and experiences and perspectives, and so forth. And I incorporated a lot of that. But it was part of a prolonged conversation, live and online, and us working in communities where there was actual resistance to the building of proposed mosques. Including the community in west suburban Chicago where the play is set, Naperville, Illinois. Naperville had been home to two cases of proposed mosques that were initially denied permits. So by working with the local Muslim communities, and with their friends and foes, and with those, who, you know, were somehow indifferent, but not really indifferent, we were able to build a story that's ultimately about belonging and not belonging in today's America. So to me, *Mosque Alert* is a Middle Eastern American play that heavily emphasizes the American, in that it's about finding one's place in a society that hasn't fully embraced you, and that asks you to prove your American-ness, or at least disprove your anti-American-ness, or your foreign-ness. It also examines how Islamophobia gets racialized and, in a way, universalized, to the extent that it also targets, and doesn't distinguish between, Hindus, Sikhs, Latinx communities, Eastern Christians, Mizrahi Jews, and so forth. And that was always very important to me, demonstrating that this is an ideology that (a) relies on othering and foreignizing, and (b) has proven to be a very effective tool politically within the American electoral landscape; one that is easily exploitable. So, scapegoating Middle Eastern Americans, scapegoating Muslims, becomes convenient and useful for folks with, well, really insidious politics.

MMN: Now, one of the inherent problems is who are we writing for? Because inevitably we will have somebody who's from the Middle East stand up and say, "We know all of this! Why are you telling us this?" And you'll also have an American, or non-Middle Eastern audience member saying, "Oh, I learned so much, coming to this play!" So, how do we deal with that dichotomy, and how do you personally deal with it both as playwrights and as artistic directors?

TY: As a playwright, I think the story, I'm personally drawn to stories that bring multiple communities together, so I often have people of different backgrounds in the play so that their various perspectives can . . . so that different people in the audience can relate to different characters in the play. So I don't necessarily think about, or consciously think about, "Oh, who's representing what perspective or what segment of my audience can relate to what?" But just naturally I'm drawn to stories that bring different kinds of people together and often it results in plays that have, that provide multiple points of entry to the audience. Having said that, it happens all the time that Iranians or Armenians in the theater have opinions about my choices in the plays, and cultural opinions. They make major broad statements like "An Iranian woman would never do that," "An Iranian mother would never say that," "An Iranian man blah blah," you know, so it happens all the time and my answer to that is, "In this play, they do." Or they try to rewrite the play for you, and I'm like "Hey, you have a great story! You should sit down and write it!"

JK: Well, I just want to start by saying that Torange and I have so much in common, both as artists and as producers, in that we strive to create landscapes that include lots of different people with different perspectives and experiences. Also we both dramatize discourse, debates, and ideas in ways that aren't about directing you as an audience member to think in a particular way, or arrive at a particular conclusion, but rather affording you the integrity and intelligence to arrive at your own conclusions. But certainly, having people of different cultural backgrounds somehow relating to each other, be they in conflict, be they romantically involved, you know, whatever the case may be. But in that same space, I think that some segments of our Middle Eastern audiences bring a certain cultural insecurity to the table, or to the conversation, and a degree of fear. And sometimes it's a very, you know, understandable or justifiable fear of . . . airing dirty laundry, or how such and such depiction of such and such idea or behavior is going to reflect poorly upon the broader community. The burden of representation that falls on so many of us who deign to create Middle Eastern American stories is enormous and frankly unfair. It's like we're supposed to represent everyone's story in one two-hour play and, God forbid, our people not "look good" every step of the way. It's this impossible expectation that certain members of our communities cannot seem to forgive us for not adhering to. But you know, by and large, as Torange said, this idea of "Well then, tell your story, tell your story the way you want to hear it told!" I mean, I have often found that to be an effective way to at least shut someone up, without sacrificing politeness and decorum, diplomacy, but also as a way to say "You too can tell a story, you too can write a play, you too . . . ." And we see ourselves, certainly with our education program, as facilitators of just that. And if you have a specific idea of what an Iranian woman does or says, then that is the Iranian woman you need to depict, but Torange is going to go in a different direction, and God love her for it. I will always maintain when people say, "Well, now that person doesn't exist in our community," "Really? I happen to know five versions of that person, no, ten versions of that person," you know what I mean? Generally speaking, the characters that live in my head are a composite, like with all writers, of the many people we know and the many parts of ourselves.

TY: I would also just add, there is the burden of representation, there is the burden of countering stereotypes. So it is true that I'm drawn to plays that counter stereotypes. So while you know a father beating up his daughter for marrying the wrong person happens all the time, it's probably unlikely that I will produce that play. So I do, as a producer, I make choices, and it is my intention to show stories that counter what most Americans already think of the Middle East.

MMN: Now, as much as we want coalition building, and we desire it and we work toward it, what do we do with problematic counter-narratives such as the Armenian Genocide or the Israeli-Palestinian conflict, where you will produce a play that maybe is very charged? Say a pro-Palestine play that's very charged against the Israeli occupation, or a pro-Armenian play that is very strongly saying that Turkey did commit such atrocities? What do you do when you have to, on the one hand, bring Middle Eastern communities together and, on the other, knowing that these plays are very divisive in certain ways, and perhaps *need* to be divisive in certain ways? Or do you just avoid that altogether and try to find the play that finds commonality rather than conflict?

JK: That's a very important question, and I just want to go back a moment to the politics of countering stereotypes. And I too think the act of countering, consciously and intentionally, very much informs a lot of our decision making and a lot of how we view plays. This idea of Middle Eastern people as human beings, that radical notion, is like this irrefutable fact that we constantly need to reiterate. Think about it. I mean, it's tragic. It's heartbreaking. It's testimony to how "successful" Orientalist, racist, and colonial discourses have been. We're talking centuries. And now it's somehow incumbent upon us as artists and storytellers to show that Middle Eastern peoples are neither demons nor angels, but rather complicated, complex people like everyone else. And that we, as a theater company, demand the right to explore those complexities, and those contradictions of the human condition, warts and all. I agree with Torange about the father who beats up his daughter, unless there's a story that absolutely warrants that depiction. Because the idea of feeding into stereotypes, the idea of confirming peoples' worst assumptions about Middle Easterners, is such a . . . it's a minefield and it can be very dangerous. Because on the one hand, if it's the daughter who comes to us with a story about being abused by her father, then there's an urgency and an importance ascribed to her story by virtue of the fact that she's coming forth, and that the telling of her story becomes part of her own catharsis, her own healing. So, we of course stand with her. Which isn't to deny that these are difficult conversations and difficult balancing acts.

Look, colonial feminism is real, and it's waiting in the wings eager to exploit authentic feminist expression.

I think when it comes to issues like the Armenian Genocide and Palestinian dispossession and Israeli occupation, we need to take a nonnegotiable stance. There was a genocide of over two million Armenians, Assyrians, and Greeks committed by Turkey. Full stop. Turkey committed those crimes and we're not going to debate that. We're not going to allow historical facts to reside in a contested arena. We know that Japanese Americans were incarcerated en masse by the US government. The US government committed a racist crime against American citizens. Not the first time, not the last, and no, I'm sorry, we're not debating the "virtues" of mass incarceration. We know that Palestinians were forcibly displaced from their land, from their homes, by Israeli forces, and that Palestinians today live under a cruel, draconian military occupation. It's incontestable. And artists have a responsibility to recognize and honor collective trauma.

TY: To everything Jamil said, I would build on that two examples. So, for us, the ReOrient Festival has been an opportunity to actually present plays from different perspectives, not ones that debate the fundamentals but show the impact from different perspectives. So, for example, we famously produced Motti Lerner's *Coming Home*, so an Israeli, the impact of the occupation on an Israeli family. And in the same evening we had *Tamam* by Betty Shamieh, and *Baggage* and *Sahmata*. So, the first year that we produced those plays we had like three Palestinian plays and Motti's play in one ReOrient. And I don't know if you know *Sahmata*, but it's about the [Palestinian] village and the destruction of the village and the grandfather telling his stories. And, you know, because of Motti and his stature we had people from the Israeli Consulate in the audience one night, the night that Motti was participating in the post-play discussions. And the same night I had invited—it accidentally happened, it wasn't an intentional thing—I had invited the singers from Aswat Arabic Music Ensemble and their founder to attend. I think they were performing at ReOrient earlier that afternoon, so many of them stayed and came to see the play, came to see the performance, the ReOrient performance, that evening. And the post-play conversation after that play was chilling, I would say, because . . . Motti is probably one of the most vocal critics of the occupation, and in his conversation after the play, he didn't hold back, he was very open. He shared his fears, essentially, for the future of Israel if the occupation continues. And the Israeli Consul who was in the audience stood up and said, "I really loved the play and I love that it's being produced here, but I have to say that I don't share your perspective and I love my country and I think it's a great country and has a lot to offer." And then one of the Palestinian singers in the audience stood up and said, "Yes, but I hope it didn't cost my humanity" or, something to that effect, and there was a back and forth between them, and it was . . . they were both very respectful to each other. It's rare for those two people to be in the same space together to begin with, and then to be actually able to have a conversation, I think is rare. And I think they were both surprised that they were in fact able to have a conversation. Of course, it got heated, and of course it got emotional, and we concluded on a note of agreeing that it's difficult and how wonderful that we are able to gather in this cultural space and have this conversation. But I think ReOrient is one place where we are able to bring in people from different communities together. And often in post-play conversations we have those kinds of opposing perspectives that may clash. Another experience that was interesting was when we produced *A Girl's War* by Joyce Van Dyke, who's an Armenian playwright in Massachusetts. It's about a love affair between an Armenian and Azeri during the Karabakh War, the border conflict there. And it was difficult for, I mean we have deep roots in the Armenian community in the Bay Area, and we've produced a number of plays that deal with the aftermath of the genocide. But it was a difficult play to pitch to the Armenian community because many people were uncomfortable with this idea of a love affair between and Armenian and an Azeri, and we were promoting it that way. And the feedback that I got was that if it hadn't been promoted that way, more people probably would have come. But it felt a little, I don't know that it felt propaganda-y, but it felt like a foregone conclusion without room for conversation, so anyway, that was a learning experience for me.

MMN: Have either of you had to deal with a playwright who's given you a play whose politics you absolutely do not agree with and that you had to reject for that reason?

JK: Well, you know, Motti Lerner's play *Pangs of the Messiah*, which we're very proud to have produced, the first time I read the script—and I very distinctly remember sitting at a gate at an airport, I think it was Washington National, and my flight had been delayed and I thought, "Well, I'll read the first few scenes, see if I like it," and I literally couldn't put it down. I read it start to finish and the flight still hadn't arrived! *Pangs* really disturbed me. It really shook me up, and in large part because Motti had created these characters who were religious Zionist settlers, we're talking leaders of an illegal West Bank settlement, who were complicated and likeable and detestable and yes, relatable. And I'm not supposed to relate to these guys. I worked for a UN agency on the West Bank with Palestinian refugee communities. The Israeli settlers and soldiers were uniformly the bad guys, and any interaction with them was negative. And to enter the world of that story, and to do so knowing that Motti is a secular, atheist Israeli Jew who's opposed to the settlement movement . . . the play took me to a very uncomfortable place, but in a way that convinced me we needed to produce it. My political discomfort greenlighted the project for me. And a number of Arab audience members who came to see *Pangs of the Messiah*—and most of our Arab audience avoided that production altogether—they too professed feeling a deep discomfort, because on the one hand they really liked the play, they found themselves relating to the characters, and yet felt torn, guilty even, about attaching humanity to people who inflict harm and suffering on fellow Arabs. And of course that's part of what Motti—that's part of the point that he was making—we can critique their world view, we can critique their politics, we can even critique aspects of their religious beliefs or how they interpret those beliefs, but we can't deny the fact that these are people who live and breathe their belief system and put their bodies on the line for a cause that they consider to be moral and just and even redemptive. Motti's not endorsing their views—to the contrary—but in putting a human face on those views, he's reminding us just how black and white the world is not. And so, that play stands out as an example, a very vivid example.

TY: I think similarly because agenda-driven plays tend to be very, you know, transactional or very direct in what they're trying to do, and that's not interesting theater. We did have one experience with playwright Ken Kaissar, whose play we chose to do a stage reading of, and then later he had a short play that we included in ReOrient. I think we did the reading first and then his short play was included in ReOrient and as part of our ReOrient promo. I knew that Ken is Jewish and he's a practicing Jew, so I knew that, but in his interview he self-identified as a Zionist so that came as a surprise to me and it was . . . . So, I had to have a conversation with him, I'm like, "Uh, what is this and how come we haven't had this conversation before?" And he said he defines Zionism as just believing that Israel has a right to exist, and I said, "Well, that's technically not what Zionism is," [*laughing*] and so we had to have a further conversation. And there was a whole . . . not even a debate, I don't know a major reaction to that, a rant by one of our Palestinian actors in ReOrient. He posted a long opinion piece on his Facebook page. I had to explain the playwright's perspective to the actor and vice versa and invite them to use the opportunity to establish dialogue, which they did. But I mean it all worked out and it was fine, but I think it did leave a bad taste in some of our Palestinian audience members' mouth, just the way he the playwright self-identified. If we're going to produce Israeli or Jewish playwrights who write about "The Conflict," I think to *only* say we will produce anti-Zionists would be very difficult and would probably . . . is problematic in a way. I think that most of the playwrights, Israeli playwrights, Jewish playwrights, that we're going to interact with, understand themselves as liberal, progressive, leftists, you know however that . . . but have this fundamental belief that there needs to be or should be . . . a Jewish state. And I don't want to engage necessarily in that debate so much as, you know, it's important to me that they recognize that Palestinian self-determination is a baseline in terms of resolution to this conflict. I would say in general again it goes back to countering dominant stereotypes, you know? I'm interested in plays that challenge the dominant perspective, that challenge those narratives regardless of where it comes from.

MMN: Let's talk about the idea of "balance." Because as you know, we often feel that if we give one half of a narrative, we must give the other half of the same narrative. But some of our colleagues feel that is extremely unhelpful and downright equivocating. So, what do we do about that? What do we do about this notion that we must balance these contested narratives in order to come to a more fair or equitable understanding?

TY: I don't feel I have to balance the narrative. [*laughs*] I reject that question.

MMN: So, with ReOrient, you don't feel the need to have a balance of ideas based on certain topics?

TY: I think with ReOrient I look at how to put the plays in dialogue with each other, not necessarily to balance the perspective but to create a more provocative conversation. So, I think this idea of fair and balanced, I mean maybe the news media or some news channels can do it, but it's really . . . it's like people saying "I'm very objective." Nobody's objective, everybody's subjective. So, I reject the notion of fair and balanced.

JK: Or people who say that they're logical and not emotional. [*laughs*] And yet, everything that comes out of their mouths is based on emotion and fear and reactionary impulses. I think that with *Semitic Commonwealth* we stated early on, including in our promotional and dramaturgical materials, that it was not about balance and that we were consciously rejecting the idea of balance and that if you read into the choice of three Jewish playwrights and three Arab playwrights a sort of balance, or an attempt at balance, you were missing the point. *Semitic Commonwealth* was about addressing imbalance and an asymmetrical power relationship between Israelis and Palestinians. If anything, we were "off-balancing" the dominant narratives. And to Torange's point about dominant narratives, we too understand ourselves as subverting and challenging a lot of the orthodoxies that get baked into narratives that are rooted in power. I mean obviously, Malek, you directed my play *Precious Stones*, Silk Road's inaugural production, and it was premised on a kind of symmetry of voices, embodying and theatricalizing multiple perspectives, and I do know that different people left the play, thinking that it was leaning one way or another. And I was quite surprised to hear that, particularly from people who thought it leaned pro-Israel and actually thanked me for that [*laughs*], you know? Because I know that wasn't our intent. Our project was essentially an exercise in getting into the minds of people we disagree with, and people we agree with, and affording them integrity and believability and complexity and fallibility. And so, I see great value in the multiplicity of perspectives approach. I'm not interested in propaganda. I don't want to write it and I don't want to produce it. I think that when we reduce conflicts down to two overriding narratives, "I'm pro-Israel" or "I'm pro-Palestine," we do audiences a disservice, and we do a disservice to ourselves as artists who are looking to grow and learn and to expand and, you know, be somehow political and relevant in this world. Basically, I reject the whole notion of balance because it seeks to establish moral equivalency, and once again false symmetry, and allows you to skirt injustice and equivocate on power and powerlessness.

MMN: I've noticed a lot of the plays I've been finding are very much from large communities, such as Arab American, Turkish American, Iranian American, and Jewish Israeli American. But what about some of the narratives from some of the very small minoritarian groups in the Middle East? For instance, have you come across a Yazidi American play, or a Kurdish American play, or an Amazigh American play? Have you come across many of those, and why aren't they more prevalent than perhaps they are?

TY: For the first time, we produced a play by a Kurdish playwright from Turkey in ReOrient, so that was a first I would say that I know, for us. And then, the Yazidis, I mean, what, there are 5,000 Yazidis in the world? So I don't think any of them are playwrights. So part of it is just numbers and access. But I do try, I agree with you, that it's important to represent more of the Middle East, and I actively search for plays that have not, perspectives that haven't been presented at Golden Thread. For example, with Yemen, I really wanted plays that deal with Yemen or tell us something about Yemen, so I had to actively seek that out. I do have access to, for example, Assyrians, and I know we have produced an Assyrian playwright, although her play did not deal with that layer of her identity. But the smaller minorities, I think it's just a matter of numbers. Having said that, you know, for example, I haven't produced a play by a playwright from Tunisia, which I think is a major shortcoming. I mean we've done Algerian plays but not Tunisian plays so . . . I mean we've done a Moroccan play many years ago, so like Tunisia, Libya, we've never done anything about Sudan. So I would be interested in those voices for sure. It's just a matter of looking for it and actively seeking it out.

JK: First of all I would love to get my hands on an Assyrian play, and we have not really had much luck. Ironically, because Chicago has a huge Assyrian population and we feel a responsibility to tell Assyrian stories. With the Yazidis, and I do want to say there are more than 5,000 of them, but yes, it's a very small community and it's been devastated in recent years. I personally don't know of a Yazidi migration to the US, but of course there are Yazidis living in this country. And if there are Yazidi houses of worship or organizations here, I just don't know of them. We worked with a Baha'i playwright some years ago who wrote a play about her experiences as an abused wife and her eventual escape. It was an absolutely beautiful play, painful as it was, very poetic very powerful. And, you know, some members of the local Baha'i community were upset that this was the one quote, unquote "Baha'i" story that we chose to tell. So the argument was, "we're already under siege, we're already a persecuted minority, we're already . . . and now you add this to the mix?" And like I said, it's really hard to have that conversation. We made a commitment to an artist who wrote a courageous and impactful play that, organizationally speaking, won us no friends in the local Baha'i community, and won us quite a few friends in the anti-domestic violence activist community. Would we do it again? Yes. But do we want to be allies to the Baha'i community? Oh my God, absolutely. But when we align our politics and aesthetic choices with the most vulnerable in our communities, which more often than not means women and queers, we're told that we're not being allies. Once again, it's the whole dominant narrative thing.

MMN: What about collaborators, such as hiring directors, designers, and other theatre professionals? What are some of the criteria you're looking for as far as their connection to the play, and how necessary are those connections for you when hiring someone?

TY: I mean in our community we don't really have many designers that are of Middle Eastern heritage. Here and there, there may be a costume designer, or maybe we're working with an Iranian video artist now. But there aren't any, and so I've always been the one providing the cultural competency information to the designers and helping them with their research. Directors we have a few more options but again, locally, there aren't that many. So, it's difficult . . . we just don't have that many options. So, again I try to, you know, steep my director in as much cultural information as possible and really work with them closely on those aspects.

JK: I think oftentimes in the absence of a director or a design team that is somehow culturally connected to the playwright and the play, dramaturgy becomes all the more important. If you want to do justice to the story that you're telling, then you need to understand the world of that story. I mean, don't get me wrong, dramaturgy is always important, but it takes on even greater stakes when cultural knowledge, context, nuance aren't immediately available, shall we say, to many of the artists involved. I mean, you want to avoid glaring mistakes that are later called out, but even more importantly, you don't want to change or undermine the story. I think that there are all these debates, and certainly in Chicago theater and beyond, about who gets to tell whose story and why and so forth. And from the beginning we identified, we defined, a playwright-protagonist alignment, so we've always been very clear about that, it's a subjective choice on our part, it's about authorial voice, but does the "who gets to write the story" extend to who gets to direct and who gets to act and who gets to design, etcetera? And those can be very, you know, contentious and prickly conversations. They can be very hurtful conversations. And, you know, there is something to be said for a director who is culturally connected to the world of the play. There's also something to be said, particularly when you have the playwright in the room, for a director who's not culturally connected to the world of the play. And I think what oftentimes gets lost in many of these conversations, particularly these very absolutist conversations, which are, in fact, not conversations at all, is that playwriting is an empathic art and there are many ways to create and leverage and activate empathy in workshops, in production meetings, in rehearsals, in collaborative processes. And if we've managed to somehow change our non-culturally specific artistic partners, imagine what that work will do when it touches our audiences. There are plenty of great arguments to make for an all Arab or all Turkish cast and production team and there are great arguments to be made for a diverse cast and production team. Now, if there's someone involved who is trying to steer the vision of the play in directions that are somehow antithetical to the intentions of the playwright, then we don't want that person in the room. We don't want that toxicity. . . . It's kind of funny for me to hear all these heated conversations today, because back in 2003, when we started Silk Road, we weren't aware of any of these conversations taking place, in fact they may not have been taking place, and yet we were adamant that our first production, my play *Precious Stones*, be directed by an Arab American director: Malek. And that we needed a Palestinian actor to play the main Palestinian character, and a Jewish actor to play the main Jewish character and, I'll tell you, for that story and that production and for that moment in Chicago theatre, those choices were spot on. They were absolutely integral to the success of our inaugural production. . . . Now, I think when we talk about directors and designers of Middle Eastern backgrounds in Chicago, yes, they're very small pools. But they will continue to grow and frankly, we have a responsibility to assure that they grow.

TY: I would say that specifically with plays that are set in the Middle East, it becomes even more important to really dig deep and have someone in the room with cultural competency, who can provide the nuances that we may not be aware of or think about. With certain plays, if there is a specific language in the play, then it's important to have someone in the room, from my perspective if at all possible the director, but if not someone else in the room who is fluent who can address linguistic questions, not from a scholarly perspective but from an everyday life perspective. So, for example, with *We Swim, We Talk, We Go To War*, even though that wasn't really set in the Middle East, but it did have Arabic in it. And having Hala Baki in the room who is Lebanese and fluent in Lebanese-Arabic, I think that was really useful. With *Scenes from 71* Years*, Malek, having you direct, and obviously having Palestinian actors in the room, was invaluable. And with the plays that we're doing next year, they're all set in the Middle East. So it's really important to have as much cultural competency in the room as possible.

MMN: So if you have a choice between two actors, one who is extremely culturally competent to the point of speaking the language, maybe they're from the culture but they're not a "great actor," as opposed to hiring somebody who is a highly trained, highly polished actor, who do you cast? Which would you rather have playing that role?

TY: For me it's never abstract. It's always case by case, depending on the play, depending on the actor, depending on who else is in the room, who else is in the cast. I think I can't answer that theoretically. It's a very practical call, and I would make that call on a case by case basis.

JK: I'm going to agree with Torange. I will also say that we often defer to the playwright, particularly when it's a world premiere, and most of our productions have been world premieres. But, you know, that conversation, because it has shifted so much over the years, I cannot be oblivious to or ignore the arguments of those, oftentimes actors, who say "I have a right to play this role," as opposed to this other person who is not of the culture. And I cannot deny or discredit or ignore that argument. Casting in general is hard. It's complicated. It changes depending on the circumstances, who's in the room at what given time. But there is something to be said for providing opportunities for artists in our communities. And even if a particular actor is a little more "green" than this other actor who isn't Middle Eastern, we also have to take the long view, we have to think in terms of how this experience will enable this actor to grow and evolve in their craft. We need to make that investment in their future and ours. We never said we were an actor training school. That's not what we set out to be. The actors rise to the occasion when given the chance, and then some. But we have a responsibility to nurturing and cultivating Middle Eastern American artists, and to creating opportunities for them that may not otherwise be there.

TY: I would add that, as theatre companies devoted to the community, we take it as part of our responsibility to nurture talent within the community. I think that goes without saying. We often discover nascent talent within our community and nurture it and support it until they become very desirable to larger theater companies and are never available to work with us again. [*laughs*]

JK: You know, we can claim that as a contribution.

TY: Building careers of our artists in our communities is part of our mission, so we do that without reservation. But I don't subscribe to the philosophy that, because an actor is from a particular community or culture or background, they automatically are a better fit for a role. I do believe that there is something about cultural body language, about cultural knowledge, that is unspoken and unexplainable, and when you see it, you recognize it, and when it's valuable to a particular play, then that's how you should make your call, you know? So, really, I think it varies from play to play, production to production.

MMN: What about funding? It's a perpetual problem, of course, so the question is why aren't companies like yours getting the kind of massive funding that other American theater companies producing the repertoire of canonized American plays get? What have you experienced, and what do you think is behind that?

TY: We get a lot of local funding and we are grateful for the support of the local foundations and California Art Council, National Endowment for the Arts . . . I don't know, some of the larger foundations that are national, part of it I think is just budget, being even eligible for, because they have a minimum budget requirement and just being visible to them. And it doesn't help that some of the larger foundations have recently changed their guidelines and shifted away from the arts. I do think that our work is social justice and being able to make that argument in an environment where everybody's trying to make that argument [is] not an easy thing. So, I've kind of given up trying to worry about funding. I cling on to those who support us and recognize us and continue to notify other foundations of our work, just to make sure that they are aware. But, I agree that a company like Golden Thread Productions, like Silk Road Rising, should really be funded at several levels higher than we actually are and should be recognized for the community impact that we have, like what we were talking about in terms of nurturing talent, developing audiences, developing artists.

JK: Well, I think we're in really similar places, you know, and I think that our budgets are probably similar. We are fortunate, and this is the brilliance of my husband Malik [Gillani], quite frankly, to have cultivated relationships for years within the local funding community, with local philanthropic foundations, corporate foundations. So we are disproportionately reliant on foundation support, and thank God, and kudos to them, that they see the virtue and necessity of our mission. Now, do they fund us at the same levels that they may fund "mainstream" others? In many cases no, but, some foundations have been quite generous and quite consistent, and I want to give them the credit they deserve. And there will be some companies that will say, "Oh, we wish we had what Silk Road has," to which I typically respond, "Well, then, you need a Malik, and there's only one of him, so . . ." [*All laugh*] I will say that the individual giving is where we lag behind. While we certainly have individuals who donate, and some quite generously so, one donor in particular, they tend not to be from our Asian and Middle Eastern communities. But they love our mission and they love our work. That said, I do think we'd be much larger, and I think we'd have much more impact and reach, if our communities, if the Silk Road communities, were to step up and donate more generously. Unfortunately, that remains an uphill battle. Now I'm not saying that there aren't any donors from the Silk Road communities. Of course there are. But the fact that we do work that sometimes ruffles people's feathers, or makes people uncomfortable, or disrupts dominant narratives within our communities, or challenges the social status quo, has not won us friends in many quarters. And frankly, when you're a same-sex couple doing work, in part, with socially conservative and religiously conservative communities, there's a stigma attached to that work, and there's a distancing that takes place. So that is a cross to bear, so to speak. But we're here, and we're doing work that matters, and we're making a difference and we're on the map, and we continue.

MMN: Why, in your opinions, hasn't one of the playwrights you have championed, who is writing specifically about our community and the issues we face, won a Tony Award? Do you believe that it's because we haven't achieved some sort of marker in the sort of larger American theater framework that keeps us from having that critical mass that'll take us forward to the next level? Is that what's wrong? Is it just our communities aren't as engaged as they could be? What's missing?

JK: I think historically there's been a lot of fear of Middle Eastern American work that once again threatens the status quo, or challenges or questions or disrupts it. And I've often said that if one of our playwrights is going to make it to Broadway, it should be Yussef El Guindi. Now, maybe someone else would contest that. Maybe it should be Heather Raffo or Mona Mansour? And I think one of the "problems" is that Yussef's plays, with maybe a few exceptions, are really subversive and really smart and ask audiences to grapple with some pretty uncomfortable stuff. And that's what I love about his voice, that's what we all love about his voice.

TY: I think we haven't been around very long and I think Yussef [El Guindi], Heather [Raffo], Mona [Mansour], they're well on their way to hopefully make it to Broadway. But I'm hopeful. I think in my lifetime it'll happen.

MMN: Both of you have companies that have been around for decades. What's next for each of your companies going forward, in your opinion at this point?

TY: Immediately our next season celebrates the passage of the 19th Amendment and the US women getting the right to vote with three plays from the Middle East, by Middle Eastern women. A Turkish woman playwright, Lebanese woman playwright, and Iranian woman playwright. So, three countries that are very present in the US news media in this moment. So we're really excited that next year is all about women, women's voices, women's political agency. It's an election year, and I hope the next president will be a woman, so I'm very focused on that at the moment. And I'm hoping that I can retire soon. With the new generation coming up, I'm very encouraged and energized that I can pass on the torch.

JK: Well, we have been talking about moving from a season model to a festival model and to exploring what a three-play rotating rep kind of festival would look like for us. My ideal festival would have one play by a MENA American playwright, one play by an East Asian American playwright, and one play by a South Asian American playwright. That way we'd get to unite three geographic regions of the Silk Road, and I'd also want them to be plays that somehow speak to each other. So I'm increasingly attracted to the idea of turning us into an annual festival, one that would grow incrementally. In terms of the more immediate future, we're thrilled to be working with playwrights Nahal Navidar and

Yussef El Guindi in 2020, and to continue our uber popular playwriting program and short play showcases in Chicago public schools, senior centers, and the city's West Ridge neighborhood. West Ridge is one of the most ethnically, racially, religiously, linguistically, and economically diverse communities in the United States. Activists from the community invited us to partner with them to help build social cohesion through storytelling. My God, talk about a welcome learning curve! You know Torange mentions retiring, and I too think about the next chapter. I mean, I'm fifty-four years old, I think by now I have some skills and experience. [*laughs*] I do think a lot about the next generation and am mindful of the fact that the politics of many Middle Eastern American artists who are younger than us have different politics. Some of the conversations they're having are conversations we don't necessarily find ourselves in or on some level even relate to. So I do think that whatever generational shift is happening . . . . Look, we define this as our life's work, as our most significant contribution perhaps. But at the same time, I don't want to get fossilized or stuck in place. I don't want to be perceived as old, as old news gone stale. The hope is to always remain dynamic and flexible. So yes, there will be another chapter, and no, I'm not writing my Silk Road obituary for quite some time. [*laughs*]

MMN: Is there anything either of you wish to add that we haven't covered?

JK: I think one of the things . . . I'm going back to the Middle East America convening at The Lark a few years back, where it really dawned on me that we're creating these radical spaces where Turkish artists and Armenian artists, Israeli artists and Palestinian artists, Iranian artists and Arab artists, can effectively remove ourselves from the dictates of our community gatekeepers, and imagine new ways of relating to each other and of relating to history, and new ways of negotiating identity and power, where at least there's the possibility of trust, and that the really, really hard work of atonement and healing can maybe happen. It was pretty mind blowing, you know. To be in a space where we could imagine relationships beyond our prescribed enmities, our prescribed hatreds and suspicions, our distrust. And I want to be very careful and establish that I'm not calling for a colonial model in which Middle Eastern Americans save the Middle East, okay? But I am relishing these opportunities to be in MENA American spaces, where we allow ourselves to rethink and reconfigure our relationships to one another. I feel inherently connected to Arab and non-Arab peoples of the

Middle East. Regardless of whether or not we're allowed to like each other. I want to build on that potential. And Middle Eastern American, sure, it's a construct, it might even be artificial, but so are a lot of things, until we endow them with meaning and vitality and longevity. How many times have I said that the artists must lead, the storytellers must lead, and I think we're becoming an example of precisely that. I also want to say that on a local level, as Torange was speaking about the Bay Area, I think that Chicago has been absolutely critical to our success and our ability to not only dream but to realize our dreams. And being part of a theater-making ecology that is detached from Broadway and Hollywood—that isn't about "I'm gonna be cast in the next Spielberg film"—but is about taking risks and creating new work and growing and experimenting and learning. We've been able to find our place in that ecology and have been pretty much embraced by the larger community. I think we're seen as an important piece of the Chicago theater mosaic. And I'm really proud of that, and I'm really grateful for how well we've been received. And I'm not saying that we couldn't exist somewhere else. But there was this convergence of time and place and need that's worked so beautifully for us.

TY: Yeah, I would love to talk a little bit about the role of community, because in the San Francisco Bay area, we have really invested in developing relationships with community, as artists, audience members, donors. We've tried to convey this message of investing in our stories. That these are our stories and invest in them and take part in them and be a part of changing the American narrative about the Middle East. And I think that when I look back to let's say five years ago to today, I think it has made a difference and we have had some successes in building a community, both of artists and of donors, board members. Again, these are things that I think to our community, it's new, you know? Theater is not . . . in a way it's a new kind of art, which to some people is attractive because of it. But to others, maybe not. They'd rather go with music or poetry or something they have a more, a deeper cultural connection with? You know, this kind of modern theater, the realistic theater, or devised theater that has emerged in the twentieth century or late nineteenth century to now, this is new. In the Bay Area, I think we have benefited from the Iranian theater company here [the Darvag Theater Group] having developed an audience already since the 1960s. We've also benefited from the Bay Area itself being open to new ideas and being . . . and encouraging risk-taking programming. The counterculture here is very strong. So these are the elements in our environment that have supported Golden Thread over the years and have been instrumental in our ability to grow and sustain our work. So I think it's important to remind ourselves that we are not isolated. That we work within a community that gets us, and supports us, and helps us thrive. And as we thrive, the community thrives as well.

REFERENCES AND
FURTHER READING

"A Community of Many Realities." Pangea World Theater, accessed May 29, 2020, https://www.pangeaworldtheater.org/about-us.

Abboud, Victoria M. (2009a), "(Trans)Planting Cedars: The Lebanese Diaspora" in Layla Maleh (ed.), *Arab Voices in Diaspora: Critical Perspectives on Anglophone Arab Literature*, Cross/cultures; 115, 371–93. Amsterdam: Rodopi.

Abboud, Victoria M. (2009b), "(Trans)Planting Cedars: Seeking Identity, Nationality, and Culture in the Lebanese Diaspora" in Layla Al Maleh, *Arab Voices in Diaspora: Critical Perspectives on Anglophone Arab Literature*, 371–93. Amsterdam: Rodopi.

Abdoh, Reza and John Bell (1995), "'To Reach Divinity through the Act of Performance.'" *TDR* 39, no. 4 (Autumn): 48–71.

Abdoh, Reza and Gautam Dasgupta. (2018), "Theatre Beyond Space and Time." *PAJ: A Journal of Performance and Art* 40, no. 3 (September): 16–28.

"About." United States Census Bureau, census.gov.

"About Mosaic" Mosaic Theater Company, accessed May 29, 2020, https://mosaictheater.org/about.

"About." Theater J, accessed May 29, 2020, https://theaterj.org/about/.

Abusrour, Abdelfattah, Lisa Schlesinger, and Naomi Wallace. (2015), *Twenty One Positions: A Cartographic Dream of the Middle East*. New York: Broadway Play Publishing Inc.

Adjmi, David. (2015), *Stunning* in Sarah Benson (ed), *The Methuen Drama Book of New American Plays*. London: Bloomsbury.

"ADL Audit: U.S. Anti-Semitic Incidents Surged in 2016–2017." Anti-Defamation League. https://www.adl.org/sites/default/files/documents/Anti-Semitic%20Audit%20Print_vf2.pdf.

Ajyal Theater Group. http://www.ajyal.us/aboutus.html.

Aker, Melis. *Dragonflies: A Memory Play* (unpublished manuscript, April 26, 2019), Adobe Acrobat file.

Aker, Melis. *Field, Awakening* (unpublished manuscript, April 26, 2019), Adobe Acrobat file.

Aker, Melis. *Gilded Isle* (unpublished manuscript, April 26, 2019), Adobe Acrobat file.

Aker, Melis. *Manar* (unpublished manuscript, June 3, 2016), Adobe Acrobat file.

Aker, Melis. *When My Mama Was a Hittite* (unpublished manuscript, April 26, 2019), Adobe Acrobat file.

Allen-Ebrahimian, Bethany. (2017), "64 Years Later, CIA Finally Releases Details of Iranian Coup." *Foreignpolicy.com*, June 20. https://foreignpolicy.com/2017/

06/20/64-years-later-cia-finally-releases-details-of-iranian-coup-iran-tehran
-oil/.

"Alliance for Jewish Theatre Presents 2019 Chicago Conference." (2019),
Broadwayworld.com, November 19. https://www.broadwayworld.com/chicago/
article/Alliance-For-Jewish-Theatre-Presents-2019-Chicago-Conference-2019
1119.

Alsultany, Evelyn, and Ella Shohat. (2012), *Between the Middle East and the
Americas: The Cultural Politics of Diaspora*. Ann Arbor: University of Michigan.

Altschiller, Donald. "Turkish Americans." https://www.everyculture.com/multi/Sr
-Z/Turkish-Americans.html/.

Ameri, Anan. (2000), *Arab American Encyclopedia*. Detroit: U X L.

Ameri, Anan, and Holly Arida. (2007), *Etching Our Own Image: Voices from
Within the Arab American Art Movement*. Cambridge Scholars Publishing.

Anderson, Benedict R. (2006), *Imagined Communities: Reflections on the Origin
and Spread of Nationalism*. London: Verso.

Asser, Martin. (2010), "Obstacles to Arab-Israeli Peace: Palestinian Refugees." *BBC
News*, September 2.

Atefat-Peckham, Susan. (2014), *Talking Through the Door: An Anthology of
Contemporary Middle Eastern American Writing*. Syracuse: Syracuse University
Press.

Ayeesh, Farhad. (n.d.), *Suitcase/The Baggage*. Bella Warda (trans). Unpublished
manuscript.

"Background on Christians in the Middle East." (2010), *United States Conference of
Catholic Bishops*, August. http://www.usccb.org/issues-and-action/human-life-
and-dignity/global-issues/middle-east/christians-in-the-middle-east/upload/
mideast-christians-background-2010-08.pdf.

Bagatourian, Bianca, (2010), *March!* (unpublished manuscript), Adobe Acrobat File.

Bagatourian, Bianca, and Misha Shulman. (2016), "A Closer Look: Bianca
Bagatourian and Misha Shulman." *Larktheatre.org*, April 29. https://www.lar
ktheatre.org/blog/closer-look-bianca-bagatourian-and-misha-shulman/.

Bagatourian, Bianca. *March!: A Short Play Based on Armenian Genocide Oral
Histories*. www.genocidepreventionnow.org.

Bakalian, Serge. (2008), "Profile: Golden Thread Productions." *PAJ: A Journal of
Performance and Art* 1, no. 2 (Fall): 87–90.

Balgamis, A. Deniz, and Kemal H. Karpat. (2008), *Turkish Migration to the United
States: From Ottoman Times to the Present*. No. 5. Madison, WI: Center for
Turkish Studies at the University of Wisconsin.

Barone, Michael. (2017), "The Census Bureau's Dubious Proposal." *The Washington
Examiner*, March 14. http://www.washingtonexaminer.com/the-census-bureaus
-dubious-proposal/article/2617378/.

Bazian, Hatem. (2004), "Virtual Internment: Arabs, Muslims, Asians and the
War on Terrorism." *The Journal of Islamic Law and Culture* 9, no. 1 (Spring/
Summer). www.hatembazian.com/content/virtual-internment-arabs-muslims
-asians-and-the-war-on-terrorism/.

Bell, John. (1995), "AIDS and Avantgarde Classicism: Reza Abdoh's 'Quotations
from a Ruined City.'" *TDR* (1988–) 39, no. 4: 21–47. doi:10.2307/1146482.

Bell, John. (1995), "Reza Abdoh: 1963–1995." *TDR* 39, no. 4: 9. Gale Academic Onefile. https://link-gale-com.libproxy.uoregon.edu/apps/doc/A17903607/ AONE?u=euge94201&sid=AONE&xid=3b181c0d.

Benshoff, Harry M., and Sean Griffin. (2009), *America on Film: Representing Race, Class, Gender, and Sexuality at the Movies.* 2nd ed. Malden, MA: Wiley-Blackwell.

Berry, Maya. (2016), "A New MENA Category: The Reality and the Headlines." *The Hill*, October 13. http://thehill.com/blogs/congress-blog/the-administration/30 0737-a-new-mena-category-the-reality-and-the-headlines/.

Bial, Henry. (2005). *Acting Jewish: Negotiating Ethnicity on the American Stage and Screen.* Ann Arbor: University of Michigan Press.

Bolton-Fasman, Judy. (2016), "The Play's the Thing: Jewish Playwriting Contest On Stage," jewishboston.com, April 29. https://www.jewishboston.com/the-plays-t he-thing-jewish-playwriting-contest-on-stage/.

Birthright Israel. "40 Friends 10 Days A Free Israel Adventure," accessed May 30, 2020, Birthrightisrael.com.

Bryck, Danny, email message to author, June 5, 2019.

Bryck, Danny. *Quixote in Kabul* (unpublished manuscript, 2015), Adobe Acrobat file.

Bryck, Danny. *The River and the Sea* (unpublished manuscript, 2016), Adobe Acrobat file.

Buck, Leila. *Hkeelee—Talk to Me* (unpublished manuscript, November 19, 2008), Adobe Acrobat file.

Buck, Leila. *In the Crossing* (unpublished manuscript, April 30, 2010), Adobe Acrobat file.

Buck, Leila. (2014), *ISite* in Michael Malek Najjar (ed.), *Four Arab American Plays: Works by Leila Buck, Jamil Khoury, Yussef El Guindi, and Lameece Issaq & Jacob Kader.* Jefferson, NC: McFarland.

Caplan, Debra. (2018), *Yiddish Empire: The Vilna Troupe, Jewish Theater, and the Art of Itinerancy.* Ann Arbor, MI: University of Michigan Press.

Cermatori, Joseph. (2018), "Reza Abdoh Today: Posthumous Reflections Fifty-Five Years after His Birth." *PAJ: A Journal of Performance and Art* 40, no. 3 (September): 1–15.

Chow, Kat. (2017), "For Some Americans of MENA Descent, Checking a Census Box is Complicated." *NPR Code Switch: Race and Identity, Remixed*, March 11. https://www.npr.org/sections/codeswitch/2017/03/11/519548276/for-some-arab-americans-checking-a-census-box-is-complicated/.

Colleran, Jeanne M. (2012), *Theatre and War: Theatrical Responses since 1991.* New York: Palgrave Macmillan.

Considine, Allison. (2017), "Middle Eastern-American Artists Ask: Who Gets to Speak for 'The Profane'?" *American Theatre*, May 5. http://www.americantheatr e.org/2017/05/05/middle-eastern-american-artists-ask-who-gets-to-speak-for-the-profane/.

Cote, David. (2009), "David Adjmi: Will his Newest Play be Stunning?" *Time Out New York*, June 10. https://www.timeout.com/newyork/theater/david-adjmi.

Culcasi, Karen. (2010), "Constructing and Naturalizing the Middle East." *Geographical Review* 100, no. 4: 583–97.

Cummings, William. (2019), "Trump Tells Congresswomen to 'Go Back' to the 'Crime Infested Places from Which They Came.'" *Usatoday.com*, July 14. https://www.usatoday.com/story/news/politics/2019/07/14/trump-tells-congresswomen-go-back-counties-they-came/1728253001/.

Daydé, Emmanuel. (2013), "Wajdi Mouawad: The Fire This Time." *Artpress* 398, March.

Davidman, Aaron, Dylan Kussman, Erik C. Andersen, Nicole Whitaker, and Bruno Louchouarn. (2016a), *Wrestling Jerusalem*. Indiecan Entertainment.

Davidman, Aaron, Dylan Kussman, Erik C. Andersen, Nicole Whitaker, and Bruno Louchouarn. (2016b), *Wrestling Jerusalem*. CreateSpace Independent Publishing Platform.

Dine, Ranana L. (2017), "The Age of Messianic Reproduction: The Image of the Last Lubavitcher Rebbe in Chabad Theology." *Journal of the American Academy of Religion* 85, no. 3: 775–805.

"DOJ, DHS Report: Three Out of Four Individuals Convicted of International Terrorism and Terrorism-Related Offences were Foreign-Born." (2018), *The United States Department of Justice*, January 16. https://www.justice.gov/opa/pr/doj-dhs-report-three-out-four-individuals-convicted-international-terrorism-and-terrorism/.

Donovan, Sandy. (2010), *The Middle Eastern American Experience*. Minneapolis: Twenty-First Century Books.

Dossa, Parin. (2004), *Politics and Poetics of Migration: Narratives of Iranian Women from the Diaspora*. Toronto: Canadian Scholars' Press Inc.

Ehya, Hamid. (2018), "Darvag and the Theatre of Iranian Diaspora." *Ecumenica* 11, no. 2 (Fall): 55–62.

Eid, Paul. (2007), *Being Arab Ethnic and Religious Identity Building among Second Generation Youth in Montreal*. Canadian Electronic Library. Canadian Publishers Collection. Montreal: McGill-Queen's University Press.

El Guindi, Yussef. (2006), "Author's Introduction." *Back of the Throat: TheatreForum*. Summer/Fall: 29.

El Guindi, Yussef. (2019), *Back of the Throat* in Michael Malek Najjar (ed), *The Selected Works of Yussef El Guindi*. London: Methuen Drama.

El Guindi, Yussef. (2017), *Collaborator*. New York, NY: Broadway Play Publishing Inc.

El Guindi, Yussef, and Salwá Bakr. (2006), *Such a Beautiful Voice Is Sayeda's; and, Karima's City: Two One-Act Plays*. New York: Dramatists Play Service.

El Guindi, Yussef. (2014), *Jihad Jones and the Kalashnikov Babes*. New York, NY: Dramatists Play Service.

El Guindi, Yussef. (2019), *Language Rooms* in *The Selected Works of Yussef El Guindi*, ed. Michael Malek Najjar. London: Methuen Drama: 133–90.

El Guindi, Yussef. (2003), *The Monologist Suffers Her Monologue* in *Altar Magazine*, 4.

El Guindi, Yussef. (2014), *Our Enemies: Lively Scenes of Love and Combat*, in Michael Malek Najjar (ed), *Four Arab American Plays: Works by Leila Buck, Jamil Khoury, Yussef El Guindi, and Lameece Issaq & Jacob Kader*. Jefferson, NC: McFarland & Company, Publishers.

El Guindi, Yussef. (2015), *Picking Up the Scent*, in *Arab Stages* 1, no. 2 (Spring).

El Guindi, Yussef. (2019), *Pilgrims Musa and Sheri in the New World* in Michael Malek Najjar (ed), *The Selected Works of Yussef El Guindi*. London: Methuen Drama.

El Guindi, Yussef. (2019), "Rosencrantz and Guildenstern Meet Abdallah and Ahmed: Musings about Arabs and Muslims in American Theater" in Michael Malek Najjar (ed), *The Selected Works of Yussef El Guindi*. London: Methuen Drama: 311–18.

El Guindi, Yussef. (2013), *The Bird Flew In* in *Mizna* 14, no. 1: 6–10.

El Guindi, Yussef. *The Review* in *MadHat* 15.

El Guindi, Yussef. (2009), "Stage Directions for an Extended Conversation" in Pauline Kaldas and Khaled Mattawa (eds), *Dinarzad's Children: An Anthology of Contemporary Arab American Fiction*. Fayetteville: University of Arkansas Press: 183.

El Guindi, Yussef. (2010), *Ten Acrobats in an Amazing Leap of Faith* in Holly Hill and Dina A. Amin (eds), *Salaam, Peace: An Anthology of Middle Eastern-American Drama*. New York: Theatre Communications Group.

El Guindi, Yussef. (2019), *Threesome* in Michael Malek Najjar (ed), *The Selected Works of Yussef El Guindi*. London: Methuen Drama.

El Guindi, Yussef. (2015), *The Tyrant* in *Rowayat: A Literary Journal Emerging from Egypt* 4.

Eliezer, Debórah. *(dis)Place[d]* (unpublished manuscript, August 26, 2019), Adobe Acrobat file.

"Eligibility." Birthright Israel. http://taglitww.birthrightisrael.com/visitingisrael/Pages/Eligibility.aspx.

Etehad, Melissa. (2016), "The Fear That's Keeping Iranian Americans from Visiting Their Homeland." *Los Angeles Times*, December 5. latimes.com/local/lanow/la-me-in-iran-dual-citizen-arrests-20161116-story.html/.

Fadda-Conrey, Carol. (2014), *Contemporary Arab-American Literature: Transnational Reconfigurations of Citizenship and Belonging*. New York: New York University Press.

Fahmy, Kareem, Evren Odcikin, Megan Sandberg-Zakian, and Pirronne Yousefzadeh, E-mail interview with Michael Malek Najjar, December 2019.

Fa'ik, Ala. (1994), "Issues of Identity: In Theater of Immigrant Community" in Michael W. Suleiman (ed), *Arabs in America: Building a New Future*. Philadelphia: Temple University Press.

Fallon, Kevin. (2019), "Mena Massoud: After 'Aladdin' Made $1Billion, I Still Couldn't Get an Audition." *Daily Beast*, December 16. https://www.thedailybeast.com/mena-massoud-after-aladdin-made-dollar1-billion-i-still-couldnt-get-an-audition.

Farah, Laila. (2005), "Dancing on the Hyphen: Performing Diasporic Subjectivity." *Modern Drama* 48, no. 2: 316–43.

Farah, Laila. (2002), "Living in the Hyphen-Nation." *Counterpoints*, January 169: 179–95.

Farfan, Penny, and Lesley Ferris. (2013), *Contemporary Women Playwrights: Into the Twenty-first Century*. New York: Palgrave Macmillan.

Farhoud, Abla. (1996), *Game of Patience*, trans. Jill Mac Dougall in Françoise
 Kourilsky and Valérie Vidal (eds), *Plays by Women: An International Anthology,
 Book Three*. New York: Ubu Repertory Theater.
Farhoud, Abla. (1994), *Game of Patience*. Translated by Jill MacDougall, in *Plays
 by Women. Book Two: An International Anthology*. New York: Ubu Repertory
 Theater.
Faris and Yamna Naff Arab-American Collection, Archives Center, National
 Museum of American History, Smithsonian Institution.
Feldman, L M. *A People: A Mosaic Play* (unpublished manuscript, March 7, 2019),
 Adobe Acrobat file.
Fleishman, Jeffrey. (2016), "Forget Playing Terrorist No. 3. Middle Eastern Actors
 Seek Roles Beyond Hollywood Stereotypes." *Latimes.com*, August 5. https://ww
 w.latimes.com/entertainment/movies/la-ca-mn-middle-eastern-actors-2016
 0727-snap-story.html/.
Fletcher, Gregory. (2011), "Off Broadway Interview: Sinan Ünel—Writer and Director
 of *A Mad Person's Chronicle of a Miserable Marriage.*" *stageandcinema.com*,
 November 16. https://www.stageandcinema.com/2011/11/16/sinan-unel-interview/.
Fractured Atlas, website. http://www.fracturedatlas.org.
Friedman, Lauren F. (2010), "A Peaceful Coexistence Remains, Despite Student
 Turnover." *Forward*, August 18. https://forward.com/culture/130141/a-peaceful
 -coexistence-remains-despite-student-tur/.
Furlanetto, Elena. (2017), *Towards Turkish American Literature: Narratives of
 Multiculturalism in Post-Imperial Turkey*. New York: Peter Lang.
Furlanetto, Elena. (2016), "'Resident Aliens': Locating Turkish American Literature
 Beyond Hyphenated American Fiction." *Amerikastudien / American Studies* 61,
 no. 2: 181–202. www.jstor.org/stable/44982286.
Gabler, Neal. (1988), *An Empire of Their Own: How the Jews Invented Hollywood*.
 New York: Crown Publishers.
Girmay, Weenta. (2010), "Jennifer Jajeh and I Heart Hamas." *Pittsburgh City Paper*,
 October 20. https://www.pghcitypaper.com/Blogh/archives/2010/10/20/jenni
 fer-jajeh-and-i-heart-hamas/.
Goldberg, Jill. (2014), "The Art of Revolution: The River and the Sea, A
 Documentary Play by Danny Bryck." *Tikkun Daily*, April 10. https://www.tik
 kun.org/tikkundaily/2014/04/10/the-art-of-revolution-the-river-and-the-sea-a
 -documentary-play-by-danny-bryck/#more-46882.
Golden Thread Productions. http://goldenthread.org/about/history/
Goldman-Sherman, Emma. *Abraham's Daughters* (unpublished manuscript,
 November 22, 2019), Adobe Acrobat file.
Gonzalez, Mike. (2017), "Conservatives Must Understand the Role of 2020 Census
 in Government Bloat." *The Hill*, December 10. http://thehill.com/opinion/cam
 paign/364115-conservatives-must-understand-the-role-of-2020-census-in-
 government-bloat/.
Goodstein, Laurie. (2017), "New Israel Law Bars Foreign Critics From Entering the
 Country." *The New York Times*, March 7. https://www.nytimes.com/2017/03/07/
 world/middleeast/israel-knesset-vote-boycott-bds-reform-judaism.html.

Grabowski, John J. (2008), "Forging New Links in the Early Turkish Migration Chain: The U.S. Census and Early Twentieth Century Ships' Manifests" in A. Deniz Balgamiş and Kemal H. Karpat (eds), *Turkish Migration to the United States: From Ottoman Times to the Present*. Madison: The Center for Turkish Studies at the University of Wisconsin and the University of Wisconsin Press.

Grassian, Daniel. (2013), *Iranian and Diasporic Literature in the 21st Century: A Critical Study*. Jefferson, NC: McFarland.

Green, Emma. (2019), "The Impossible Future of Christians in the Middle East." *The Atlantic*, May 23. https://www.theatlantic.com/international/archive/2019/05/iraqi-christians-nineveh-plain/589819/.

Greenblatt, Natasha. (2016), *The Peace Maker* in Stephen Orlov and Samah Sabawi (eds), *Double Exposure: Plays of the Jewish and Palestinian Diasporas*. Toronto: Playwrights Canada Press.

Greene, Sevan K. *This Time* (unpublished manuscript, April 29, 2016), Adobe Acrobat file.

Gualtieri, Sarah M. A. (2009), *Between Arab and White Race and Ethnicity in the Early Syrian American Diaspora*. Berkeley: University of California Press.

Guzman, Richard. (2016), "Arab-American Theater Group Pokes Fun at Everyday Life." *Press Telegram*, November 23. https://www.presstelegram.com/2016/11/23/arab-american-theater-group-pokes-fun-at-everyday-life/.

Haddad, Kathy. *Zafira and the Resistance* (unpublished manuscript, May 9, 2019), Adobe Acrobat file.

Hamami, Tariq. *Smail* (unpublished manuscript, November 11, 2019), Adobe Acrobat file.

Hashemi, Seyed Afshin. (2002), *The Anniversary Present: A Soliloquy* (unpublished manuscript, July 2002), Adobe Acrobat file.

Hashemi, Seyed Afshin. (2014), *Flying into Darkness*. Buna Alkhas (trans) Tehran: Afraz Publications.

Hashemi, Seyed Afshin. (2011), *Four Scenes of One Play*, Ayeh Solouki, Mehrnoush Hamzelouian, and Afshin Hashemi (trans), (unpublished manuscript), Adobe Acrobat file.

Hashemi, Seyed Afshin. (2014), *Hassan and the Giant/The Narrow Mountain Pass*, Buna Alkhas (trans), (unpublished manuscript, November 15, 2014), Adobe Acrobat file.

Hashemi, Seyed Afshin. *The Most Honest Murderer of the World: A Soliloquy* (unpublished manuscript, 1996), Adobe Acrobat file.

Hashemi, Seyed Afshin. *Speech* (unpublished manuscript, September 16, 2009), Adobe Acrobat file.

Haslam, Nick. (2017). "Cultures Fuse and Connect, So We Should Embrace Polyculturalism." *The Conversation*, June 6. https://theconversation.com/cultures-fuse-and-connect-so-we-should-embrace-polyculturalism-78876.

Hassanpour, Amir. (2005), "Kurds" in Dinah L. Shelton (ed), *Encyclopedia of Genocide and Crimes Against Humanity*, Vol. 2. Macmillan Reference USA: 632–7. Gale Ebooks. https://link.gale.com/apps/doc/CX3434600213/GVRL?u=euge94201&sid=GVRL&xid=2929ca98. Accessed November 25, 2019.

References and Further Reading

"Hate Crimes & Discrimination Issue Brief." *Arab American Institute*. http://www
.aaiusa.org/aai_issue_brief_hate_crimes#_ftn2/.

Hill, Holly. (2009), "Middle Eastern American Theatre: History, Playwrights and
Plays." http://inclusioninthearts.org/projects/middle-eastern-american-theatre
-history-playwrights-and-plays/.

Hill, Holly, and Dina A. Amin. (2009), *Salaam, Peace: An Anthology of Middle
Eastern-American Drama*. New York: Theatre Communications Group.

"Historical Overview." Archives of Baháʼí Persecution in Iran, accessed May 30,
2020, https://iranbahaipersecution.bic.org/historical-overview.

"History." New Arab American Theater Works, accessed May 29, 2020, https://ww
w.newarabamericantheaterworks.org/history.

"History." New York Arab American Comedy Festival, accessed May 28, 2020,
http://arabcomedy.com/pages/history.

Hondius, A.J., et al. (2000), "Health Problems among Latin-American and Middle-
Eastern Refugees in The Netherlands: Relations with Violence Exposures
and Ongoing Sociopsychological Strain." *Journal of Traumatic Stress* 13, no. 4
(October): 619–34.

Hooglund, Eric J., ed. (1987), *Crossing the Waters: Arabic-Speaking Immigrants to
the United States Before 1940*. Washington, DC: Smithsonian Institution Press.

Houssami, Eyad. (2012), *Doomed by Hope: Essays on Arab Theatre*. London: Pluto
Press.

Huffman, Elizabeth. *Not My Revolution* (unpublished manuscript, January 15,
2019), Adobe Acrobat file.

Ibrahim, Denmo. *Baba* (unpublished manuscript, December 20, 2019), Adobe
Acrobat file.

Ibrahim, Denmo. (2020), "Gathering to Define Community: On the National
Convening for Artists of Middle Eastern, North African, and Southwest Asian
Descent." Howlround.com, March 5. https://howlround.com/gathering-define-
community.

"Incidents and Offenses." *FBI*: UCR. https://ucr.fbi.gov/hate-crime/2015/topic-pag
es/incidentsandoffenses_final.

İpek, Nedim, and K. Tuncer Çağlayan, eds. (2008), "The Emigration from the
Ottoman Empire to America" in A. Deniz Balgamiş and Kemal H. Karpat (eds),
Turkish Migration to the United States: From Ottoman Times to the Present.
Madison: The Center for Turkish Studies at the University of Wisconsin and
the University of Wisconsin Press: 29–43.

Issaq, Lameece and Jacob Kader. (2014), *Food and Fadwa* in *Four Arab American
Plays: Works by Leila Buck, Jamil Khoury, Yussef El Guindi, and Lameece Issaq &
Jacob Kader*, ed. Michael Malek Najjar. Jefferson, NC: McFarland.

Irani, Kayhan. *There is a Portal: A Solo Show* (unpublished manuscript, December
31, 2018), Adobe Acrobat file.

Irani, Kayhan. *We've Come Undone* (unpublished manuscript, 2003), Adobe
Acrobat file.

Jacobs, Louis. (1999), "Lubavitch" in *A Concise Companion to the Jewish Religion*.
Oxford University Press. https://www.oxfordreference.com/view/10.1093/acref
/9780192800886.001.0001/acref-9780192800886-e-417.

Jacobs, Louis. "Lubavitch." *Oxford Reference*, Accessed May 29, 2020. https://www
.oxfordreference.com/view/10.1093/oi/authority.20110803100117426.

Jajeh, Jennifer. *I Heart Hamas: And Other Things I'm Afraid to Tell You*
(unpublished manuscript, May 21, 2013), Adobe Acrobat file.

"Jewish Play Project Announces 2020 Top Seven Plays; Starts National Tour."
(2020), *Broadway World*, January 21. https://www.broadwayworld.com/off-off
-broadway/article/Jewish-Plays-Project-Announces-2020-Top-Seven-Plays-Sta
rts-National-Tour-20200121.

Joelle, Lindsay. *TRAYF* (unpublished manuscript, December 9, 2019), Adobe
Acrobat file.

Joelle, Lindsay. E-mail message to author, November 28, 2019.

Joseph, Rohit. (2019), "Play with Blackface Cancelled in Surrey, B.C., After
Complaints." *cbc.ca*, November 1. https://www.cbc.ca/news/canada/british-c
olumbia/surrey-double-trouble-1.5345465.

Kaissar, Ken. (2014), *The Victims or What Do You Want Me to Do About It?* in
Jamil Khoury, Michael Malek Najjar, and Corey Pond (eds), *Six Plays of the
Israeli-Palestinian Conflict*, 177–225. Jefferson, NC: McFarland.

Kaplan, Debra. (2018), *Yiddish Empire: The Vilna Troupe, Jewish Theater, and the
Art of Itinerancy*. Ann Arbor: University of Michigan Press.

Karim, Persis M., and Nasrin Rahimieh. (2008), "Introduction: Writing Iranian
Americans into the American Literature Canon." *MELUS* 33, no. 2, *Iranian
American Literature* (Summer): 7–16.

Kaye/Kantrowitz, Melanie. (2007), *The Colors of Jews: Racial Politics and Radical
Diasporism*. Bloomington: Indiana University Press.

Kayyali, Randa A. (2006), *The Arab Americans. New Americans*. Westport, CT:
Greenwood Press.

Kelley, Robin D.G. (1999), "Polycultural Me." *The UTNE Reader*, September–
October. https://www.utne.com/politics/the-people-in-me/.

Khalidi, Ismail. (2016), *Sabra Falling* in Stephen Orlov and Samah Sabawi (eds),
Double Exposure: Plays of the Jewish and Palestinian Diasporas. Toronto:
Playwrights Canada Press.

Khalidi, Ismail. (2018), *Tennis in Nablus* in Jamil Khoury, Michael Malek Najjar,
and Corey Pond (eds), *Six Plays of the Israeli-Palestinian Conflict*. Jefferson, NC:
McFarland.

Khalidi, Ismail. *Truth Serum Blues* (unpublished manuscript, May 12, 2009),
Adobe Acrobat file.

Khalidi, Ismail and Naomi Wallace. 2015, "Preface" in *Inside/Outside: Six Plays
from Palestine and the Diaspora*, ed. Naomi Wallace and Ismail Khalidi. New
York: Theatre Communications Group.

Khazem, Taous Claire. *In Algeria They Know My Name*, (unpublished manuscript,
September 14, 2019), Adobe Acrobat file.

Khoury, Jamil. (2015), "MULTI MEETS POLY: Multiculturalism and
Polyculturalism Go on a First Date." YouTube video, 33:56, January 21. https://
youtu.be/lBJqAoYYw4E.

Khoury, Jamil. *Mosque Alert* (unpublished manuscript, July 18, 2016), Adobe
Acrobat file.

Khoury, Jamil. (2012), "Not Quite White: Arabs, Slavs, and the Contours of Contested Whiteness." YouTube video, 24:08, February 26. https://youtu.be/vHmbI2mnuwU.

Khoury, Jamil. (2013), "Towards an Arab American Theatre Movement." *Howlround .com*, August 18. https://howlround.com/towards-arab-american-theater-movement.

Khoury, Jamil, Michael Malek Najjar, and Corey Pond, eds. (2018), *Six Plays of the Israeli-Palestinian Conflict*. Jefferson, NC: McFarland.

Khoury, Jamil, and Torange Yeghiazarian. (2017), "Middle Eastern American Theatre, on Our Terms." *American Theatre*, September 29. http://www.amer icantheatre.org/2017/09/29/middle-eastern-american-theatre-on-our-terms/.

Khoury, Jamil, and Torange Yeghiazarian. Interview with Michael Malek Najjar. Skype Interview. December 23, 2019.

Khoury, Raja G. (2003), *Arabs in Canada Post 9/11*. Toronto: G•7 Books.

King, Charles. (2014), *Midnight at the Pera Palace: The Birth of Modern Istanbul*. New York: W.W. Norton and Company.

Kläger, Florian, and Klaus Stierstorfer, eds. (2015), *Diasporic Constructions of Home and Belonging*. Berlin: De Gruyter.

Knopf, Robert, and Julia Listengarten, eds. (2011), *Theater of the Avant-Garde 1950–2000: A Critical Anthology*. New Haven: Yale University Press.

Krasinski, Jennifer. (2018), "Loosed Threads: Jennifer Krasinski on the Art of Reza Abdoh." *Artforum International* 57, no. 2: 160–70.

Lababidi Buck, Hala. (2019), *Bridge Between Worlds: A Lebanese-Arab-American Woman's Journey*. Washington, DC: New Academia Publishing.

Laschinger, Verena. (2016), "An Introduction to Turkish-American Literature." *Amerikastudien / American Studies* 61, no. 2: 113–19. www.jstor.org/stable /44982282.

Lazour, Daniel, and Patrick Lazour. *We Live In Cairo* (unpublished manuscript, December 12, 2019), Adobe Acrobat file.

"Lebanon's Palestinian Refugees." (2009), *www.aljazeera.com*, June 4. http://www .aljazeera.com/focus/2009/05/2009527115531294628.html/.

"Lebanon 2017 International Religious Freedom Report: Executive Summary." *U.S. Department of State*. https://www.state.gov/wp-content/uploads/2019/01/Le banon-2.pdf.

Lederhendler, Eli. (2017), *American Jewry: A New History*. Cambridge: Cambridge University Press.

Lerner, Motti. (2015), "Playwriting as Resistance to War" in Domnica Radulescu (ed), *Theater of War and Exile: Twelve Playwrights, Directors and Performers from Eastern Europe and Israel*. Jefferson, NC: McFarland.

Lindencrona, F., et al. (2008), "Mental Health of Recently Resettled Refugees from the Middle East in Sweden: The Impact of Pre-resettlement Trauma, Resettlement Stress and Capacity to Handle Stress." *Social Psychiatry and Psychiatric Epidemiology* 43, no. 2 (February): 121–31.

Lis, Jonathan, Jack Khoury, and Sharon Pulwer. (2016), "Israel's Nationalistic 'Loyalty in Culture' Bill Passes Legal Test." *Haaretz*, February 25. https://ww w.haaretz.com/israel-news/.premium-culture-loyalty-bill-gets-ags-qualified-okay-1.5409115.

Maghbouleh, Neda. (2017), *The Limits of Whiteness: Iranian Americans and the Everyday Politics of Race*. Stanford: Stanford University Press.

Mahjar program. (1996). http://www.elnil.org/Mahjar.html.

Maleh, Ghassan, and Don Rubin, eds. (2000), *The Arab World*. London: Routledge.

Marvasti, Amir B., and Karyn D. McKinney. (2004), *Middle Eastern Lives in America*. Lanham: Rowman & Littlefield Publishers.

Mayer, Jane. (2007), "The Black Sites: A Rare Look Inside the C.I.A.'s Secret Interrogation Program." *New Yorker*, August 13.

Micallef, Roberta. (2004), "Turkish Americans: Performing Identities in a Transnational Setting." *Journal of Muslim Minority Affairs* 24, no. 2 (October): 233–42.

Miller, Daryl H. (1993), "Through Music, 'Ghurba' Helps Audience Find Its Way Home." *Daily News*, September 18. http://cornerstone.pbworks.com/w/page/16 506935/GHURBA#ArticlesReviewsandotherLinks/.

Milner, Arthur. (2012), *Two Plays About Israel/Palestine*. Bloomington, IN: iUniverse.

"Mission." Noor Theatre, accessed May 29, 2020, http://www.noortheatre.org/about.

Modirzadeh, Leyla. *Lubbock or Leave It!* (unpublished manuscript, September 27, 2019), Adobe Acrobat file.

Mondalek, Najee. (2013), *Me No Terrorist = Ana mush irhābīyah*. Houston: Worldwide distribution by Voice for Music Production, Inc.

Mondalek, Najee. (1995), *Ibtasim anta fī Amīrikā = Smile, you're in America*. Houston: Worldwide distribution by Voice for Music Production, Inc.

Morrow, Martin. (2008), "Wajdi Mouawad Discusses Scorched, His Searing Play about the Lebanese War." *CBC News*, September 19, 2008. https://www.cbc.ca/n ews/entertainment/hot-topic-1.701170.

Moses, Itamar, and David Yazbek. (2018), *The Band's Visit*. New York: Theatre Communications Group.

Mossalli, Marriam. (2010), "Arab Humor Hits NYC." *Arabnews.com*, May 5. http://arabcomedy.com/pages/press/.

Mufson, Daniel. (1999), *Reza Abdoh*. Baltimore: Johns Hopkins University Press.

Murphy, Maureen Clare. (2018), "Israel Destroys Gaza Cultural Center." *The Electronic Intifada*, August 10. https://electronicintifada.net/blogs/maureen-clare-murphy/israel-destroys-gaza-cultural-center.

Myers, Steven Lee. (1992), "Syrian Jews Find Haven in Brooklyn." *New York Times*, May 23. Gale Academic Onefile. https://link.gale.com/apps/doc/A174852201/AONE?u=euge94201&sid=AONE&xid=efa8bbc7.

Naber, Nadine. (2012), *Arab America: Gender, Cultural Politics, and Activism*. New York: New York University Press.

Naff, Alixa. (1985), *Becoming American: The Early Arab Immigrant Experience*. M.E.R.I. Special Studies. Carbondale: Southern Illinois University Press.

Najjar, Michael Malek. (2015), *Arab American Drama, Film and Performance: A Critical Study, 1908 to the Present*. Jefferson, NC: McFarland.

Najjar, Michael Malek. (2014), Email interview with Maha Chehlaoui, March 27.

Najjar, Michael Malek. (2013), *Four Arab American Plays: Works by Leila Buck, Jamil Khoury, Yussef El Guindi, and Lameece Issaq & Jacob Kader*. Jefferson, NC: McFarland.

Najjar, Michael Malek. (2019), *The Selected Works of Yussef El Guindi: Back of the Throat, Our Enemies: Lively Scenes of Love and Combat, Language Rooms, Pilgrims Musa and Sheri in the New World, Threesome*. London: Methuen Drama.

Najjar, Michael Malek. (2004), "Writing from the Hyphen: Arab American Playwrights Struggle with Identity in the Post-9/11 World." *Gale eNewsletters Arts & Humanities Community News*, September 2004. http://www.silkroadr ising.org/news/writing-from-the-hyphen-arab-american-playwrights-struggle -with-identity-in-the-post-911-world.

Naujoks, Daniel. (2010), "Diasporic Identities - Reflections on Transnational Belonging." *Diaspora Studies* 3 (1) (January): 1–21. http://libproxy.uoregon.edu /login?url=https://search.proquest.com/docview/862580266?accountid=14698.

Noor Theatre. "Obie Grant Award Acceptance Speech 2016." YouTube, 26 May 2016. https://youtu.be/0RvTKFC5pJ4.

Novick, Julius. (2008), *Beyond the Golden Door: Jewish American Drama and Jewish American Experience*. New York: Palgrave Macmillan.

Nu'aima, Miḫā'īl. (1974), *Kahlil Gibran: His Life and His Work*. Beirut: Naufal Publishers.

"'Oasis in Manhattan' Premieres Wednesday." (1965), *Los Angeles Times*, October 31. ProQuest Historical Newspapers: Los Angeles Times (1881–1989): B44.

Orlov, Stephen. (2016), *Sperm Count* in Stephen Orlov and Samah Sabawi (eds), *Double Exposure: Plays of the Jewish and Palestinian Diasporas*. Toronto: Playwrights Canada Press.

Oshagan, Vahé. (1986), "Literature of the Armenian Diaspora." *World Literature Today* 60, no. 2, *Literatures of the Middle East: A Fertile Crescent* (Spring): 224–8.

"Our History." Silk Road Rising, accessed May 29, 2020, https://www.silkroadrising .org/our-history/#our-history.

Ozieblo, Bárbara, and Noelia Hernando-Real. (2012), *Performing Gender Violence: Plays by Contemporary American Women Dramatists*. New York: Palgrave Macmillan.

Palti Negev, Stav. *Salim Salim* (unpublished manuscript, January 23, 2019), Adobe Acrobat file.

Palti Negev, Stav. *Elsewhere: A Play for an Audience of One* (unpublished manuscript, December 2, 2018), Adobe Acrobat file.

Parlakian, Nishan. (2004), *Contemporary Armenian American Drama: An Anthology of Ancestral Voices*. New York: Columbia University Press.

Patel, Faiza. (2018), "Why the Trump Administration is Trying to Make Muslim Immigrants Seem Dangerous." *The Washington Post*, January 29. https://www .washingtonpost.com/news/posteverything/wp/2018/01/29/why-the-trump-a dministration-is-trying-to-make-muslim-immigrants-seem-dangerous/?hpid =hp_hp-cards_hp-posteverything%3Ahomepage%2Fcard&utm_term=.6f e3c7e78480/.

Pfeiffer, Sacha. (2019), "Guantánamo Court and Prison Have Cost Billions; Whistleblower Alleges 'Gross' Waste." NPR, September 11, https://www.opb .org/news/article/npr-guantnamo-court-and-prison-have-cost-billions-whistle blower-alleges-gross-waste/.

Pinsker, Sanford. (2000), "The Mitzvah Tank and the Parking Ticket." *Midstream* 46, no. 4: 32.

"Police Identify Army Veteran as Wisconsin Temple Shooting Suspect." (2012), *CNN.com*, August 7. https://www.cnn.com/2012/08/06/us/wisconsin-temple -shooting/index.html.

Pontifex, John. (2020), "The End of Iraqi Christianity?" *Catholic Herald*, January 16. https://catholicherald.co.uk/the-end-of-iraqi-christianity/.

Poole, Ralph J. (2016), "'Built for Europeans Who Came on the Orient Express': Queer Desires of Extravagant Strangers in Sinan Ünel's "Pera Palas"." *Amerikastudien / American Studies* 61, no. 2: 159–80. www.jstor.org/stable /44982285.

Prashad, Vijay. (2001), *Everybody Was Kung Fu Fighting: Afro-Asian Connections and the Myth of Cultural Purity*. Boston: Beacon Press.

Pultar, Gönül, Louis Mazzari, and Belma Ötüş Baskett, eds. (2019), *The Turkish-American Conundrum: Immigrants and Expatriates between Politics and Culture*. Cambridge: Cambridge Scholars Publishing.

Regencia, Ted. (2018), "Chemical Attacks on Iran: When the US Looked the Other Way." *Aljazeera.com*, April 19. https://www.aljazeera.com/news/2018/04/c hemical-attacks-iran-180415122524733.html.

Raffo, Heather. *Noura* (unpublished manuscript, October 18, 2018), MS Word file.

Raffo, Heather. (2006), *Heather Raffo's 9 Parts of Desire*. Evanston, IL: Northwestern University Press.

Rida, Rashad. (2003), "From Cultural Authenticity to Social Relevance: The Plays of Amin al-Rihani, Kahlil Gibran, and Karim Alrawi" in Sherifa Zuhur (ed), *Colors of Enchantment: Theater, Dance, Music, and the Visual Arts of the Middle East*. Cairo: The American University of Cairo Press.

Roald, Anne-Sofie. (2011), *Religious Minorities in the Middle East: Domination, Self-Empowerment, Accommodation*. Leiden: BRILL. ProQuest Ebook Central.

Rohter, Larry. (2011), "Behind the Persian Veil: Theater Illuminating the Iranian Experience." *The New York Times*, March 2. https://www.nytimes.com/2011/03 /03/theater/03festival.html.

Ronson, Jon. (2015), "You May Know Me from Such Roles as Terrorist #4." *GQ*, July 27. https://www.gq.com/story/muslim-american-typecasting-hollywood.

Ross, Steven J., Saba Soomekh, and Lisa Ansell, eds. (2016), *Sephardi and Mizrahi Jews in America: An Annual Review of the Casden Institute for the Study of the Jewish Role in American Life*. West Lafayette, IN: Purdue University Press for the USC Casden Institute for the Study of the Jewish Role in American Life.

Rozik, Eli. (2013), *Jewish Drama & Theatre*. Eastbourne: Sussex Academic Press.

Sabawi, Samah. (2016), *Tale of a City by the Sea* in Stephen Orlov and Samah Sabawi (eds), *Double Exposure: Plays of the Jewish and Palestinian Diasporas*. Toronto: Playwrights Canada Press.

References and Further Reading

Sabry, Somaya Sami. (2011), *Arab-American Women's Writing and Performance: Orientalism, Race and the Idea of the Arabian Nights*. London: I.B. Tauris.

Said, Edward W., Charles Bruce, and Jimmy Michael. (1998), *In Search of Palestine*. Princeton, NJ: Films for the Humanities & Sciences.

Said, Edward W. (1994), *Orientalism*. New York: Pantheon.

Said, Edward W. (2000), "Reflections on Exile" in *Reflections on Exile and Other Essays*. Cambridge: Harvard University Press.

Said, Edward W. (1970), "The Arab Portrayed" in Ibrahim A. Abu-Lughod (ed), *The Arab-Israeli Confrontation of June 1967: An Arab Perspective*. Evanston, IL: Northwestern University Press.

Said, Najla. (2013), *Looking for Palestine: Growing Up Confused in an Arab-American Family*. New York: Riverhead Books.

Salaita, Steven. (2007), *Arab American Literary Fictions, Cultures, and Politics*. 1st ed. American Literature Readings in the 21st Century. New York: Palgrave Macmillan.

Salem, Lori Anne. (1999), "Far-Off and Fascinating Things: Wadeeha Atiyeh and the Images of Arabs in the American Popular Theater, 1930–1950" in Michael W. Suleiman (ed), *Arabs in America: Building a New Future*. Philadelphia: Temple University Press.

Sayed, Hala. (2016), "The Power of Transformation in Denmo Ibrahim's *BABA*: A One Woman Show Journey into Family, Faith and Freedom." *Annals of the Faculty of Arts, Ain Shams University* 44 (January–March): 617–38.

Sayrafiezadeh, Saïd. *Autobiography of a Terrorist* (unpublished manuscript, February 8, 2017), Adobe Acrobat file.

Schiff, Ellen, ed. (1996), "Introduction" in *Fruitful & Multiplying: 9 Contemporary Plays from the American Jewish Repertoire*. New York: Mentor.

Selim, Yasser Fouad. (2014), "Arab American Theatre Caught in Censorship: A Study of Betty Shamieh's *Roar* and *The Black Eyed*." *International Journal of Humanities and Social Science* 4, no. 3 (February): 81–8.

Semmerling, Tim Jon. (2006), *"Evil" Arabs in American Popular Film: Orientalist Fear*. Austin, TX: University of Texas Press.

Sevahn Nichols, Adriana. *Night Over Erzinga* (unpublished manuscript, April 2016), Adobe Acrobat file.

Sevahn Nichols, Adriana. (2015), "To Armenia with Love and Loss: Writing a Play about Ancestors Consumed by an Atrocity Became an Unexpected Passport to a Homecoming." *American Theatre* 32, no. 8: 134.

Seyhan, Azade. (2001), *Writing Outside the Nation*. Princeton, NJ: Princeton University Press.

Shaheen, Jack G. (2008), *Guilty: Hollywood's Verdict on Arabs After 9/11*. Northampton: Olive Branch Press.

Shaheen, Jack G. (2001), *Reel Bad Arabs: How Hollywood Vilifies a People*. New York: Olive Branch Press.

Shaheen, Jack G. (2003), "Reel Bad Arabs: How Hollywood Vilifies a People." *Annals of the American Academy of Political and Social Science* 588, no. 1: 171–93.

Shamieh, Betty. (2003), "Lives I Could Not Have Led." *American Theatre*, July/
August 20: 6; ProQuest Direct Complete.

Shamieh, Betty. (2005), *Roar*. New York: Broadway Play Publishing.

Sheikh, Irum. (2011), *Detained Without Cause: Muslims' Stories of Detention and
Deportation in America After 9/11*. New York: Palgrave Macmillan.

Sherman, Jason. (2006), *Modern Jewish Plays*. Toronto, ON: Playwrights Canada Press.

Shulman, Misha. *Apricots: A Comedy* (unpublished manuscript, 2008), Adobe
Acrobat file.

Shulman, Misha. *Desert Sunrise: A Tragedy with (Some) Hope* (unpublished
manuscript, May 22, 2019), Adobe Acrobat file.

Shulman, Misha. *Martyrs Street* (unpublished manuscript, May 24, 2019), Adobe
Acrobat file.

Stayton, Richard. (1993), "THEATER: Never More Than a Stranger: Playwright
Shishir Kurup is Constantly Grappling with Identity and Roots. His New Work
Sheds Light on the Lives and Concerns of the Little-known Arab Community
in L.A.." *Los Angeles Times*, September 5. https://www.latimes.com/archives/la
-xpm-1993-09-05-ca-31979-story.html.

Suleiman, Michael W. (2006), *The Arab-American Experience in the United States and
Canada: A Classified, Annotated Bibliography*. Ann Arbor, MI: Pierian Press.

Syler, Claire, and Daniel Banks. (2019), *Casting a Movement: The Welcome Table
Initiative*. Abingdon, Oxon; New York, NY: Routledge, an Imprint of the Taylor
& Francis Group.

Tehranian, John. (2010), *Whitewashed: America's Invisible Middle Eastern Minority*.
New York: New York University Press.

"The 'Arab Spring': Five Years On." Amnesty International. https://www.amnesty.
org/en/latest/campaigns/2016/01/arab-spring-five-years-on/. Accessed January
10, 2018.

"The Empowerment of Hate: Civil Rights Report 2017." Council on American-
Islamic Relations 2017, 2. http://www.islamophobia.org//images/2017Civil
RightsReport/2017-Empowerment-of-Fear-Final.pdf.

Tirosh-Polk, Zohar. *Six* (unpublished manuscript, 2018), Adobe Acrobat file.

Tirosh-Polk, Zohar. (2014), *The Zionists* in Jamil Khoury, Michael Malek Najjar,
and Corey Pond (eds), *Six Plays of the Israeli-Palestinian Conflict*. Jefferson, NC:
McFarland.

Troper, Harold. (2010), *The Defining Decade: Identity, Politics, and The Canadian
Jewish Community in the 1960s*. Toronto: University of Toronto Press.

Turnbull, Lornet. (2019), "Why Young Jews Are Detouring from Israel to
Palestine." *Yesmagazine.org*, May 28. https://www.yesmagazine.org/issue/travel
/2019/05/28/israel-palestine-young-jewish-activists-birthright/.

Ünel, Sinan. (2015), *Pera Palas*. CreateSpace Independent Publishing Platform.

Ünel, Sinan. *The Cry of the Reed* (unpublished manuscript, September 17, 2012),
Adobe Acrobat file.

Urquhart, Conal. (2011). "Juliano Mer-Khamis: A Killing Inspired by Drama, not
Politics." *The Guardian*, April 21. https://www.theguardian.com/world/2011/apr
/21/jenin-grievances-death-juliano-mer-khamis.

Virtusio, Jessi (2015), "'Ghashee w Mashee' Offers Look at Arab-American Life." *Chicago Tribune*, November 11. https://www.chicagotribune.com/suburbs/d aily-southtown/ct-sta-ghashee-gsu-st-1113-20151111-story.html/.

Voice of America. http://www.voanews.com.

Watkins, Eli, and Abby Phillips. (2018). "Trump Decries Immigrants from 'Shithole Countries' Coming to US." *Cnn.com.*, January 12. https://www.cnn .com/2018/01/11/politics/immigrants-shithole-countries-trump/index.html/.

"Welcome to BIHE." The Bahá'í Institute for Higher Education, accessed May 27, 2020, http://bihe.org/.

"Where We Work." United Nations Relief and Works Agency for Palestine Refugees in the Near East (UNRWA). https://www.unrwa.org/where-we-work /lebanon.

"Who We Are and What We Envision." Breaking the Silence, accessed May 29, 2020, https://www.breakingthesilence.org.il/about/qa?qa=1.

Williams, Matt. (2012). "Wisconsin Sikh Temple Shooting: Six Killed in Act of 'Domestic Terrorism.'" *The Guardian*, August 5. https://www.theguardian.com/ world/2012/aug/05/wisconsin-sikh-temple-domestic-terrorism.

Winitsky, David. (2014), "Jewish Theater: Every Good Question Deserves Another Question." *Howlround*, March 9. https://howlround.com/jewish-theater.

Yarchun, Deborah. *The Man in the Sukkah* (unpublished manuscript, 2018), Adobe Acrobat file.

Yeghiazarian, Torange. *Isfahan Blues* (unpublished manuscript, 2013), Adobe Acrobat file.

Yeghiazarian, Torange. *444 Days* (unpublished manuscript, Production Copy, September 22, 2013), Adobe Acrobat file.

Younis, Sam. (2009), "Author's Statement" in Holly Hill and Dina Amin (eds), *Salaam, Peace: An Anthology of Middle Eastern-American Drama*. New York: Theatre Communications Group.

Zaimeche, Salah, et al. (2019), "Algeria" in Adam Augustyn et al. (eds), *Encyclopedia Britannica*. Encyclopædia Britannica, Inc. https://www.britannica .com/place/Algeria.

Zhao, Xiaojian, and Edward J. W. Park. (2014), *Asian Americans: An Encyclopedia of Social, Cultural, Economic, and Political History*. Santa Barbara: Greenwood, an Imprint of ABC-CLIO, LLC.

Zillich, Tom. (2019), "UPDATE: Surrey Theatre Cancels Play Over Blackface Criticism." *Surrey Now-Leader*, November 1. https://www.surreynowleader.com /news/no-blackface-vancouver-group-wants-surrey-theatre-show-cancelled/.

Zuhur, Sherifa. (2003), *Colors of Enchantment: Theater, Dance, Music, and the Visual Arts of the Middle East*. Cairo: American University in Cairo Press.

CONTRIBUTORS

Kareem Fahmy is a Canadian-born director and playwright of Egyptian descent and is the cochair of the Middle Eastern American Writers Lab at the Lark. He has been a fellow or resident artist at the Sundance Theatre Lab, Oregon Shakespeare Festival (Phil Killian Directing Fellow), Eugene O'Neill Theatre Center (National Directors Fellow), Second Stage (Van Lier Directing Fellow), Soho Rep (Writer/Director Lab), Lincoln Center (Directors Lab), the New Museum (Artist-in-Residence), and New York Theater Workshop (Emerging Artist Fellow & Usual Suspect). He has worked at theatres around the country, including MCC, New Dramatists, the Civilians, Geva Theatre, Pioneer Theatre, Silk Road Rising, and Berkeley Rep. Kareem holds an MFA in Directing from Columbia University.

Jamil Khoury is the co-founder and co-executive artistic director of Silk Road Rising. A theatre producer, playwright, essayist, and filmmaker, Khoury's work focuses on Middle Eastern themes and questions of diaspora. He is particularly interested in the intersections of culture, national identity, and religion. Khoury has been playwright-in-residence at the Joan Mitchell Center (2019), Tufts University (2018), Benedictine University (2017), North Central College (2016), Valparaiso University (2015), and Knox College (2015). He holds an MA in religious studies from the University of Chicago Divinity School and a BS in international relations from Georgetown University's School of Foreign Service and is a Kellogg executive scholar (Northwestern University) in Nonprofit Management.

Evren Odcikin is a theatre director, adapter, translator, and producer who was born and raised in Turkey. He is the associate artistic director at Oregon Shakespeare Festival, a founder of Maia Directors, and a resident artist at Golden Thread Productions. He has worked at Portland Center Stage, Cal Shakes, Berkeley Rep, South Coast Rep, New York Theater Workshop, Kennedy Center, InterAct (Philadelphia), Cleveland Public Theatre, the Lark, Magic Theatre, Crowded Fire, Shotgun Players, TheatreFirst, and Playwrights Foundation, among many others. https://odcikin.com.

Contributors

Megan Sandberg-Zakian is a freelance director based in Jamaica Plain, MA, and a cofounder of Maia Directors. The daughter of an Armenian molecular biologist and a Jewish playwright, Megan is a freelance theatre director and the director-in-residence at Merrimack Repertory Theatre in Lowell, MA. She is passionate about the development of diverse new American plays and writers and supporting theatres to work toward inclusion and equity on and offstage.

Torange Yeghiazarian is the founding artistic director of Golden Thread Productions in San Francisco, the first American theatre company focused on the Middle East where she launched such visionary programs as ReOrient Festival, New Threads, Fairytale Players, and What do the Women Say? A playwright, director, and translator, Torange has been published in *The Drama Review, American Theatre Magazine, Amerasia Journal,* and contributed to *Encyclopedia of Women & Islamic Cultures* and *Cambridge World Encyclopedia of Stage Actors.* Born in Iran and of Armenian heritage, Torange holds a master's degree in theatre arts from San Francisco State University.

A child of Iranian immigrants, **Pirronne Yousefzadeh** is a theatre director, writer, and educator. She currently serves as the associate artistic director and director of engagement at Geva Theatre Center. She has directed and developed new work both in New York and regionally at the Public, Playwrights Horizons, New York Theatre Workshop, Atlantic Theater Company, Kennedy Center, La Jolla Playhouse, Actors Theatre of Louisville, Cleveland Playhouse, A.C.T., Pioneer Theatre Company, InterAct Theatre Company, and Hangar Theatre, among others. pirronne.com.

INDEX

Page numbers in *italics* refer to Figures.

Index

Index

Index

Index

Index

Printed in the USA
CPSIA information can be obtained
at www.ICGtesting.com
LVHW020244210324
775093LV00001B/84